MEMOIRS
1892–1969

MEMOIRS
Episodes in New Mexico
History 1892–1969

Facsimile of 1969 Edition
by
William A. Keleher

New Foreword
by
Marc Simmons

With a Preface
by
Michael L. Keleher

SUNSTONE PRESS

SANTA FE

New Material © 2008 by Sunstone Press. All Rights Reserved.

No part of this book may be reproduced in any form or by any electronic or mechanical means including information storage and retrieval systems without permission in writing from the publisher, except by a reviewer who may quote brief passages in a review.

Sunstone books may be purchased for educational, business, or sales promotional use. For information please write: Special Markets Department, Sunstone Press, P.O. Box 2321, Santa Fe, New Mexico 87504-2321.

Library of Congress Cataloging-in-Publication Data

Keleher, William Aloysius, 1886-1972.
  Memoirs : episodes in New Mexico history, 1892-1969 : facsimile of the 1969 edition / by William A. Keleher ; new foreword by Marc Simmons ; with a preface by Michael L. Keleher.
    p. cm. -- (Southwest heritage series)
  Originally published: Santa Fe, N.M. : Rydal Press, c1969. With title: Memoirs, 1892-1969 : a New Mexico item.
  Includes index.
  ISBN 978-0-86534-623-9 (softcover : alk. paper)
   1. Keleher, William Aloysius, 1886-1972. 2. Keleher, William Aloysius, 1886-1972--Childhood and youth. 3. New Mexico--History--1848- 4. New Mexico--History--1848---Biography. 5. Historians--New Mexico--Albuquerque--Biography. 6. Lawyers--New Mexico--Albuquerque--Biography. 7. Albuquerque (N.M.)--Biography. I. Keleher, William Aloysius, 1886-1972. Memoirs, 1892-1969. II. Title.
  F801.K353A3 2008
  978.9'6105092--dc22
                              2008011556

WWW.SUNSTONEPRESS.COM
SUNSTONE PRESS / POST OFFICE BOX 2321 / SANTA FE, NM 87504-2321 /USA
(505) 988-4418 / ORDERS ONLY (800) 243-5644 / FAX (505) 988-1025

The Southwest Heritage Series is dedicated to Jody Ellis and Marcia Muth Miller, the founders of Sunstone Press, whose original purpose and vision continues to inspire and motivate our publications.

CONTENTS

THE SOUTHWEST HERITAGE SERIES / I

FOREWORD TO THIS EDITION / II
by
Marc Simmons

PREFACE TO THIS EDITION / III
by
Michael L. Keleher

FACSIMILE OF 1969 EDITION / IV

I

THE SOUTHWEST HERITAGE SERIES

The history of the United States is written in hundreds of regional histories and literary works. Those letters, essays, memoirs, biographies and even collections of fiction are often first-hand accounts by people who wanted to memorialize an event, a person or simply record for posterity the concerns and issues of the times. Many of these accounts have been lost, destroyed or overlooked. Some are in private or public collections but deemed to be in too fragile condition to permit handling by contemporary readers and researchers.

However, now with the application of twenty-first century technology, nineteenth and twentieth century material can be reprinted and made accessible to the general public. These early writings are the DNA of our history and culture and are essential to understanding the present in terms of the past.

The Southwest Heritage Series is a form of literary preservation. Heritage by definition implies legacy and these early works are our legacy from those who have gone before us. To properly present and preserve that legacy, no changes in style or contents have been made. The material reprinted stands on its own as it first appeared. The point of view is that of the author and the era in which he or she lived. We would not expect photographs of people from the past to be re-imaged with modern clothes, hair styles and backgrounds. We should not, therefore, expect their ideas and personal philosophies to reflect our modern concepts.

Remember, reading their words and sharing their thoughts is a passport back into understanding how the past was shaped and how it influenced today's world.

Our hope is that new access to these older books will provide readers with a challenging and exciting experience.

II

FOREWORD TO THIS EDITION
by
Marc Simmons

It has been my privilege over many years to meet quite a few of the Southwest's leading historians. I first began seeking them out when I was in elementary school and took the measure of each one, to see what I could learn from them about the history craft.

On November 19, 1966, I visited William A. Keleher at his home not far from downtown Albuquerque, New Mexico. We sat in his living room for an hour or so, talking about New Mexico's golden past and he inscribed a couple of his books I'd brought along. After more than 40 years, the specifics of our conversation that day have dimmed. But I do recall coming away with the firm impression that I had been fortunate to spend a bit of time with a master historian.

In fact, Will Keleher spent most of his adult life as a practicing attorney and a civic leader. Yet on the side, he managed to publish four major books about 19th century New Mexico, plus a volume of his memoirs that began in 1892 and extended to the end of the 1960s. In my own *Albuquerque, A Narrative History* (1983), I relied heavily on Keleher's recollections to capture the spirit and flavor of life in the city that he had known intimately at the turn of the century.

Born in Lawrence, Kansas, William was only two years old when his family moved to Albuquerque in 1888. That was just eight years after arrival of the railroad and the founding of New Albuquerque at trackside. Thus, the boy and the town grew up together.

In 1900 at age 14, Will was hired as a Western Union messenger to deliver telegrams by bicycle throughout the business district. On his own, he began studying Morse Code and soon was able to send and receive telegrams.

"At that time," Keleher would declare later, "Albuquerque was a genuine Wild West town." Gambling was wide open and the municipal government paid its expenses by collecting fines from madams in the red light district. Hangings, legal and otherwise, were not uncommon, while fires and floods regularly troubled the community. Will Keleher saw it all growing up, and it left him with a sense of being a part of history.

William A. Keleher as a young man.
Photograph courtesy of Michael L. Keleher.

In 1907 he took a job as a reporter on the *Journal* and a few years later became city editor for the old *Albuquerque Herald*. The experience gained as a journalist would stand him in good stead when down the road he began writing history. Before that, however, he acted upon what he called "a long cherished wish to attend law school." The school was Washington & Lee in Virginia. Returning to Albuquerque with his degree in 1915, he practiced law there for much of the remainder of his life.

So what was it that turned Attorney William Keleher toward a parallel career as a New Mexico historian? Clearly, several things contributed to that end. One was his association with many frontier figures, beginning with an aging former Santa Fe Trail trader Franz Huning, to whom he had delivered telegrams as a boy, and through his long friendship with famed gunfighter Elfego Baca.

Other factors mentioned by Keleher himself were his newspaper reporting and his legal training. Owing to those things, he said, "it was only natural that the time would come when I would have the urge to write."

His first book, *Maxwell Land Grant* (1942), was published by Santa Fe's then prestigious Rydal Press. In it, Keleher led the way in sorting out the long and confusing history of that enormous grant in northeast New Mexico. His research led him to the conclusion that each one of the old Spanish and Mexican land grants had a human interest story connected with it.

Maxwell Land Grant was followed by *The Fabulous Frontier* in 1945 (revised in 1962), containing robust sketches of men like Thomas B. Catron, Sheriff Pat Garrett, rancher John Chisum, and Senator Albert B. Fall. Each left a strong imprint on New Mexico's history in the years before statehood.

Book three in Keleher's quartet of histories was *Turmoil in New Mexico, 1846-1868* (1952). In vivid and precise detail, he carved out explosive stories of the American conquest of New Mexico, the Confederate invasion during the Civil War, and the saga of the last great Navajo war that led to the tribe's exile on the Pecos river.

And finally, Keleher brought out his *Violence in Lincoln County* (1957), adding much new information on the troublous times there in the long period from 1869 to 1881.

To the dedication and self-discipline necessary for such large production must be added the reminder that William Keleher, in the midst of his scholarly labors, carried on his very active law career. He even found time to serve a term as president of the New Mexico State University board of regents.

Honored as one of the state's foremost historians, William A. Keleher died on December 18, 1972.

Sunstone Press by bringing Keleher's books back into print in its highly acclaimed Southwest Heritage Series gives a new generation of readers access to these valuable works of regional history. The author's legacy deserves to be preserved.

III

PREFACE TO THIS EDITION
by
Michael L. Keleher

William A. Keleher observed first hand the changing circumstances of people and places of New Mexico until his death December 18, 1972, surrounded by family. He was born in Lawrence, Kansas November 7, 1886, and arrived in Albuquerque two years later, with his parents and two older brothers. The older brothers died of diphtheria within a few weeks of their arrival. One quickly observes from his writings, and writings about him, he lived a fruitful and exemplary life. He was recognized as a successful attorney, being honored by the New Mexico State Bar as one of the outstanding Attorneys of the Twentieth Century. His knowledge and understanding of humankind is evidenced by his quote attributed to Sir Thomas Browne, 1686, and printed after the title page in *Turmoil in New Mexico*:

> The iniquity of oblivion scattereth her poppy and deals with the memory of men without distinction to merit and perpetuity...who knows whether the best of men be known, or whether there be not more remarkable men forgot, than any that stand remembered in the known account of time.

An insight to his character and religious belief is indicated by the last paragraph of the Foreword to his *Memoirs*, First Edition:

> The writing of this book has afforded me an opportunity for study and reflection while attempting to recall what was said or done by people in the long ago, many of whose voices are stilled forever. During this time, I have experienced a renewed consciousness of the significance and vital importance of recognition of God's eternal verity.

His dedication and love of family and New Mexico is shown by the concluding paragraph of *Memoirs* by which he bequeaths his "respect for the law and my love for New Mexico" to his children, grandchildren and nephew.

William A. Keleher in later life.
Photograph courtesy of Michael A. Keleher.

His great joy seemed to be to have someone call at his house or stop him on the street and ask him to autograph one of his books, which he did gracefully, with a twinkle in his eye and some individual remembrance or personal comment after a short visit with the admirer. On more than one occasion he remarked the changing circumstances of people and places he knew would be forgotten forever. It became his single-minded purpose to record his observations of persons and circumstances so they would not be forgotten, and avoid the "iniquity of oblivion".

Anyone who reads his books will enjoy an increased awareness of people and places of New Mexico, and they too will become an heir to his respect for the law and love for New Mexico.

IV

FACSIMILE OF 1969 EDITION

MEMOIRS:
1892–1969

Other books by the same author:

MAXWELL LAND GRANT, a New Mexico Item *1942*
THE FABULOUS FRONTIER, Twelve New Mexico Items *1945*
TURMOIL IN NEW MEXICO 1846-1868, a New Mexico Item *1952*
VIOLENCE IN LINCOLN COUNTY 1869-1881, a New Mexico Item *1957*

MEMOIRS:
1892-1969

A New Mexico Item

By WILLIAM A. KELEHER

THE RYDAL PRESS
SANTA FE, NEW MEXICO

ALL RIGHTS RESERVED
INCLUDING THE RIGHT OF REPRODUCTION
IN WHOLE OR IN PART
COPYRIGHT © 1969 BY WILLIAM A. KELEHER
PUBLISHED BY THE RYDAL PRESS
SANTA FE, NEW MEXICO 87501

FIRST EDITION

SBN 69-911292-5
MANUFACTURED IN THE UNITED STATES OF AMERICA

Dedicated with love and affection to my brother, Ralph J. Keleher, and my sister, Julia M. Keleher, and to the memory of our beloved sister, Katherine E. Keleher, 1897–1967.

Contents

Foreword		9
CHAPTER ONE	Father and Mother and the Landscape	11
CHAPTER TWO	Early Day Memories	27
CHAPTER THREE	School and Work	45
CHAPTER FOUR	Newspaper Days	68
CHAPTER FIVE	Trying to Become a Lawyer	84
CHAPTER SIX	Detour to El Paso	99
CHAPTER SEVEN	Municipal Government	112
CHAPTER EIGHT	City Water Works	123
CHAPTER NINE	Political Destinies	130
CHAPTER TEN	About Elfego Baca	153
CHAPTER ELEVEN	Bronson Cutting and Elfego Baca	165
CHAPTER TWELVE	National Bank Failure	192
CHAPTER THIRTEEN	The Gallup Coal Strike	207
CHAPTER FOURTEEN	Libraries	225
CHAPTER FIFTEEN	Eugene Manlove Rhodes	234
CHAPTER SIXTEEN	Interest in Regional Writing	247
CHAPTER SEVENTEEN	Conclusion	278
Index		285

"The wind bloweth where it listeth, and thou hearest the sound thereof, but canst not tell whence it cometh, and whither it goeth."

JOHN, Chapter 3-8

Foreword

THIS BOOK is written especially for New Mexicans of good heart, whether New Mexicans by birth, adoption or inclination. Hopefully it will be read by some readers who have read one or more of my other books, particularly "*The Fabulous Frontier, 12 New Mexico Items,*" because through such reading they may not be strangers to some of the people and characters described in this book. As will be apparent, this work is a combination autobiography, biography, narrative and memoir. The format has changed from the original concept of its form and content. In the beginning it was my intention to write a personal narrative, but this idea was early abandoned and a method employed which would exclude from my writing anything but a subject matter with which I had been personally associated or identified. The use of this method obliged me to forego including references to some people and subjects of importance. However, it has been my hope that such exclusions will be compensated for by the inclusion of other material which otherwise would have been omitted.

I wish to express my thanks and gratitude to my wife, Loretta Barrett Keleher, for much help and assistance during the many months I worked on this project; and to single out and especially thank my sister, Julia M. Keleher, for many years a teacher in the English Department at the University of New Mexico, for valuable assistance in every phase of the work; and to express my appreciation to Dr. Myra Jenkins, State Archivist, of Santa Fe, for help and many courtesies extended in connection with providing photostats and microfilm.

In reviewing the manuscript it appears obvious to me that my life has been closely identified with the use of words, spoken or written: in the telegraph office, place of my first employment, then as a reporter on various newspapers, and finally by some fifty and more years of general law practice.

The writing of this book has afforded me an opportunity for study and reflection while attempting to recall what was said or done by people in the long ago, many of whose voices are stilled forever. During this time I have experienced a renewed consciousness of the significance and vital importance of the recognition of God's eternal verity.

Respectfully submitted,
WILLIAM A. KELEHER
Albuquerque, New Mexico

CHAPTER ONE

Father and Mother and the Landscape

MY FATHER, David Keleher, was born in Dunkirk, New York, on August 29, 1850, died in Albuquerque on November 16, 1903. My father's parents, Dennis Keleher and Margaret Scannell Keleher, both born and reared in Cork, Ireland, emigrated to America in the '40's, in the wake of the potato famine in Ireland, settling first in Piermont, New York, then in Dunkirk. They moved to Kansas Territory in 1853, living in Lawrence, Douglas County, for many years. Here my father attended grade school. He was an eye witness to some incidents growing out of the Quantrill Raid on Lawrence. After finishing grade school he served an apprenticeship in the sheet metal trade, becoming a journeyman tinner. David Keleher came to Albuquerque in 1881, soon after the completion of the Santa Fe railroad into Albuquerque, largely on the recommendation of Thomas F. Keleher, an elder brother.

Thomas Keleher had arrived in Albuquerque on November 7, 1879, having traveled by railroad to Las Vegas, and on to Albuquerque by horse and buggy. Upon reaching Albuquerque he started business as a dealer in wool, hides and pelts. He had previous experience in this business while employed by Shellcuff and Williamson of St.

FATHER

DAVID KELEHER

Louis as a buyer of buffalo hides in Dodge City, Kansas, Vinita, Indian Territory, and Fort Smith, Arkansas. While working in those places Thomas Keleher became acquainted with Bat Masterson, Wild Bill Hickok and other noted characters of the day.

MOTHER

MARY ANN GORRY KELEHER

Upon his arrival in Albuquerque in 1879, Thomas F. Keleher was welcomed to the plaza and befriended by Elias S. Stover, former Lieutenant Governor of Kansas, managing partner in Stover, Crary & Co., general merchants. Soon thereafter he became acquainted with the few Anglos living in the town at the time, among them Louis Ilfeld, Edward Spitz, Franz Huning, Frederick H. Kent, and William McGuinness.

Father and Mother, David Keleher and Mary Ann Gorry, were married in the Church of San Felipe de Neri, in Old Albuquerque, on September 25, 1882, following a rather romantic courtship. Strangers, they were passengers from New Town to Old Town on the horse-drawn street car on the Albuquerque Street Railway Company tracks. The car in which they were riding, with the San Felipe Church as their destination, jumped the track as it neared Old Town. All on board alighted, and the male passengers gallantly helped the driver get the car back on the tracks. David Keleher escorted Mary Ann Gorry to her seat in the righted car, introduced himself, and the romance began.

At this time, Mary Ann Gorry, an Irish emigrant, had been in America less than two years, in Albuquerque only a few months. She was born in 1862, in Athleague, County Roscommon, Ireland where her father had been a member of the Royal Irish Constabulary. She attended school in Athleague and Kildare in Ireland, and received a fairly good grammar school education. Her "passage money" to America had been provided by two uncles, John and Thomas Gorry. Mother often told me of her crossing the Atlantic in a sailing ship of the White Star line, a crossing which took six weeks; of her arrival in New York, of her experience at Castle Garden on Ellis Island; of her trip on the rail cars from New York City to St. Louis where an aunt lived. Her aunt, through acquaintances, had found a position for her as a governess for George and Stella Smith, twelve and ten years old, the children of Mr. and Mrs. Frank W. Smith. Mr. Smith was General

Superintendent of the Atlantic and Pacific Railroad, with headquarters in Albuquerque.

After their marriage in Albuquerque in 1882, the David Kelehers went to Lawrence, Kansas, Father's home town, where they lived until their return to Albuquerque in 1888, bringing with them three sons, Franklin, Daniel and William. I had been born on Sunday morning, November 7, 1886 between 9 and 11 o'clock (Mother often told me) as the sound of the nearby St. John's Church bells rang for mass.

In 1889 Father resumed his work as a tinsmith in the Atlantic and Pacific railway shops in Albuquerque. My parents were in Albuquerque only a few months after their return, when they sustained a great misfortune in the death of their two older children, my elder brothers, both victims of diphtheria. Daniel died on January 15, 1889, and Franklin died on February 14, 1889. The death of the two boys, one month apart, was a crushing blow to my parents, from which they never fully recovered. Of this tragedy I became increasingly aware as the years passed and I was old enough to understand the significance of death, recalling now that on occasion Mother told me about the passing of her little sons, hoping desperately for a miracle of recovery. On such infrequent occasions, while Mother talked softly, crying quietly, Father always tiptoed from the room. I recall even now, so many, many years later, Mother's voice as she relived the agony of her suffering, and of her prayer recited to the Virgin Mary, a prayer she had learned in far off Ireland: "Hail Mary, full of grace, the Lord is with thee; blessed art thou among women," her little ones responding to the words she and Father had taught them: "Holy Mary, Mother of God, pray for us, now and at the hour of our death."

My first recollection of a Keleher family dwelling place in Albuquerque revolves around the year 1892 when we lived in a house at 303 West Baca (now Santa Fe) Avenue, rented from Santiago Baca, at the time Sheriff of Bernalillo County. This house, still standing, was two blocks from the Atlantic and Pacific railway shops, a half mile from the Atlantic and Pacific General Office Building. In 1893, my father, anxious to own a home of his own, bought a lot from Franz Huning on the northeast corner of Fourth Street and Atlantic Avenue for $600 and built on it a small frame house which he painted white. That house, at 323 West Atlantic Avenue, was occupied by the Keleher family from 1893 to 1911 when economic conditions made it possible to move to 501 West Fruit Avenue.

Father planted a border of cottonwood trees the length and width of the lot. These were kept alive by water pumped from a well and carried to each tree in a bucket, a duty "taken over" by me and each succeeding child, Lawrence, Ralph, Julia and Katherine when old enough to do such a job. The trees grew to great size through the years, living memorials to values held by my parents. Mother planted climbing roses and honeysuckle vines. No doubt, as she looked at the sweep of barren land extending westward for miles to the Rio Grande, she compared it with the lush green of her native Ireland, but I never heard her complain.

The dominant activity of our immediate pioneer neighborhood, and of the little town of Albuquerque, revolved around the Santa Fe Railroad Shops, located at Second Street and Atlantic Avenue, where our father worked until he died in 1903. Close to the shops were several small grocery stores, the most popular of which was one owned by an Italian named A. Bratini whose trademark for

Atlantic and Pacific Railroad General Office Building, Second Street and Atlantic Ave., Albuquerque, showing officials of the company and General office staff, from a photograph taken by W. F. Cobb in 1892 a few months before the Atlantic and Pacific was acquired by the Atchison, Topeka and Santa Fe at Special Master's Sale incident to a mortgage foreclosure proceeding.

everything from nails to licorice candy was "Bratini's Best."

The neighborhood grew slowly. Many of the settlers were German emigrants who built substantial brick houses and planted gardens. By diverting water in the *acequia madre* running north and south through the area into ditches which they dug adjacent to their homes, they were able to irrigate fruit trees and vegetable gardens, one of the nicest of which was the vegetable garden of the Joseph Beck family. Nick Metz, of Alsace-Lorraine, planted an extensive vineyard on his property and yearly made fine wine.

The most successful business man in our part of town was Byron Henry Ives, who quit his job as a carpenter in the Santa Fe Shops and planted rose bushes, and long rows of flower seeds in a vacant lot on the corner of Baca Avenue and Fourth Street. Such was the beginning of the Ives Greenhouse which for years supplied the flowers for weddings, funerals and social functions throughout New Mexico and parts of Arizona. Byron Ives had a fine baritone voice and sang every Sunday in the Lead Avenue Methodist Church Choir. On one occasion he sang the leading role in an Albuquerque production of Gilbert and Sullivan's *The Pirates of Penzance*. Many students at the University of New Mexico have through the years been recipients of the Ives Scholarships established at this institution by this pioneer citizen.

Mother's best friend was Mrs. S. W. White, whose sons Charles and William became executives in The First National Bank of Albuquerque, and whose grandson, William, is carrying on the banking tradition in the Santa Fe National Bank. Mrs. White often took Mother riding in the family horse and buggy. The most exciting expedition for them, however, was the collection of baked foods

FATHER, MOTHER, LANDSCAPE 19

for the annual Bazaar given by the Ladies' Altar Society of the Immaculate Conception Church. This event, of which they were co-chairwomen year after year, was held during Fair Week.

A few doors from the White home was a pretentious three-story brick house built by James Gorman on the corner of Iron Avenue and South Second Street. Today, that house is a refuge for homeless men of any age, race or creed—the House of the Good Shepherd.

While living on Baca Avenue, it had been my habit, although only about six years old, to go on exploring expeditions, walking alone about town, taking in the sights. This custom was continued after the move to 323 West Atlantic. Apparently I had demonstrated to Mother that I could be trusted to go and come at will, but there was always the possibility that harm might come to me. I walked freely in and out of the railroad yards, exposed at times to death or injury by switch engines in the yards and passing trains on the main line. There was danger also from swimming in the Rio Grande, and from quicksand along the river bottom. With the exception of the railway yards and the river, the possibilities for accident and injury were not great, and my wanderings became more or less casually accepted at home. The huge, as it then appeared, General Office building, the largest *adobe* structure in New Mexico as I learned later, was in our immediate neighborhood. Another all important landmark in 1893 was the three-story brick San Felipe Hotel, which had been built in 1884 at a cost of $103,000, on the southwest corner of Fifth Street and Gold Avenue, today the site of a thirteen-story federal building. The San Felipe, as I learned in later years, had been built by Contractor Edward Medler, father of the late District Judge Edward L. Medler, of Las Cruces and Truth or Consequences, N. M., through the promotion efforts of M. F. Thompson and Colonel G. W. Meylert. Colonel Meylert was a temperance advocate in a day of much drinking of hard liquor in Albuquerque. Meylert would not allow intoxicating liquor to be sold on the San Felipe premises. Instead of space to be used as a club or saloon in the hotel he had a room available for use as a library.

The San Felipe had 80 guest rooms. Its rates, American plan, for room and board, were $2.50 and $3.00 a day. When the legislature of New Mexico in 1889 established the University of New Mexico in Albuquerque, Colonel Meylert arranged for the first meetings of the Board of Regents to be held in the San Felipe Hotel library room. Later Meylert helped to induce owners to donate tracts of land for the University campus. In the '90's I was in and out of the San Felipe Hotel lobby many times, attracted there perhaps by the mineral exhibits displayed in glass enclosed cabinets. There was at the time a band stand on a vacant lot north from the San Felipe, from which, on Sunday evenings in the summertime, the First Regimental Band of the New Mexico Territorial Militia gave concerts, most of the players being from Old Town. The San Felipe Hotel was located half a mile west of the Santa Fe Railway depot and the Hotel found it necessary to transport some of the guests to and from the hotel.

My somewhat casual interest in the San Felipe Hotel building became more meaningful on August 18, 1899. While playing with other boys at Fourth Street and Lead Avenue about 4 p.m., I noticed clouds of heavy black smoke pouring from the roof of the San Felipe Hotel at Fifth and Gold, only three blocks away. There was a Gamewell fire alarm box on a pole adjacent to the very spot where I was standing. Taking one more look to be assured that there would be no reason to have me arrested for turning in a false fire alarm, all as spelled out in a cautionary printed warning inside, I broke the glass on the box, pulled the lever, and set in motion a chain of events visualized by every small boy, but seldom realized in actuality. Then there was the immediate response. The mournful wail of the "mocking bird" fire whistle screeched its shrill alarm. I well knew of my own knowledge that the whistle was attached to a contraption on the steam boiler at the water plant near Tijeras and Broadway. My part in the drama having been played, and now past history, I hurried to the scene of the fire. Fire Chief Bernard Ruppe of the Albuquerque Volunteer Fire Department was already there, with several firemen, shouting orders and commands for more lines of hose, more water. By dark the fire had been pretty well extinguished, the remaining skeleton-like walls of the building silhouetted against the western skies.

The San Felipe Hotel was vacant at the time of the fire, having been closed for lack of business. The property had been purchased by Frank E. Sturges, long time proprietor of the Sturges European Hotel, First Street and Railroad Avenue. Sturges at the time of the fire was having the San Felipe remodeled and refurbished. The Elks Lodge bought the San Felipe property from Frank Sturges, converting it into a theater, which offered Weber and Fields, arriving in Albuquerque on a special train, enroute from Los Angeles to New York, as the attraction on opening night. With the coming of motion pictures, ending a grand and glorious chapter in the theater, the Elks converted the building into a home for brother Elks. The Elks Lodge sold the property to the federal government as the site for an office building.

Some two miles north and west of the San Felipe Hotel was another landmark, attractive to boys, the Territorial

Fair Grounds, where in the fall of each year since its establishment on October 3, 1881, there had been offered to the public spectacular events, including balloon ascensions, high diving, baseball tournaments, horse racing, and once in 1895, a program of real bullfighting which Territorial Governor W. T. Thornton had ordered Sheriff Jacobo Yrisarri to stop, and which order had been ignored by the Sheriff, who contended that bullfighting was not prohibited by law in New Mexico. In later years I learned that the Territorial Fairground had once been the headquarters for troops during the Civil War. The site had been the scene of many events of historic interest.

Adjacent to the Territorial Fairgrounds, several hundred yards from the west fence there were in my boyhood the remnants of Tom Post's once famed toll bridge over the Rio Grande. The bridge connected Old Town and Atrisco with the outside world. In early days Atrisco was an important community, the architecture and streets of which had been patterned after home land recollections of far off Spain. In later years I learned that Tom Post had built the toll bridge across the river hopeful of making a fortune out of the traffic. The venture was a commercial success in the beginning, but flood waters tumbled down in late May in 1891 from the mountains of northern New Mexico and Colorado, smashed the bridge timbers into kindling wood, carried the structure downstream, and Tom Post's dreams of greatness perished, leaving him the recollections of an old-time stage driver, and ownership of Tom Post's Exchange, adjacent to the plaza in Old Town.

To the south on the Rio Grande, two miles below the wrecked Tom Post bridge, near today's Barelas Street Bridge, there were in my boyhood days attractive but dangerous holes patronized by swimmers from late May until early September. Reports of drownings and narrow escapes from drownings, and rumored hazards of quicksands, failed to deter boys bent on water-sports pleasures. The Rio Grande was only a mile or so from home. In summer months I spent much time in and about the river, swimming and playing. Pat Murphy, a much older boy, had given me my first lesson in swimming at the age of ten years, when he picked me up and threw me into the river, clothes and all, and in response to my frantic cries for help, shouted, "Swim, kid, or you'll get drownded."

Several miles west of the Rio Grande there were the volcanoes, then and now a landmark on the horizon, where sky and the blue-black ridge of the volcanoes seemed to meet at sunset, too far away for walking, accessible only to boys fortunate enough to be able to ride there on a pony. It was a prize worthy of the efforts of boys to explore the terrain adjacent to the huge volcanic boulders balanced on hilltops east of the several craters, millions of years old we were told. The entire fascinating panorama of the volcanic scene was overshadowed by Mount Taylor, over 10,000 feet above sea level, one hundred miles to the west near the edge of the east boundary of the Navajo Indian reservation. The high mountain had been named after President Zachary Taylor, we were also told, not long after the American Occupation of 1846. The volcano country was a stimulating source of interest for boys ambitious to know more about scientific values in the fields of geology, archaeology, or anthropology. In the Rio Grande Valley could be found bits of Indian pottery, arrowheads and artifacts carried down from the upper regions in times of flood. Imbedded in the windswept sands in the volcano country these were precious prizes and rewards for finders.

Away from the volcanoes and across the Rio Grande, and east of Old Albuquerque, there was the new town of

Albuquerque, depending upon the railroad shops almost entirely for support and maintenance. A cement sidewalk in the business section of the town was a novelty seldom encountered. Plank sidewalks, not too carefully nailed down, afforded the most convenient means of pedestrian traffic. There was no street paving in Albuquerque until 1903, when public-spirited citizens banded together, and with the cooperation of the mayor and city council organized an improvement district which resulted in pavement being laid by the El Paso Bitulithic Company, from Silver to Tijeras Road on Second Street and from First to Sixth Streets on Railroad (now Central) Avenue.

Beyond the eastern approach to the Sandia Mountains, there was the Estancia Valley, a vast cattle and sheep breeding and grazing country, hundreds of square miles in extent, where on many occasions the six-shooter was recognized as the final, ultimate authority. Since the time when the "memory of man runneth not to the contrary," livestock growers had ranged their herds of cattle and sheep rent free. It was not until 1908 that free grazing became a thing of the past with the creation of the United States Forest Service following the establishment of the National Forests created under President Theodore Roosevelt's administration. Hugh H. Harris was the first Supervisor of the Manzano National Forest, followed soon in the management of the Third district offices by many disciples of Gifford Pinchot. Among them were: A. C. Ringland, T. S. Woolsey, Jr., A. O. Waha, E. H. Clapp and many other dedicated men.

The denial of free and unlimited pasturage in the Estancia Valley country proved disastrous for William McIntosh and other men of Scotch ancestry, who had settled in the valley, established vast sheep ranges and prospered under the open range policy. In a way McIntosh was an institution. Successful in his sheep and wool-growing ventures in the Estancia Valley, he invested heavily in Albuquerque enterprises. He was for several years owner of the town's all important baseball team, the Albuquerque Browns, renamed the McIntosh Browns in McIntosh's honor, in consideration for his agreement to finance the team. When Bill McIntosh came to town to deliver his lambs or market his wool crop, the town was turned inside out for days at a time. He was the most honored guest at the Sturges European Hotel and paid without questioning all items on the statements of account. Albuquerque at the time of the McIntosh heyday, between 1895 and 1905, was the nearest Estancia Valley railway shipping point. Forty wagons, some drawn by oxen, others horsedrawn, transported the McIntosh produce to Albuquerque markets; McIntosh money went into Albuquerque business channels. E. J. Post & Co. became the McIntosh Hardware Co. Trusted friends saw to it that McIntosh acquired blocks of stock in the Bank of Commerce, and the bank elected him a director.

The fighting and feuding between "New Town" and "Old Town" which had been waged between the years 1880 and 1893 as to which community was entitled to the use of the name of Albuquerque had begun to subside, and the die hards in both camps had indicated a willingness to bow to the inevitable and accept the fact that the "New Albuquerque," built up around the railway depot and tracks was to be a permanent community, separate and apart from the old town of Albuquerque, located two miles to the west. The squabble had been settled as between the new town and the old town over the right to use the postmark "Albuquerque" in the respective post-offices. A ruling from Washington provided that neither one should use the word "Albuquerque." Letters mailed in Old Town were to be postmarked "Old Albuquerque" and letters mailed in new town were to be postmarked "New Albuquerque." This arrangement continued for a number of years until a new ruling gave the new town the exclusive right to the Albuquerque postmark.

CHAPTER TWO

Early Day Memories

BROWSING THROUGH bound volumes of the *Albuquerque Times* a few years ago, I read an article published in the issue of July 23, 1892, written when I was nearing the age of six. The article related the killing of Nicholas J. Sanchez, and recalled to my memory my first conscious recollection of events of the outside world. The Kelehers in 1892 lived at 303 West Baca (now Santa Fe) Avenue. Nick Sanchez had a grocery store at 1009 South Second Street, in the next block. I was one of his casual customers, spending a penny with him occasionally at the candy counter, to me the all-important place in his store. So it was that I had more than a passing acquaintance with Nick Sanchez, and was very much interested when Mother, having been awakened quite early one morning, told me that Nick Sanchez had been killed during the night. She told of the noises that had awakened her, of the going and coming of men on horseback, of the yelling and shouting. I was disappointed that I had slept through all the excitement. The Nick Sanchez killing was an incident in my childhood, recollected for many years; consequently I was glad to learn the date of the murder and some of the details. According to the *Times*:

> The City of Albuquerque was startled Wednesday night, July 21, 1892, by the announcement that N. J. Sanchez,

prominent groceryman, had been shot and killed in his store on South Second Street, about 10:30 p.m. His body had been found lying behind the counter. Held in his hand was a half-cocked pistol. Four gun shot wounds told the story of his death. The murderers were apprehended after some days and two of the ring leaders were hanged.

On October 17, 1895, in the Cathedral of St. Francis in Santa Fe, I witnessed the ceremonies incident to the conferring of the pallium upon Archbishop Placidus Louis Chapelle, Archbishop of Santa Fe, by James Cardinal Gibbons of Baltimore. My father had taken me to Santa Fe for the occasion. We arrived in Santa Fe late at night, passengers on an excursion train from Albuquerque carrying more than a hundred people. Most of the excursionists became guests of relatives and friends during their stay in Santa Fe. Father and I, without hotel reservations, were guests of the kind-hearted proprietor of a billiard hall on the plaza, who generously kept the doors of his business open all night and welcomed those who would otherwise have had difficulty finding a place to sleep. I stretched out on the billiard table and was soon fast asleep. After covering me with his overcoat, Father sat up all night in a chair by the table. We were up and about soon after daylight, had breakfast at a nearby cafe, and hurried to the Cathedral, arriving about 5:30, just as the front doors were being opened. We were given good seats, just behind the rows and rows of pews reserved for special guests.

Cardinal Sattoli, papal delegate to the United States, had been scheduled to go to Santa Fe from Washington to take part in the ceremonies incidental to conferring the pallium upon Archbishop Chapelle. He was unable to be present in Santa Fe on October 17, 1895, but visited there on February 21, 1896. On February 23, 1896, Cardinal Sattoli was in Albuquerque, and attended a reception tendered in his honor at the Commercial Club. I went to the reception and managed to get a place where I could see and hear his Eminence. The Cardinal, speaking in Italian, responded to an address of welcome.

One Sunday in 1896 my father took me on a trip to Old Town to call on two men, Thomas Hughes and William McGuinness. Father and I rode to the end of the line in Old Town on the horse-drawn car, visited first at Tom Post's Inn, which I learned later was where stage-drivers had lived in stagecoach days, before the coming of the railroad. At Tom Post's father treated me to a bottle of strawberry soda pop. We then crossed the street and entered the Bernalillo County jail, where Thomas Hughes, editor of the *Albuquerque Daily Citizen*, was serving a sixty-day sentence. Father introduced me to him, and then handed him several cigars, explaining to me that Mr. Hughes was a "great smoker." They talked for what seemed to me to be a long time. Father told me later that Tom Hughes was in jail because he had been found guilty of contempt of court. Many years later, when a lawyer, I read the Supreme Court opinion of December 20, 1896, reported in 8 N.M. 225, entitled "In the matter of Contempt vs. Thomas Hughes, Respondent," which told why Tom Hughes had been punished.

Thomas Hughes was serving out a jail sentence because he elected to stand fast and adhere to the code of the press, refusing to divulge the identity of the man who had inspired publication of an editorial in the *Citizen*, which the court experts found to be contemptuous. Thomas Hughes was the father of Miss Lena Hughes, married several years later to Charles O. Cushman in Albuquerque. Of the Hughes-Cushman marriage there was born Austin Thomas Cushman, in Albuquerque in 1901. The latter was elected chairman of the Board of Directors and

Chief Executive Officer of Sears, Roebuck and Co., serving in these capacities from 1962 to 1967. On the Cushman side of the family, Austin Thomas Cushman is the great-grand-nephew of Elias S. Stover, founder of Stover, Crary & Co., general merchants of Old Albuquerque in 1879. Elias S. Stover had served as Lieutenant Governor of Kansas in 1867. He served in 1889 as the first president of the regents of the University of New Mexico and was elected in 1910 from Bernalillo County as a member of the Constitutional Convention.

Following the visit with Tom Hughes, father took me to call on William McGuinness who lived in an *adobe* house just off the *Rancho Seco* in Old Town. Mr. McGuinness appeared to me to be a very old man. Father told me he wanted me to meet Mr. McGuinness because he was an old timer in New Mexico who had, in his day, taken a prominent part in its affairs. Later I learned that Mr. McGuinness, born in Ireland, had emigrated to America in 1850. He had joined the army in New York City, and had been sent to Utah to help the military suppress the Utah Rebellion after which he had served as a private in New Mexico throughout the Civil War. After the war, McGuinness lived in Old Albuquerque, where he worked for Ash Upson, colorful early day itinerant printer and peripatetic publisher. Upson was publisher in the late 60's of the *Albuquerque Review*, a weekly newspaper. Judge Hezekiah S. Johnson of the Second Judicial District at the time, owned an interest in the *Review*. When no ordained clergyman of his faith was available, Judge Johnson conducted religious services for the Episcopal Church each Sunday in the Tom Post Exchange Hotel dining room.

Established in 1860 by Thomas S. Greiner, the *Albuquerque Review* was originally a Spanish language newspaper. Years after visiting William McGuinness with my father, I became acquainted with two of his several sons, the late Michael McGuinness, an Albuquerque lawyer, and John, a court reporter, who married a daughter of the Elfego Bacas. Some twenty-five years ago I asked Michael McGuinness concerning the whereabouts of the bound volumes of the *Albuquerque Review*, once owned by his father, intending to offer to buy them if available. McGuinness told me that he had inherited the bound file from his mother and had retained them for many years, but only recently had given them to the New Mexico Museum in Santa Fe.

On the night of October 19, 1896, near my tenth birthday, I was one of many people on the board sidewalk in front of the John D. Torlina Shoe and Carpet Store, 222 West Railroad (now Central) Avenue. I have no present recollection as to how or why I happened to be near Torlina's store. Perhaps I had been alerted by John Jacoby or his brother, Harry, our next door neighbors, of 305 West Baca (now Santa Fe) Avenue, to watch for an important parade scheduled for that very night. There was ample reason for me to respect the predictions of the Jacoby brothers. John was mascot for the Albuquerque Browns, in my eyes a marvelous baseball team, and his younger brother Harry was a lantern boy for Fergusson Hook & Ladder Company No. 1. Both were places of honor and trust, far beyond the attainment of most boys of our neighborhood.

As the head of the parade reached Third Street, the buzzing sounds of the crowd reflected the prevailing suspense and excitement. I made my way to the front of the crowd lining the sidewalk, trying to get to a place where I might see and hear to better advantage. From the front line I saw a man, later identified as John Braden, who was trying to control a team of horses that he was driving. The horses were hitched to a wagon near a float drawn by four horses, on which I learned years later was seated Margaret Otero Harrison, the young and beautiful daughter of Mariano S. Otero, wife of Dr. George W. Harrison. Mrs. Harrison was queen of the Territorial Fair and had as her guests on the float several young ladies, members of her court. Braden finally managed to stop his horses, but had suffered burns which caused his death several hours later. More than seventy years after the incident, I can recall witnessing Braden's heroic attempts to control the horses as flames burned his hands, arms, shoulders, and other parts of his body. Long afterwards I learned from newspaper accounts that a planned spectacular parade and fireworks display marking the successful end of the Territorial Fair had turned out to be a ghastly tragedy. One newspaper account was as follows:

> As the parade turned into Copper Avenue at Fifth Street, the Flambeau Club started to shoot off fireworks. Immediately, an explosion occurred, shaking the very earth's foundation, sparks and dangerous missiles ignited in Braden's ammunition wagon, went off in all directions; several rockets shot out of the wagon and struck the horses. Terror-stricken, the horses dashed away, separating members of the Flambeau Club and the band boys; running down and knocking over several of them. By this time the ammunition wagon was a mass of flames, but Braden stayed at his post, trying to stop the horses and save the lives of the crowd that lined the streets. At Third and Railroad, the horses came to a standstill after colliding with the Scott-Moore Hose Company cart. The wheels of the two vehicles had locked together. Braden still had hold of the reins, his body enveloped in flames. Overcome by exhaustion, Braden fell to the ground from his seat, crawling on his hands and knees to the sidewalk, calling out to the spectators "take off my clothes," and holding his hands to his mouth to prevent suffocation. Town Marshal Fred Fornoff

EARLY DAY MEMORIES 33

expressed the sentiment of the community when he said: "No doubt that John Braden saved the lives of Mrs. Harrison and the other young ladies in the Queen's float from death or serious injury. I never saw or heard of such heroism as was displayed by John Braden. He could have jumped from the wagon when the explosion occurred and saved himself, but he stayed at his post and prevented the frightened horses from running away and trampling upon and doubtless killing a number of people."

Public spirited citizens of Albuquerque arranged for an appropriate community funeral service for John Braden. Archie Hilton, Bob Reagan, Sandy Wardwell, and other old-time stagecoach drivers recalled Braden's background. He had been a stagedriver for the Ben Holliday Stage Company as early as 1862, driving between Fort Kearney and Fort Bridger out of Salt Lake City; he had worked at times for Holliday as messenger, armed guard and wagonmaster. When Holliday sold out to Wells, Fargo & Co., Braden worked for that concern for two years; then he had served for a time as Town Marshal of Pueblo, Colorado. In Albuquerque he had worked as a driver for Olmstead & Dixon.

Funeral services for John Braden were held in Grant's Opera House, on the second floor of the Grant Building, northwest corner of Third and Railroad Avenue, almost on the spot where he had been fatally burned. Rev. T. C. Beattie, pastor of the Congregational Church, conducted the services, assisted by Rev. Mr. Foulkes, and Rev. Mr. Welch. Mrs. Thomas J. Shinick, one-time soprano soloist in St. Patrick's Cathedral in New York City, sang "Angels Ever Bright and Fair." H. J. Emerson, marshal of the parade in which Braden had lost his life, served as Marshal-of-the-Day. On the morning of the funeral he distributed handbills about town, on which the message was printed: "Let's all pay tribute to a true hero." Postmaster A. M. Whitcomb flew the American flag at half mast over the postoffice, 117 West Gold Avenue, on the afternoon of the funeral. The fire bell, at the northeast corner of First and Railroad, tolled its mournful message before and after the funeral service.

Grant's opera house was crowded with people gathered to mourn John Braden's death. The procession to Fairview Cemetery was a lengthy one. Many men walked alongside the hearse, including several units which had been in the parade on the night of the tragedy, among them: First Regimental Band, Company G, First Regiment, New Mexico Militia; Scott Moore Hose Company No. 1; Fergusson Hook & Ladder Company; the Flambeau Club, and a committee from the Grand Army of the Republic.

Citizens subscribed the necessary money to pay for John Braden's funeral and to pay for a monument to be erected in his memory. The Braden memorial, a fountain, was placed in Robinson Park, the only park then in Albuquerque. On the memorial were carved his name and the dates of his birth and death. John Braden was Albuquerque's first publicly acclaimed hero.

More than seventy years have come and gone since John Braden sacrificed his life that others might live. The monument, erected to commemorate his deed of valor, still stands in Robinson Park. Not one word, however, remains engraved on the monument to declare why it was erected, or whose memory it was designed to perpetuate.

On March 10, 1896, many people in Albuquerque were excited because of the arrival of Francis Schlatter, a strange and truly mysterious man, who appeared first in New Mexico in the Taos Valley. The people of northern New Mexico had called him *El Sanador,* the Healer or Curer, and had urged him to remain with them. He told them, however, that his time was not really his own; that he was under the "guidance of the Father," and must press on to an undisclosed destination. Schlatter was called "the Healer" by the Spanish-speaking people of northern New Mexico because it was reported that he had worked many cures through prayer and the laying on of hands.

When the Healer left Taos for Embudo, he was accompanied for twenty miles along the highway by hundreds of people, traveling on foot, on horseback, in buggies and wagons. Great crowds of people from Bernalillo, Alameda, Duranes and other nearby settlements accompanied Schlatter on his way to Albuquerque. Enroute to Albuquerque from the Taos Valley, Schlatter had stopped in Santa Fe, Peña Blanca and Cabezon. Every place he went the people welcomed him as a holy man. Some followers of the Healer, emotionally upset because of the miracles he was reported to have performed, heralded him as another Christ who had come to save the world from destruction. Schlatter's fame preceded him into Albuquerque, where he lived for some days with a Spanish-American family in Barelas at 1520 South Third Street.

I was very much interested in Schlatter because I was anxious to have him undertake the cure of my younger brother, Lawrence, eight years old, who had been afflicted with a lame leg since he was four years old. In later years, the medical doctors would probably have said his condition was due to an attack of infantile paralysis. During Lawrence's childhood and later years, Albuquerque doctors had failed to adequately diagnose his ailment or to prescribe a curative treatment, much to the sorrow and despair of our family.

After his arrival in Albuquerque, newspapers reported that Schlatter would meet afflicted people and their relatives and friends at the Mutual Protection Society Hall on Third Street, just south of Cromwell Avenue. I went to the hall, with my brother Lawrence, long before the time set for the meeting. Hundreds of people were gathered outside the building, competing to gain admission. Peace officers fought back the crowds in their attempt to control them. Taking Lawrence by the hand I got to the place in the hall near a raised platform on which the Healer was to stand. The hall was crowded with people leading the lame and the blind. The Healer entered the hall from a rear door, and began at once to bless hands extended to him. He also blessed handkerchiefs and other tokens extended to him by his followers. I had a close-up view of the Healer, and I can recall a picturesque figure wearing a long white garment, sandals on his feet. His hair was brown and hung down his back to his waist. It seemed to me that Francis Schlatter looked very much like a healer, a holy saintly man. After waiting for more than an hour, it was Lawrence's turn to be treated by the Healer. I walked beside my brother as he approached the Healer, and watched him as he placed his hands on my brother's head, praying and blessing him, it seemed to me, with the zeal of a priest and the fervor of a long-time friend. I was hoping for an immediate miracle to be performed by the Healer, right there and then. As Lawrence walked away from the holy man, he limped just as before. I realized that I had expected too much. Believing that I had done everything I could for my brother, I helped him out of doors through the crowd and we went to our home only a mile or so away. My brother received no benefit from our visit to Francis Schlatter, and he was a somewhat downcast boy for several days. Lawrence continued to be lame, with a noticeable limp until his death twelve years later, on May 8, 1908.

His mission in Albuquerque completed, according to

EARLY DAY MEMORIES 37

his public statement made in the newspapers, Francis Schlatter left Albuquerque on a cold, windy day in March, 1896. He was escorted to the boundary of the Isleta Indian reservation by dozens of people from Isleta Pueblo, the villages of Atrisco, Tomé, Los Padillas, and other nearby settlements. At last, in a scene reminiscent of one depicting the Saviour in Biblical days, the Healer bade his followers farewell, blessed them and then struck out across country, alone, scantily clad, arriving in Seboyeta, Valencia County, in three days. Newspaper versions told of his later activities. After resting in this village for several days, during which he continued in his missionary work of praying and healing, Schlatter announced that he was leaving for "the mining camps" and started toward Mogollon. Disregarding the protests of those who predicted he would perish in the deep snow and cold weather, the Healer started on his journey again. He traveled alone, through a vast country of mountain and plain where there were but few roads and trails. It was believed at first that Schlatter had perished on the way, but Silver City newspapers, on April 14, reported that he had reached a mining camp in safety, had started down the Gila River, was reported as finally having been seen 100 miles south of the San Carlos Indian reservation. Weeks later word filtered through the Mexican border that the Healer had arrived in Cananea, Sonora, Mexico. Months later Schlatter was reported to have died in Mexico, at an unknown time and place. (In a chapter entitled "The Healer Comes to Datil," in her book, *No Life for a Lady* [1941] Agnes Morley Cleaveland gives her recollections of Francis Schlatter. Dr. Myra Ellen Jenkins, Senior Archivist at the State Records Center, Santa Fe, recalled recently that Dr. E. L. Hewitt, prominent New Mexico archaeologist, became interested in the story of the Healer, and wrote about him in *Camp*

Fire and Trail, U.N.M. Press, 1943. Dr. Hewitt claimed to have discovered Schlatter's place of death, and to have recovered the rod or staff Schlatter carried on his journeys, which Hewitt presented to the New Mexico Museum.)

In 1895 New Mexico was a Territory, without a vote in the electoral college. Nevertheless, William Jennings Bryan of Nebraska, then 36 years old, not too well known at the time, visited Albuquerque on January 20, 1895, and delivered a speech.

Mr. Bryan came to Albuquerque as a gesture of friendship for Harvey B. Fergusson, a prominent lawyer, with whom he had served in Congress of the United States when Mr. Fergusson was the delegate in Congress from New Mexico. On July 10, 1895, some six months after his speech in Albuquerque, Bryan was nominated for president of the United States on the Democratic ticket. In Albuquerque the distinguished visitor spoke from a platform erected for the occasion on the vacant lots on the southeast corner of Fourth Street and Railroad Avenue, on which Rosenwald Brothers, years later, built a three story building to house Albuquerque's first department store. I went to the Bryan Day celebration, heard Mr. Bryan speak to a large crowd. I was too young to understand his speech on free silver, or his explanation of the 16 to 1 theory. However, I was sufficiently impressed by his oratory and magnetic personality to become and remain a Bryan admirer for many years. At the end of Mr. Bryan's speech, Mr. Fergusson invited all those who wished to do so, to come to the speaker's platform to be introduced to the city's guest. I joined the crowd, shook hands with Mr. Bryan and then went to the end of the line. I ascended the platform once more and shook hands with Mr. Bryan. After I had repeated this routine several times, I found that I was the only person remaining, that in fact I was the line. Mr. Bryan must have observed the same situation because when he shook my hand again, he smiled down at me and said: "Young man, it seems to me that some place, some time, I've seen you before."

Months later, the newspapers stated that William McKinley, Republican candidate for president, would be in Albuquerque for several hours, that he would speak from the rear of a private car at the Santa Fe Railway depot. Mr. McKinley was to arrive in Albuquerque from the east on Santa Fe train No. 1, at 7:10 p.m., was to confer with Territorial leaders and prominent citizens, address the people, and leave at 11 o'clock on the El Paso train for Deming. His car was to be attached in Deming to a Southern Pacific train for a tour of Pacific Coast states. Having seen Mr. Bryan, by now the democratic candidate, I was anxious to see Mr. McKinley. I was at the depot well in advance of the time scheduled for arrival of the McKinley train but it was reported late. The large crowd which had gathered at the depot to greet Mr. McKinley at the station began to dwindle in numbers as more up-to-date arrival times were reported on the bulletin board. Finally, at 11 o'clock those still waiting at the depot were told that the telegraph office had just given out the information that the train had just then left Lamy, that Mr. McKinley had retired for the night, would not make an appearance in Albuquerque. Disappointed because I had not seen Mr. McKinley, I went home.

Among my early day recollections is one about a picket fence-gate, carried away by Hallowe'en pranksters in 1897, from the home of Otto Dieckman, 801 South Third Street, two blocks distant from my home at 323 West Atlantic Avenue. The day after the gate disappeared, Dieckman let it be known among the boys of the neighborhood that he would give a prize to anyone who would return the gate. The prize was to be a pass to a prize fight film being shown for two nights at the National Guard Armory, First Street and Gold Avenue. Upon learning the interesting news, I hurried to the Dieckman home, rang the bell and when Mr. Dieckman came to the door I told him that I believed I could find the missing gate for him. Following me a short distance to an alfalfa patch in the John D. Torlina orchard, I pointed out the missing gate, maintaining a discreet silence when Mr. Dieckman, looking suspiciously in my direction, remarked, "Now, if we could only find the boys who took the gate."

True to his promise, Otto Dieckman, who was agent for the Armory, gave me a pass to the film show. The next night I saw the first motion picture to be shown in Albuquerque, the boxing contest between Bob Fitzsimmons and James Corbett, for the championship of the world, fought at Carson City, Nevada, on March 17, 1897. My present recollection of the film, although somewhat hazy, is that it was jumpy and sketchy, probably a number of still pictures shown in rapid sequence, but nevertheless a thrilling experience.

On May 27, 1898, barefoot and scantily clad because of the almost summer weather, I was seated comfortably in front of the Eight Spot Saloon, on the wooden sidewalk on the southwest corner of the junction of First and Second Streets with Atlantic Avenue, thinking regretfully perhaps, that I had missed the runaway of the preceding day in which the Balling bakery wagon had been demolished and pies and cakes scattered to the four winds on a nearby street, "all up for grabs." I was almost twelve years old and am relying on the date of May 27, 1898, as being correct, having taken it from Albuquerque newspapers, and from the opinion of the Territorial Supreme

Court Reporter in the case of Territory of New Mexico vs. Ruiz, 10 N.M. 120.

My reverie on that occasion was interrupted by sounds of shouting and yelling, coming from a cloud of dust enveloping two galloping horsemen riding "hell for leather" south on Second Street, squarely in my direction. Both riders were brandishing six-shooters, firing recklessly as they neared the Atlantic Avenue intersection. In a matter of seconds, the horsemen had galloped south on Second Street. Within a few moments the gathering crowd of people became aware of the cause of the excitement. One of the horseback riders, whose name I learned later was José P. Ruiz, had killed Patricio O'Bannon, five years old, who had been shot while playing with several children in the street near the O'Bannon home at Barelas Road and Bridge Street. I knew Patricio O'Bannon by sight and became well acquainted in later years with Daniel O'Bannon, a brother, once a cigarmaker for Kirster Brothers factory, and for several years Assessor of Bernalillo County.

Within a short time word came back to the neighborhood of Second Street and Atlantic Avenue that Undersheriff Ed Newcomer had arrested Ruiz, the alleged killer, who, it was reported, had been drinking in downtown Albuquerque and had decided on a "shoot-'em-up" spree, with fatal results.

On June 1, 1900, I was up early and rode my bicycle to Pat Gleason's Gold Star Saloon in Old Town, located on the south side of that part of the road known today as Central Avenue, midway between the courthouse, in which Ruiz had been convicted, and the county jail in which he had been held prisoner. The jury found Ruiz guilty of first degree murder. The Supreme Court upheld the verdict of the lower court.

I never learned how or why Pat Gleason's "Gold Star"

had been chosen as the place of execution. Long since torn down, the Gold Star, as of 1900, was not considered a very attractive place. Tradition had it that Billy the Kid at one time had patronized the Gold Star bar on at least one occasion, a fable encouraged and perpetuated by no less an authority than Elfego Baca. Baca seriously claimed to have become acquainted with Bonney at the Gold Star and to have hobnobbed with him about Old Town. Pat Gleason and "Gunnysack" Riley, his head porter, had cleaned up the Gold Star premises, and built a wooden fence enclosing a pasture area in the rear of the saloon, and made the place as presentable as possible for the accommodation of the people Sheriff Thomas S. Hubbell had invited to witness the hanging.

By eight o'clock, an hour before the time fixed for the hanging, I presented myself for admission at the execution corral gate. A deputy sheriff refused to allow me to enter, as might have been expected. Long years later, a friend gave me the original printed pass that had been issued to Dr. Pearce, the official physician for the execution, which read as follows:

> Pass Dr. John F. Pearce to witness the execution of José P. Ruiz on June 1, 1900, for the murder of Patricio O'Bannon, on May 27, 1898. T. S. Hubbell, Sheriff.

The invitations issued by Sheriff Thomas Hubbell of Bernalillo County, could not hope to compare favorably with the more elaborately worded invitations sent out several months before by a brother sheriff bidding guests to attend a hanging in adjoining Navajo County, Arizona. On November 28, 1899, Sheriff F. J. Wattron had mailed out the invitations from Holbrook, Arizona. J. Lorenzo Hubbell, of Ganado, Arizona, years later a celebrity among artists and sculptors, brother of Sheriff Thomas

Photostats of early day "hanging passes."

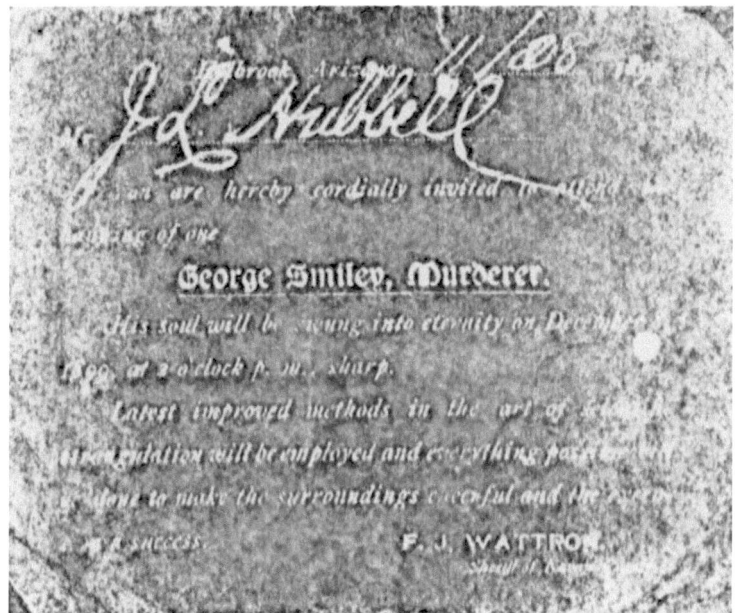

Pass *Dr. J.B. Pearce*
To witness the execution of Jose
P. Ruiz, on June 1, 1900, for the
murder of Patricio O'Bannon, on
May 27th, 1898.

J. L. Hubbell
SHERIFF.

Holbrook, Arizona

J. L. Hubbell

You are hereby cordially invited to attend
the hanging of one

George Smiley, Murderer.

His soul will be swung into eternity on December
8, 1899, at 2 o'clock p. m., sharp.

Latest improved methods in the art of strangulation will be employed and everything possible will be done to make the surroundings cheerful and the event a success.

F. J. WATTRON,
Sheriff.

Hubbell, received one of the invitations. A photostat of the original was shown to me by a member of the Hubbell family many years after the soul of the unfortunate George Smiley, on whose behalf the invitations had been issued, had been "swung into eternity." The typographical gem read as follows:

> Holbrook, Arizona, November 11, 1899. Mr. J. L. Hubbell: You are hereby cordially invited to attend the hanging of one George Smiley, murderer. His soul will be swung into eternity on December 8, 1899 at 2:00 p.m. sharp. Latest improved methods in the art of scientific strangulation will be employed and everything possible will be done to make the surroundings cheerful and the execution a success.
> F. J. Wattron, Sheriff of Navajo County

Having been turned away at the admission gate on June 1, 1900, and prevented from witnessing the Ruiz hanging, I had mingled with the crowd gathered in the street in front of the Gold Star and found that some of the would-be spectators of the hanging intended to attend funeral services for the deceased at the nearby church of San Felipe de Neri. Upon entering the church, I was given a seat in the middle aisle, managed to get in line at the conclusion of the requiem mass, and with the other mourners viewed the body in the casket, noticing as I walked along, the blue strangulation marks on the throat of the deceased.

More than a score of years later, I mentioned the O'Bannon incident to Felix Gianotti, the embalmer, who had prepared the body of José P. Ruiz for burial. Gianotti told me: "They hanged the wrong man that day. They should have hanged the men who made the rot-gut whiskey sold to José Ruiz by those saloon keepers."

CHAPTER THREE

School and Work

IN SEPTEMBER 1892, I applied for admission at a temporary parochial school located in a one-story *adobe* building (still standing) at the southeast corner of Sixth Street and Railroad Avenue (524 Central Ave., SW), taught by Sisters St. Claire and Isabella. The Sisters told me they had no first grade in the school and advised me to await the opening of the new St. Mary's, then being built a short distance to the north. The school at Sixth and Railroad was called the "switch school" because there was a street car passing-track in the middle of Railroad Avenue. The switch school numbered among its pupils several tough boys, including Pat Foy and Pat Murphy, both of whom I knew, although they were much older. So, in September, 1893, within two months of being seven years old, I became a first grade pupil in St. Mary's Parochial School. St. Mary's was located in a recently completed brick building, trimmed with sandstone, on North Sixth Street, between Copper Avenue and Tijeras Road. The school was under the management of the Sisters of Charity of Cincinnati. Sister Mary Alacoque taught the first, second and third grades. Sister Seraphine was the teacher of grades four to seven, and Sister Ildefonse eight to twelve. My mother had taught me to read before I started to school, so I was in advance of some members of the class.

Some thirty boys were enrolled in the first, second and third grades at the newly established St. Mary's. I recall several boys about whose background I learned more in the years ahead. There was George Collier, son of the Hon. Needham C. Collier, Judge of the Second Judicial District Court, appointed to the court through the friendship of Edward Douglas White, at the time United States Senator from Louisiana, and later Chief Justice of the Supreme Court of the United States. Collier and White had served in the same regiment in the Confederate Army during the Civil War. Robert Crichton, author of *The Secret of Santa Vittoria,* a best-selling novel published in 1966, is a grandson of Judge Collier. Robert Crichton's mother, May Collier, a daughter of Judge Collier, and his father, Kyle Crichton, also a writer, lived in Albuquerque for many years.

In St. Mary's of my day Henry F. Connelly was a boy about my age, whom I got to know fairly well in grade school. Quite likely I would have paid more attention to Connelly if I had then known what I learned years later, that he was a grandson and namesake of Henry F. Connelly, Governor of the Territory of New Mexico throughout the Civil War years.

Tranquilino Armijo was another member of the first grade class whom I recall in retrospect. He was the younger brother of George W. Armijo, in later years a prominent political figure in New Mexico, a veteran of many party battles, sometimes serving the Republican party, sometimes a valiant soldier in the Democratic organization, serving each cause faithfully.

I also recall in the first few grades at St. Mary's a boy named Damas Provencher, who with his brother Hector,

SCHOOL AND WORK 47

rode to school each day astride a burro. The Provenchers stabled the animal in the school yard several hours each day, fed him a few wisps of alfalfa hay at noon, and rode away in the late afternoon to a home several miles distant from town. In retrospect it appears that his school companions might have treated the Provenchers with more consideration if they had known more of their background, of which I was ignorant until many years had elapsed. In 1892 Damas Provencher's father, also named Damas Provencher, a merchant, had been murdered at El Gallo, a settlement in the old Fort Wingate-San Rafael area, three miles south of Grants, Valencia County, New Mexico, while serving as an election judge. Provencher had been killed while counting ballots on election night, by a shot fired through a window pane at the precinct polling place. The assassination was probably the culmination of a quarrel among politicians.

Sister Seraphine, one of my teachers at St. Mary's, organized St. Mary's Cadet Corps of some forty boys. They drilled with wooden guns, marched in the Territorial Fair parade in 1897, and were awarded a silver medal at the Fair for proficiency in military tactics. On one occasion Gen. Eugene A. Carr, retired U.S.A., reviewed the Corps. In later years I learned that the General, at the time a resident of Albuquerque, had served as a major officer during the Civil War and commanded Fort Wingate in the latter years of his military career. General Carr's grandchildren, Clark M. Carr, of Carco Aviation, and Virginia Carr Van Soelen, were born in Albuquerque. Great grandchildren, Theodore and Don Van Soelen, sons of the late Theodore Van Soelen, nationally known artist, and the late Virginia Carr Van Soelen, are native residents of New Mexico.

Sister Seraphine also organized a Sanctuary Society

composed of thirty altar boys, and on Holy Thursday the members read aloud in the parish church the twenty-sixth chapter of St. Matthew. Sister alternated the principal character speaking parts to various boys, the part of Christ being assigned to me several times. For many years thereafter I could recite the entire chapter almost word for word and at the present time with a bit of prompting can do so.

I left St. Mary's School on June 1, 1900, and went to work as a messenger for the Western Union Telegraph Company, 207 South Second Street. I had passed the eighth grade examinations and was confident of being promoted to the ninth, the first year of high school. However, it was all too apparent that my father's health, slowly but steadily deteriorating following a siege of pneumonia the previous year, would prevent him from being physically able to carry on. In a day when there were no such benefits as workmen's compensation, and pensions and sick leave with pay were benefits of the distant future, there was no alternative but to look to me to take over in his place, and to the extent possible become the bread winner of the family. The Western Union furnished me with a messenger regulation cap and a badge reading: "Western Union Telegraph and Cable Co. Messenger No. 2." Maurice Vaughan, the Western Union manager helped me on my way by introducing me to Henry Brockmier, agent for the Phoenix bicycle, who had a shop at 120 West Gold. I bought a Phoenix bike from Mr. Brockmier, price thirty-five dollars, no down payment, monthly installments of five dollars, without interest. Maurice Vaughan resigned within a few months to manage a Logan and Bryan stockbroker's office on the second floor of the Cromwell Building. The office, probably the first of its kind in Albuquerque, was owned by W. P. Metcalf, of Metcalf and Strauss, merchandise house.

Western Union Telegraph office Albuquerque where the author standing behind the counter to the left was employed in 1900.

In 1900, when I started to deliver Western Union telegrams, the intersection at Gold and Second was the hub of the business section of the town. The principal entrance way to the Santa Fe depot, at the dead end of First Street and Gold Avenue on the east and the San Felipe Hotel at Fifth and Gold on the west, were largely responsible for this situation. Railroad Avenue, the name of which was changed to Central Avenue in 1912, was a comparatively quiet and unimportant street in 1900, when contrasted with Gold Avenue, on which were located the First National Bank, the Albuquerque *Daily Citizen,* Wells, Fargo & Co. Express office, Albuquerque *Journal-Democrat,* the Commercial Club building and other important establishments. In 1900, however, the post office, located for some years at 117 West Gold, had moved to a building at Second and Silver, built for and leased to the government by Joseph Barnett.

According to the official United States government census in 1900 Albuquerque had a population of 6,326; Old Town a population of 1,191; suburbs immediately adjacent to Albuquerque 4,613. The total population for Albuquerque and immediate suburbs was 12,130.

In my first few days in the Western Union everything in the office seemed strange and alien to me, particularly the clickety clack noises made by a dozen or more telegraph instruments all ticking away simultaneously it seemed, and apparently all in conflict and utter confusion. I discovered, however, within a few months, that order could be developed out of apparent chaos, and that the telegraph signals could be made readily understandable. I studied the Morse Code, with its dots and dashes representing letters of the alphabet and figures numbering from 1 to 0. Within a few months I could send and receive telegrams. I learned telegraphy, I fear, at the expense of

SCHOOL AND WORK

ruining the disposition of James Merchant, the operator at Bland, now a ghost town, but at the time a thriving gold mining camp sixty miles from Albuquerque, forty miles by Santa Fe Railroad to Wallace, now Domingo, and twenty miles north from the rail head at Wallace. The stage line was operated by W. L. Trimble using six-horse conveyances between Wallace, Bland and Albermarle, site of the richest ore producing mine in the Cochiti district.

The Western Union had built the combination telegraph and long distance telephone line from Albuquerque to Bland, perhaps the first attempt to establish long distance telephone service between Albuquerque and the outside world. The Michael Pupin coil was as yet a thing of the future, and the Albuquerque-Bland line was unsuccessful for all practical purposes. As a result the telegraph was used almost exclusively between Albuquerque and Bland. After serving an apprenticeship in the, to me, magical world of the Morse code, I noticed that the operators in the Albuquerque office were reluctant to "work" with Bland, probably because most of the telegrams sent over the wire were in code. The Bland wire was ignored in the Albuquerque office to the extent that Merchant, the Bland operator, would call and call, repeatedly trying to get Albuquerque to answer. Anxious to learn how to telegraph, I capitalized on the situation, answering the Bland call, spelling out the words, "send slow." Before long there was established a routine arrangement with the Bland operator, to "send slow" and I learned to send and receive telegrams. Most of the telegrams were addressed to concerns in Boston, Mass., which owned the mines operated in the Albermarle area.

Many telegrams sent over the Bland wire were addressed to Albuquerque concerns, among them the San José Market, owned by G. L. Brooks and associates, the Southwestern Brewery and Ice Company owned by Jacob and Henry Loeb, First National Bank, the Bank of Commerce, and W. L. Trimble, stage line owner, whose son, William Lawrence Trimble, for many years a TWA pilot, is presently a TWA executive at Orly Field, Paris. Because of the traffic on the Bland line I soon became conscious of the extent of a considerable Bland "trade" which flowed into Albuquerque. As a messenger for the Western Union, delivering telegrams every day, from 7 a.m. to 9 p.m., I soon learned the location of the streets and avenues of the town, which was bounded at the time on the east by High Street, on the north by Mountain Road, on the south by Cromwell Avenue, and on the west by a line intersecting Huning Castle.

Franz Huning's Glorieta flour mill, located in 1900 at today's Central Avenue and Laguna Boulevard, was still in operation. Franz Huning received several telegrams each week. On several occasions I delivered telegrams to Mr. Huning, then an old man, in person at his residence, the Huning Castle built in 1883, torn down and demolished in 1955. I always knew what to expect on such occasions in the way of conversation. The ritual hardly ever varied. Franz Huning in person, generally with "Grossmutter" Huning hovering in the background to observe the fun, would answer the doorbell. "Young man," he would begin, "I presume you have a telegram for me, and wish to deliver it?" The reply, "Yes, Mr. Huning." "Young man," he would continue, "I understand that if you deliver the telegram to me in Old Town instead of New Town, there will be a ten-cent delivery charge. Is that correct?" The reply: "Yes, Mr. Huning." Then: "Young man, I don't know whether you recognize it or not, but if I stand here (placing himself behind the west

Castle Huning in Albuquerque from a photograph taken in 1897 showing Franz Huning near the entrance to his 700 acre estate, patterned after his recollections of castles on the Rhine in his native Germany.

Courtesy: W. Haussamen

door of the double door entrance) I am in Old Town, but if I stand here (placing himself behind the east door of the entrance) I am in New Town." The reply: "Yes, Mr. Huning, I understand that to be the case." The ending of the skit was always satisfactory and acceptable to the messenger boy. Franz Huning would take a telegram in Old Town or New Town, as he chose, but always rewarded the boy with a twenty-five cent tip.

In the course of my work as messenger I got to know by name or by sight most of the prominent business and professional men of the town. I got sufficiently acquainted with Fred Fornoff, the town marshal, to ask for permission to ride my bicycle on the sidewalk when the streets were muddy. Fornoff was in the news in 1908 as the first law officer to talk to Wayne Brazil after he admitted killing Pat Garrett, slayer of Billy the Kid, on February 29, 1908. He gained further national notice when he jumped into the ring at Las Vegas, New Mexico, on July 4, 1912, and stopped the Jack Johnson-Jim Flynn heavyweight championship fight.

Albuquerque in 1900 was a genuine Wild West town, supporting numerous saloons and many gambling houses, in which roulette, fan tan, chuck-a-luck, poker, keno and other gambling games were operated on a wide-open basis day and night, gambling being legal and lawful at the time. The town police knew about the red light district, located in the heart of the business district, because the town authorities relied largely on the "fines" collected each month to support and maintain the municipal government.

On or about November 5, 1900, I was sent by the Western Union office to the First National Bank to get several large bills changed into bills of smaller denominations. I went direct to the bank, only a short distance away, at

Second and Gold, had the bills changed at the cage of Cashier Frank McKee. Returning to the Western Union office, Manager Fred Tuohy counted the currency in my presence, then told me I was short five dollars. I returned to the bank at once, told my troubles to Mr. McKee, who was sympathetic and promised to count the cash in his cage at 3 o'clock, at which time he could then tell whether he was $5.00 over or just even. Mr. McKee warned me: "Whenever you cash a check or make change always wait until you see if you receive the correct amount, or are being shorted. If you think there has been a mistake, make your protest known at once, there and then." I have always remembered and acted on Mr. McKee's advice. Back at the First National Bank promptly at 3 o'clock, Mr. McKee told me that his cash balanced to the penny. I then realized that the five dollars was my loss. Sorrowfully I relayed the word to the boss at the Western Union, who told me he would deduct the money from my pay at the end of the month. A few days later I was riding my bicycle on Gold Avenue, between First and Second Streets, almost opposite Brockmier's bicycle shop. Coming in the opposite direction were a horse and wagon, being driven by a rancher who I learned later was from Alameda. The horse was jogging along at a moderate rate of speed in the center of the street. All of a sudden my bicycle and I had collided with the horse and wagon. I emerged from the collision with the spokes and rim of the front wheel of the bicycle smashed. I took the bicycle the few steps to Brockmier's shop, where it was repaired the next day at a cost of $3.75. Financially the week had been disastrous for me.

    I continued to work as messenger for a year, then was promoted to be counter clerk, a job that entailed waiting on customers, helping to keep the messenger boys busy, finding out why they had failed to deliver telegrams. One of my star messenger boys of the period was Willie Haney. On several occasions Willie brought with him to the Western Union office Fred Haney, his brother, then three years old, in the years to come one of the great baseball players and managers of all time (long time manager of the Milwaukee Braves). Fred Haney has been perhaps Albuquerque's greatest contribution to professional baseball.

My salary as counter clerk was twenty-five dollars a month. Another year went by and in June, 1902, I was promoted to be what W. T. McCreight, one of the publishers of the Albuquerque *Daily Citizen*, described in a squib in his paper as a "full fledged operator." Part of my work was to copy a pony Associated Press report for the *Citizen* each week day, sent out from Denver, copied by telegraphers in Pueblo, Las Vegas, Santa Fe, Albuquerque and El Paso.

As a "full fledged telegraph operator" my salary was fifty dollars a month, by far the most money I had ever earned. By working two Sunday nights a month I was paid $5.00 additional, bringing my wages up to $55.00 a month. The Sunday shift was from 4 p.m. to 6 p.m. and from 7 p.m. until 2:30 a.m. on Monday, by which time "30" was generally sent over the wires from Denver which carried the night A.P. report for the Albuquerque *Journal*.

In August, 1902, the Western Union sent me to Santa Fe to work in the office there during the illness of Miss Clara Zimmer, the manager. One of the interesting sights in Santa Fe in the summer of 1902 was the promenade in the plaza, accompanied by the music of the First Regimental Territorial Band. As a result of the custom then prevailing in Santa Fe, the men and women, boys and girls all participated in the promenade. The males prome-

SCHOOL AND WORK 57

naded in one direction, the females in the opposite direction, all participants finally sorting out and promenading as couples at the culmination of the promenade, a gala custom still observed in some towns in Mexico. Miss Zimmer resigned as manager of the Western Union in Santa Fe in 1905, and was married to Richard H. Hanna, an attorney, who later became Chief Justice of the Supreme Court of New Mexico.

On April 18, 1906, the San Francisco fire and earthquake paralyzed the Bay Region telegraph facilities. As a result many telegrams were routed through the El Paso office, acting as a relay station for Los Angeles, Dallas and Denver. The Western Union sent me to El Paso to work as a relief operator, at a salary of seventy dollars a month, plus a dollar an hour for unlimited overtime. In the El Paso office I was first assigned to work for a time on the Juarez wire sending and receiving messages, mostly in Spanish, to and from Chihuahua, Torreon, Durango and other cities in Mexico. At other times I sent and received telegrams for hour after hour on all available wires, most of them to or from Oakland or San Francisco. Becoming ill while employed in El Paso, partly from overwork at the key and sounder, I went to a physician who examined my chest and rendered the verdict: "Quit your job as telegraph operator and get work that will keep you out of doors." I took a day off (*"Cinco de Mayo,"* May 5, 1906, a national holiday in Mexico at the time) crossed the Rio Grande on the street railway, and went to the plaza opposite the cathedral in Juarez. I found a bench in a secluded spot, stretched myself out on it, hopeful for a bit of rest. I was dozing away nicely after a few moments. Then a Mexican *rurale* appeared, a policeman's club in hand. He gave the soles of my shoes a couple of whacks with the club, and issued an ultimatum in Spanish, the English equivalent of which was: "Get out of here at once or you will find yourself in jail."

Returning to El Paso, I explained my health problem to Chief Operator Joseph W. Brooks, an understanding man, a brother of Belvidere Brooks, soon thereafter elected President of the Western Union, and made arrangements to go home. Once again in Albuquerque, I took a thirty-day leave of absence, hopeful of recuperating sufficiently during that time to resume work permanently. I discussed my problem with Dr. Walter G. Hope, my physician, always to me a kind and sympathetic friend. Dr. Hope confirmed the diagnosis of the El Paso physician, which was again confirmed later from X-ray pictures taken by Dr. J. R. Van Atta, my good friend of many years, a pioneer physician who established the first X-ray clinical laboratory in Albuquerque on November 17, 1914.

By August 1, 1906, I was back at work in the Albuquerque office, but pondering over the prospects of quitting my job and getting an out-of-doors one as my doctors had recommended. One afternoon I answered a call from Bluewater, a station on the Santa Fe railway between Grants and Gallup, and took down a telegram on the typewriter addressed to George G. Anderson, Alvarado Hotel, Albuquerque, signed G. C. Scharf, Resident Engineer, which read: "Garrett and Alarid quitting to return to school, send replacements at once." I knew the background of the situation. Garrett and Alarid, both from Santa Fe, had been doing summer work on the Bluewater Development Company surveying corps; Garrett was going back to the New Mexico Military Institute at Roswell, and Alarid was returning to St. Michael's College in Santa Fe, where he was a star athlete. Without thinking too much of the consequences if my action was called to the attention of Western Union officials, I wrote the following note on my typewriter: "Dear Mr. Anderson. I would like to apply for one of the positions mentioned in the telegram from Mr. Scharf." Enclosing the telegram and note, to which I had signed my name, in an envelope addressed to G. G. Anderson, I sent them by a messenger boy to the Alvarado Hotel. Within the hour Mr. Anderson was in the Western Union office. I knew him by sight, knew that he was from Denver and was Consulting Engineer on the Bluewater project. "Young man," Mr. Anderson began at once after his arrival, "I must say you have adopted a novel method of applying for a job." I told Mr. Anderson that I was very anxious to get out of doors, giving him the background of my situation. After a brief discussion, he said: "When could you go?" I left for Bluewater, 112 miles west of Albuquerque, the next night, taking with me Robert E. McCabe, another young man anxious to get out-of-door work. I had assembled a bed roll, a few articles of clothing, including a slicker, and had bought, on Mr. Anderson's recommendation, a pair of surveyor boots.

My new job, as rear chainman with the surveying corps, paid sixty dollars a month, ten dollars more than my Western Union salary. My work at Bluewater made possible the realization of my dream for a life out of doors, in a country that held much magic for me; bracing air, the heavy scent of pine and cedar trees on the nearby mountains and hills, glimpses on the far horizon of a magnificent valley, were factors of that magic.

In 1906, Bluewater had a population of fewer than a dozen people. The settlement had been built around and about Welcome Chapman's General Store. I soon learned from Chapman that the Bluewater country was being settled by members of the Church of Latter Day Saints of Jesus Christ. Through Chapman and his neighbors I became better acquainted with the beliefs of the members of that church. I learned much about the Angel Maroni, bantered good naturedly with my newly found friends about the merits and demerits of the Book of Mormon, and argued concerning the facts and legends associated with the lives of Joseph Smith and Brigham Young. I grew to respect the sincerity with which the members of the colony adhered to and practiced their religion. Forty years later it was my good fortune to form a friendship with J. Reuben Clark, long one of the Twelve Apostles of the Church, while serving with him as a Director of The Equitable Life Assurance Society of the United States.

Bluewater was located in a valley containing some 12,000 acres of agricultural land on the western slope of Mount Taylor. Bluewater Canyon, to the north and west of the valley, had been a challenge to men with an urge to build a dam which would impound the water accumulated at the junction of Bluewater and Cottonwood creeks. U.S. Army Engineers based at nearby Fort Wingate had dreamed of having the government build for the Navajo Indians a dam at the head of Bluewater Canyon which would irrigate all land in the Bluewater Valley. As early as 1885 an earthen dam had been built by private enterprise which was washed away by flood waters in 1899. By 1906 engineers were again in the field, surveying for the dam site, for main canals and laterals. I was glad to be a member of the 1906 engineering corps. The corps surveyed and resurveyed every acre in the valley, checked and double checked the figures. In tramping over the Bluewater area, all members of the crews had undoubtedly walked repeatedly over the Paddy Martinez country, many years later found to contain priceless deposits of uranium ore. The atomic bomb and demand for uranium ingredi-

SCHOOL AND WORK 61

ent products eventually altered the face of the Bluewater Valley. The irrigation project on which I worked was eventually completed in 1910, and in favorable years the harvest yielded annually an average of 1,200 carloads of vegetables, mostly carrots and lettuce, shipped to market over the Santa Fe railroad. The time came, however, after the atomic explosion in 1945 when water rights in the Bluewater Valley were of a greater value for mining and milling than for agricultural use. As a result, the Bluewater Valley today is not the horticultural empire envisaged by its early-day promoters, but instead supplies a vital product for an industry not dreamed of in 1906. The Grants-Milan area, tributary to the Bluewater Valley, is dotted with important mining and milling enterprises.

I spent my birthday, on November 7, 1906, in a driving rain storm, holding the rear end of a surveyor's chain, happy in the thought that my health was improving and encouraged by the hope that my prospects for the future were not too dismal. However, by December 1, the fall rains had turned to sleet and snow. The surveying crews, unable to continue work in the deep snow, were laid off until spring.

After leaving my job with the Bluewater Development Co., I worked at several occupations during the next year. For a brief time I was employed at Vaughn as a concrete bridge inspector by the Eastern Railway of New Mexico, a subsidiary of the Santa Fe Railroad, which was building the Belen cut-off. Later I worked for a time for the Santa Fe in the Belen yards, helping on industrial trackage surveys. Returning to Albuquerque after completing the work with the Santa Fe Engineering Corps in Belen, I learned that the Clerk of the Board of Education had resigned. I applied for the position calling personally on all eight members of the Board of Education, among them

R. W. Hopkins, George R. Craig, A. A. Sedillo, and Frank H. Strong. The Board gave me the position at a salary of sixty dollars per month, and I glady accepted.

The bookkeeping for the Board of Education was rather a simple task. I had learned something of accounting while working for the telegraph company and I put such knowledge to use in the city-schools work; writing out checks, filling in the stubs, posting the journal, writing up the ledgers, and reconciling bank balances of public funds; all such funds were produced through ad valorem tax receipts and proceeds of poll taxes.

The school system in the Albuquerque of 1907 consisted of a Central High School, a two-story white brick building of eight classrooms, and several administrative offices, located on the northeast corner of Third Street and Lead Avenue, and four ward-schools of six classrooms each. The First Ward building was located on the southeast corner of North Edith Street and Grand Avenue; the Second Ward building in the 700 block on South Edith Street; the Third Ward building on the southwest corner of Fourth Street and Iron Avenue, and the Fourth Ward building on the southwest corner of Sixth Street and Fruit Avenue. Not a trace of any one of these buildings remains today. All the ward buildings were built in 1893 from the proceeds of a $90,000 bond issue.

During my time as Clerk of the Board in 1907 and part of 1908 the school staff consisted of a superintendent with a monthly salary of $383.33; a clerk at $60.00; five janitors, each paid a monthly salary of $80.00; five principals with salaries ranging from $125.00 to $135.00. There were forty-three grade school teachers with starting salaries of $55.00 per month, with maximum salaries of $85.00 per month. High school teachers of history, Latin, science and mathematics were paid from $83.33 to $125.00 per month,

SCHOOL AND WORK 63

depending on the years of service. Music and art supervisors were paid $133.33 per month. One of my duties was to make out and deliver the pay checks to the employees on the first of each month. On paydays the teachers appeared to be pleased to have me knock on classroom doors, ordinarily forbidden, and deliver the payday checks.

Occasionally a pupil from one of the five schools would knock on Superintendent Sterling's office door and hand him a note, which I knew from experience was a request from a principal's office that corporal punishment be administered to the notebearer. It was Superintendent Sterling's practice to have a heart to heart talk with the culprit, at the conclusion of which he would summon me, using always the same formula: "Mr. Keleher, this young man has been judged incorrigible by his principal, and I have been asked to punish him. I want you to be a witness and be prepared to testify, if necessary, that the punishment was not excessive." Superintendent Sterling would then take from a drawer of his desk a length of garden hose and give the offender a few whacks. This formality having been complied with, he would send the culprit back to his school principal with a note saying he had been properly punished and authorizing reinstatement in his class.

While working in Superintendent Sterling's office in 1908 I became acquainted with John Milne, teacher of mathematics in the Central High School, who told me that he was from Scotland. (John Milne and I then began a friendship which continued steadfast over the years until his death on September 5, 1956. He succeeded W. D. Sterling as superintendent of the Albuquerque City Schools, a position he held with great success until his death.)

One of the unexpected rewards connected with my

work as clerk of the Board of Education was that it afforded me the opportunity to read at will in the Central School library, located in a room next to my office. I can recall only a few titles of the many books I read, among them the *Autocrat of the Breakfast Table,* by Oliver Wendell Holmes. I remember discovering A. Conan Doyle. Reading the adventures of Sherlock Holmes marked the beginning of long-time interest in Doyle.

During the time I was working for the Board of Education, Rev. A. M. Mandalari, S.J., pastor of the Church of the Immaculate Conception, told me that he had arranged to have Rev. Thomas E. Sherman, Jesuit, son of General William T. Sherman of Civil War fame, come to Albuquerque and deliver a series of lectures. Father Mandalari asked me if I would write articles on the lectures for the *Journal,* saying he had already arranged with Mr. Macpherson to publish them. I accepted at once.

I attended the Sherman lectures faithfully each night, made notes, hurried to the *Journal* office to type out the report. Father Sherman lectured on social and economic problems of the day, touching only indirectly on Catholic doctrine, and his lectures were well attended. As a mark of respect and evidence of good will toward a son of an old comrade-in-arms, a delegation of some twenty members of G. K. Warren Post No. 1, Grand Army of the Republic, attended one lecture in a body, accompanied by a delegation from the Women's Relief Corps, an affiliate organization.

In my boyhood in Albuquerque, the members of the Grand Army of the Republic held an important place in the life of the community. Its members appeared to be welded together by invisible bonds of patriotism, loyalty to country and devotion to the American flag, cemented

SCHOOL AND WORK 65

by ties which stretched from the hearts of comrades to long extinguished campfires on almost forgotten battlefields. However unimportant the organization and its members might be in the everyday life and affairs of the community, the Civil War veteran became all-important at G.A.R. encampments, and on May 30, Decoration Day, and July 4 in each year. In my early days I knew most Union Veterans by sight and many by name. As the years went by I became quite well acquainted with some of them, gladly spent time among those veterans with whom I was personally acquainted, listening to their wartime narratives.

Among the Civil War veterans with whom I was acquainted I recall particularly William M. McClellan, of Pennsylvania, a neighbor of the Keleher family, who lived for many years on the northwest corner of Third Street and Hazeldine Avenue. McClellan had seen much service during "the War of the Rebellion," as he called it. He had fought at Winchester, Virginia, had been wounded and left for dead on the field in the second battle of Bull Run; was in the fight at Fredericksburg, in which Stonewall Jackson met his death; was in a decisive battle at Gettysburg; had helped take Atlanta; had accompanied Sherman on his march to the sea; and taken part in the battles of Chattanooga and Lookout Mountain. In addition to McClellan, I was fairly well acquainted with: Adolph Harsch, Rev. Thomas Harwood, Edward Johnson, Elias S. Stover, W. W. McDonald, James Seibert, B. A. Jones, Zenas H. Bliss, John C. Murphy, Willis Lawrence, Harry B. Stewart, Leverett Clark and William Burnside. Burnside had enlisted in the Union Army at Atlanta and was the only Negro member of G. K. Warren Post No. 1.

Marcus P. Kelly, business manager for the *Albuquerque Journal,* a member of the Immaculate Conception Church parish, had attended the Sherman lectures and had also read the articles I had written about them. Believing that the lectures had been accurately reported for the *Journal,* Marcus Kelly inquired of Mr. Macpherson as to the identity of the writer of the articles. Told that they had been written by Bill Keleher, Clerk of the Board of Education, Kelly went to Horace B. Hening, managing editor of the *Journal* and urged him to "keep an eye on Keleher; he might make you a reporter some day." Hening asked me within a few days if I would like to go to work for the *Journal* as a reporter, and I promptly told him that for years it had been my ambition to work on a newspaper. There and then he employed me as a reporter for the *Journal.*

Delighted with the prospects of my new job as a reporter for the *Journal,* and confident that he would rejoice with me, I hurried to the postoffice to tell R. W. Hopkins, Albuquerque Postmaster, of my good fortune. Mr. Hopkins was president of the Board of Education, and I felt it my duty to notify him at once of my intention to resign. Mr. Hopkins was not enthusiastic about my plans. He told me I was about to make the mistake of a lifetime, and urged me to remain as Clerk of the Board, saying that newspaper reporters were heavy drinkers as a general rule; that in fact he knew several Albuquerque reporters who drank too much for their own good. He predicted that if I became a reporter, I would likely wake up to find myself dead drunk rolling in the gutter within a few months. Disregarding the kindly meant advice offered by Mr. Hopkins, I took the job as reporter, a most fortunate happening, which opened up for me an entirely new world. At the end of my first month, Mr. Macpherson asked me how much salary he had promised to pay me and I told him $65.00. He made out my check for $75.00, which was the largest salary I had been paid up to that time. Eventually, in 1910, when I was promoted to be City Editor of the *Journal,* Mr. Macpherson paid me $150.00 a month, more money than I had expected to earn.

CHAPTER FOUR

Newspaper Days

WILLIAM S. BURKE, long time editor of the *Journal,* had a private office in a somewhat dilapidated brick building at 314 West Gold connected to the main Journal building by an entranceway. In this office there were a few odds and ends of furniture including an old-fashioned rolltop desk and swivel chair, a six-foot varnished pine table in the center, the top cluttered with big-city newspapers and daily and weekly New Mexico exchanges. Mr. Burke wrote most of his editorials in longhand on newsprint with a stub pencil, but at times he wrote them on a Smith-Premier typewriter of ancient vintage. Editor Burke at the time was about seventy years old. He had been a printer and hard working newspaper man since boyhood. He knew a great deal about the Civil War at first hand, having served as a Union soldier in several important campaigns; in one major battle he had been wounded in action. He knew all about Kansas politics because he had been an editorial writer on the Leavenworth, Kansas, *Times* during the years when it was owned by D. R. Anthony.

While editor of the *Leavenworth Times,* Burke wrote *Military History of Kansas Regiments During the War for the Suppression of the Great Rebellion,* published in

1870, even to this day an important book of Kansas Civil War history. Burke came to New Mexico from Leavenworth in 1881 when the new town of Albuquerque was a year old, and soon became editor of the *Albuquerque Journal.* Following Grover Cleveland's election as President in 1885, Burke started a campaign to have the President-elect nominate Edmund G. Ross to be Governor of the Territory of New Mexico. The President sent the Ross nomination to the Senate and he was confirmed. Burke and Ross had been for many years personal friends and fellow political workers in Kansas.

During one municipal campaign in Albuquerque, brought on by the alleged failure of the Water Supply Company to comply with the obligations of the city franchise, Burke wrote editorials for the *Journal,* defending the company's position. The *Daily Citizen,* the afternoon paper, published several editorials critical of the Water Company. The *Citizen* published a lead editorial in one issue calling attention to Burke's physical deformity, saying that he had become crippled in mind and body because of constant stooping to do dirty work for his political masters. In an answering editorial Mr. Burke said he had become deformed as the result of wounds sustained in honorable battle during "the late war, in defense of his country," while the editor of the *Citizen* had skulked and hidden out in the backwoods of Missouri, avoiding military service, too cowardly to fight.

It had seemed to me that the *Citizen's* editorials were unfair and unjust. I talked to Burke about possible retaliation. He told me: "Will, I don't want you to be concerned, and I hope you won't be. I must tell you in confidence that by arrangement with the publishers of the *Citizen,* I am writing the editorials for that paper, and at the same time writing the *Journal* editorials. I wrote the editorial published in the *Citizen* yesterday, directing attention to my physical deformity. It was designed to divert the minds of the people from thinking too much concerning the complaints about the water supply and franchise rights. We wanted the people to think about me and my personal physical affliction, and in this I think we have succeeded."

Burke also told me on this occasion that his wife, ignorant of the arrangement with the *Citizen*, had been fearful that he would be beaten up on his way home from the office late at night or early in the morning. To calm her fears, he had employed a deputy sheriff to protect him.

I was a pallbearer at Mr. Burke's funeral when he died in 1910. The services were held at First Presbyterian Church, long since torn down, located at the time on the southeast corner of Fifth Street and Silver Avenue. Burial was in Fairview Cemetery. Many years later, at my request, Senator Sam G. Bratton, succeeded in having the Congress enact a bill providing for payment of a Civil War Veteran's pension to Abby U. Burke, the editor's widow.

I went to Mrs. Burke's home to tell her personally the good news. At the time ninety-three years old, she told me on this occasion that she had recently begun to study French because she wanted to read Molière's plays in the original. When I refused to accept payment from Mrs. Burke for services rendered in connection with the pension claim, she insisted upon giving me a file of *The Log Cabin* published in New York City and Albany, by Horace Greeley & Company, covering the period from May 16, 1840, to October 31, 1840. *The Log Cabin* supported William Henry Harrison for President and John Tyler for Vice-President in the campaign of 1840. I had the file of papers bound and have kept them these many years in remembrance of two fine friends, William Smith Burke and Abby U. Burke.

Several months after I went to work as a reporter for the *Albuquerque Journal* in 1908, a new daily newspaper began publication, providing the big excitement of the day, startling to the publishers of both the *Albuquerque Daily Citizen* and the *Albuquerque Journal,* and the subject of much gossip among the editorial and mechanical staffs of both papers. In the back shop of each paper there was much speculation as to how long "the new rag" would last. Volume 1, No. 1 of the *Albuquerque Sun,* the name of the new paper, was published on May 18, 1908, by Sun Publishing Co., a New Mexico corporation, which had received a charter from the Territory of New Mexico on May 7, 1908. The incorporators were Mrs. H. M. Bennett, of Pittsburgh, Pennsylvania, owner of 410 shares of stock, Willis McConnell, her son, owner of 10 shares, and Marcus P. Kelly, 10 shares. A very handsome man, Marcus Kelly, former business manager of the *Albuquerque Journal,* had been lured away from the *Journal* to become business manager of the *Sun* at a promised salary of $10,000 a year, an arrangement which later became the subject of a lawsuit, in the course of which the *Sun* referred to Kelly in news articles and editorials as "the $10,000 beauty." Dr. C. C. Hendricks, a medical doctor, who had recently arrived in Albuquerque from Pittsburgh, Pennsylvania, after serving in the United States Army Medical Corps in the Philippine Islands, became the editor and administrative head of the *Sun.* Dr. Hendricks, so it was reported by men employed on the *Sun,* had studied law in the Philippines, had been admitted to the bar in Manila and had also practiced law in Pennsylvania.

Mrs. Bennett, so it was also reported, was well known in Pittsburgh, where as Laura Biggar Bennett, she was a prominent actress.

In establishing the *Albuquerque Sun,* Dr. Hendricks let it be known that no stock would be offered for sale, no financial assistance would be asked locally; and it was announced that although a modern and complete newspaper printing plant would be purchased later, the new paper for the time being at least would be printed on the press of Albright and Anderson. Hendricks rented a storeroom at 114 South Fourth Street, in the recently completed Charles E. Glecker building, arranged for the Western Union Telegraph Company to run a loop to the *Sun* office, subscribed for the Hearst leased wire service, employed a press telegraph operator who started work at 5 a.m. because of the time differential, and within a few days the third daily newspaper, publishing in the afternoon six days a week, was on the streets.

Although he was said to have had no previous experience in the newspaper field, Hendricks wrote surprisingly good editorials and managed his staff in the editorial room with much skill, producing from the first a newspaper which offered keen competition to the two rival dailies. After the initial burst of enthusiasm had subsided, the *Sun* front office, like all newspaper executive offices, small and large, began to discuss production costs, to talk about advertising revenue and soliciting new subscribers. In order to help the front office by stimulating reader interest, editor Hendricks began to publish editorials attacking prominent men of the community, so worded that they deliberately provoked and infuriated those against whom they were directed. Hendricks wrote editorials critical of friend or foe, striking out blindly. Apparently he wrote regardless of personal relationships. In one or more editorials, Hendricks attacked Horace Brand Hening, the managing editor of the *Albuquerque Journal,* and Hening's close friend, William H. Gillenwater, Republican leader of Bernalillo County. On or about September 10, 1908, the *Sun* published a particularly vicious editorial about Hening. He considered the content of the editorial a below the belt blow. In the late evening of September 10, I saw Gillenwater as he drove in front of the *Journal* office at 310 West Gold, stopping his horse and buggy long enough for Hening to leave the office and climb into the buggy and take his seat beside Gillenwater. I asked James S. Black, my boss: "Mr. Black, what's going on?" Black replied, "Hening and Gillenwater are both sore at Hendricks. They are going out to his place. Gillenwater is going out to kill Hendricks. He is taking Hening along as a witness to prove that he shot Hendricks in self defense." When Hendricks had taken up residence in Albuquerque he rented the J. F. Sulzer ranch home situated on a large parcel of land adjacent to the University of New Mexico campus, today the site of the Monte Vista public school at 3211 Monte Vista Boulevard NE. Returning to the *Journal* office in an hour Gillenwater stopped his horse in front of the *Journal* office, Hening got out of the buggy and entered the *Journal* office. Shortly afterward I asked Black: "What happened?" He replied that Hening had told him that when Gillenwater had rung the bell at the Sulzer place, a maid had come to the door and told them that Hendricks was not home, so they left.

Hendricks continued his editorial writing, shooting at targets promiscuously, apparently hopeful of hitting a bull's eye. From attacking individuals, Hendricks transferred his attacks to public institutions. The Regents of the University of New Mexico were soon involved in a fight with Hendricks, following a particularly vicious attack on the then President, William G. Tight. The Tight controversy became rough and tough, so much so that Tight, a nationally known geologist, who had gained some notoriety as a mountain climber in South America, decided that the game was not worth the candle, wrote out a letter of resignation, effective at the end of the school year.

Having won his fight with the Regents of the University of New Mexico, as he saw it, Hendricks began a fight with the Police Department, consisting at the time of fewer than a dozen policemen. "A reign of terror" existed in the City of Albuquerque Hendricks declared editorially and in news stories. An editorial published on June 3, 1909, was typical: "Men and women of this community are held up on the highways of the City almost at the whim of our executives, who hold high court and try the case without jury, without complaint, without even hearsay evidence to base the charge on." The following day Hendricks said in a lead editorial: "There is not a woman in this town who is safe in leaving her home, either alone or with her husband or brother. She is liable to arrest at the whim of any officer of the law."

Hendricks' editorials attacking the Albuquerque Police Department grew in number and intensity. William Phillips, on the force only about a year, chafed, like all his brother officers, under the Hendricks accusations, and promised revenge. He worked a twelve-hour shift, from 7 p.m. until 7 a.m. Not long after midnight on June 4, 1909, Officer Phillips asked me if I would like to see some fun. Scenting a possible story for the *Journal*, I gave him an immediate answer "Yes." He then told me confidentially of his plans. That very day, soon after 7 o'clock, when he would be off duty, Phillips had decided to "beat the hell out of that fellow Hendricks," and urged me to get a ringside seat for the event. Phillips was at the police station shortly before 7 o'clock. He placed his badge, gun and billy club on the desk, then changed from his police uniform to civilian clothes, went to the *Sun* office on South Fourth. I was at the place of rendezvous ahead of time, sat down on the street curbing across the street from the *Sun* office, in the rear of which the federal government was to build in 1912 a new postoffice building. Phillips made his appearance as scheduled, waving nonchalantly to me as much as if to say: "Watch out; this is going to be good."

Phillips was a tall man, over six feet in height. He was built somewhat along the rangy type. He was not too powerful a man, it seemed to me, for the type of endurance contest contemplated. Hendricks, soon to be his opponent in physical combat, was a stoutly built man, and as after events demonstrated, a man of strength and fearlessness. My personal hope and expectation was that after a preliminary tussle spectators would interfere and that the contest would be declared a draw. My personal sympathy, with misgivings, was with the policeman. I admired his courage, at the same time questioning his judgment. Within a short time after Phillips had encountered Hendricks in the *Sun* office, spectators heard the noise of overturning desks and tables, ripping electric light and power wires, the echoes accompanying the thud of body blows. Within a few moments after Phillips had made his grand entry into the *Sun* office, he was obliged to endure a humiliating and ignominious exit. Hendricks soon demonstrated that he was not only in good physical condition, but an expert in the manly art of self defense, quite familiar with the rules of the late Marquis of Queensberry. Landing a right cross to the jaw, Hendricks saw his opponent crumple up in a heap on the floor. Wiping the dust off his hands, Hendricks picked Phillips up from the floor by the seat of the pants, took him to the door, tossed him out on the sidewalk.

On June 4, 1909, the *Sun* published a modest account of the fight between Officer Phillips and Editor Hendricks. A 24-point headline told the story from the Hendricks viewpoint: "Cowardly assault on Editor of Sun by Police Officer." The article in full read as follows:

> Police Officer William Phillips invaded the editorial offices of the *Sun* this morning and assaulted Editor Hendricks of the *Sun,* threatening to kill him, while Hendricks was sitting at his desk writing editorials. Phillips rushed into the room and waving an editorial of yesterday's issue of the *Sun,* assaulted the editor and an altercation ensued. District Attorney Frank W. Clancy, who has a law office next door, tried to restrain the combatants.

Following the advice of friends, Phillips resigned from the police force within a few days and resumed work as a carpenter. Later, through his attorneys, Hickey and Moore, Phillips filed suit against the *Sun* and Hendricks, asking $25,000 for injuries suffered in the encounter and for damages to his reputation. The *Sun* "folded" within a few weeks after the Phillips-Hendricks episode. Hendricks returned to Pittsburgh, forfeiting for all time as it subsequently developed, any and all illusions he may have entertained looking toward a seat in the United States Senate as a man from New Mexico eager to champion the cause of the common people.

In the early spring of 1910, Edward Payson Weston, world famed pedestrian of his day, stopped overnight in Albuquerque on a walk across the continent from the Pacific Ocean in California to New York City. Then a reporter on the *Albuquerque Journal,* I walked several miles south of town to meet Weston, and was one of the dozen or more men to escort him along the Santa Fe track to the Santa Fe-Fred Harvey Alvarado Hotel. Early the next morning I was Weston's only companion for a mile or two as he resumed his journey to the east. Weston told me that he had decided to follow the Santa Fe route from Los Angeles to Chicago, and wrote to Edward Payson Ripley, President of the Santa Fe Railroad, telling him that his, Weston's mother, had told him many times that he and Mr. Ripley had been named after Edward Payson, a New England Presbyterian clergyman. In his letter Weston asked Ripley for a permit to allow him to walk on the Santa Fe right of way, explaining that on former cross country walks he had been chased off railroad property by cops, sometimes had been arrested and detained by railroad detectives as a trespasser. Mr. Ripley sent him the requested permit and sent him also a red flag attached to a wooden handle, telling him to use it in his discretion. By using it he would be privileged to stop any train on the system and ask for food, water, or help of any kind. President Ripley sent a copy of his letter in bulletin form to all agents on the Santa Fe between Los Angeles and Chicago.

Weston told me that he had found it necessary to use the letter several times and had been particularly glad to exhibit it to watchmen and "bulls" who had threatened to arrest him. Because of the letter, Weston had been furnished food and shelter in railroad depots, section houses and Fred Harvey hotels and eating houses. Weston told of one experience in which he had incurred the wrath of trainmen on the desert near Barstow, California. On this occasion Weston found himself in 120-degree heat of midday on the Mojave Desert. There was not a drop of water remaining in his canteen and he was without food. In desperation Weston unrolled his red flag, waved it frantically while standing in the center of the main line track as a fast passenger train thundered toward him. Weston said that the engineer blew the whistle frantically and the fireman rang the bell incessantly. When the train came to a standstill, Weston said that the entire crew, engineer, fireman, conductor, brakeman and flagman, rushed toward him. Some members of the crew, watches in hand, appeared angry enough to kill him on the spot. Nervously, Weston exhibited President Ripley's letter and pointed to his red flag. Then the conductor, in a rather conciliatory voice, said, "Mr. Weston, we are at your service. What can we do for you?" Weston explained his needs. The entire crew, acting as a bodyguard, accompanied him to the dining car. Weston told the steward: "Cracked ice, please, and fill my jug with water. Give me also some fruit juice, some sliced bread, a bit of meat and cheese." The dining car steward, trained in European courtesy and quickly sensing the situation, made up a basket of eatables and handed it down to Weston.

Weston asked me if the Associated Press had as yet taken him up. On being told that the A.P. covered his walk each day, Weston said, "Watch the A.P. on the fifteenth of this month. If everything goes all right, I expect to be going through Kansas. I will be 71 years old on that day, and am planning to celebrate my birthday by walking 71 miles, a mile for each year of my life. I will do it by getting up at 2:30 o'clock in the morning and walking until I have covered the 71 miles." I watched the papers and true to his prediction Weston walked 71 miles along the track in Kansas on March 15, 1910. The Associated Press carried the story which told of the achievement.

On February 7, 1912, William G. McAdoo, of New York

City, at the time and in later years very much in the news, was registered at the Alvarado Hotel in Albuquerque. I was then a reporter on the *Albuquerque Journal,* and telephoned to Mr. McAdoo asking for an interview; he came downstairs to the lobby within a few moments. He told me that he was in Albuquerque with his daughter, Harriet, who was to marry Charles Martin of Yonkers, New York. He said that Martin was arriving that afternoon from Prescott, Arizona, where he had been living as a health seeker.

With apparently little else to do but await the arrival of the train from Prescott bearing his future son-in-law, Mr. McAdoo told me about his early years in Chattanooga where he had been Clerk of the United States District Court, and of a period during which he had practiced law in New York City. He spoke of the many hours he had spent in daydreaming, looking down from the windows of his skyscraper office toward the Hudson River.

He also told me of the growth and development of the plan for a tunnel to be constructed beneath the Hudson River which he considered feasible and practicable, although many engineers whom he consulted differed from him. Financiers had shaken their heads when asked to put up the money for the tunnel. It was difficult to get publicity favorable to his project, Mr. McAdoo recalled, but he praised Arthur Brisbane, a prominent writer for the Hearst papers, for his interest. Mr. Brisbane wrote a series of articles laudatory of the enterprise.

Charles Martin arrived in Albuquerque as scheduled. Within an hour after his arrival the county clerk issued a marriage license to Charles Taber Martin of Yonkers, N. Y., born October 9, 1882, and Harriet Florette McAdoo, Irvington, New York, born October 7, 1886 in Chattanooga, Tennessee. They were married in Albuquerque on February 9, 1912 in St. John's Episcopal Church, by Archdeacon W. E. Warren.

Twelve years later I met McAdoo under somewhat different circumstances. In 1924 he had apparently been rejected from the national political arena following the symbolic bruising, knockdown and drag-out fight with the Al Smith forces at the Democratic National Convention in New York which brought about the nomination of John W. Davis.

Regardless of the reasons, political or otherwise, which had prompted him to change his place of residence from the Atlantic coast to the Pacific, in the fall of 1924 McAdoo was a Californian, practicing law in Los Angeles with William H. Neblett, under the firm name of McAdoo & Neblett, with offices in the then named Bank of Italy Building at Eighth and Olive. William Neblett, Bachelor of Arts from William & Mary, was a senior in Washington and Lee Law School in 1913, when I, a junior law student, became acquainted with him, a first cousin of Colin Neblett, United States District Judge in New Mexico. William Neblett and I became friends at Washington and Lee, and have retained that friendship unbroken.

Neblett had practiced law briefly in Silver City, Grant County, New Mexico, beginning in 1915, then moved in 1920 to Los Angeles where he began to practice his profession following extensive military service with the AEF in France. Reading in a Los Angeles newspaper in 1924 that William Gibbs McAdoo was in town, and that he planned to practice law in that city, Neblett impulsively decided to seek an interview with him. Although he was a stranger Neblett called on McAdoo, introduced himself and persuaded him that together they would make an ideal law firm.

I went to Los Angeles in 1924 planning to become associated in the law practice of the McAdoo-Neblett office. I was admitted to the California bar on December 8, 1924, on motion made by H. D. Lillie, Clerk of the Court, before a court composed of Frank Finlayson, Presiding Judge, and Louis R. Works and Gavin W. Craig, Associate Justices of the District Court of Appeals, Second Appellate Division.

After a trial of two months in the McAdoo-Neblett office I was convinced that my roots were too deeply imbedded in New Mexico soil to make a change, and that whatever destiny had in store for me, my future and my duty lay in New Mexico, not in California. As a result, I returned to Albuquerque and resumed my practice.

Some ten years elapsed between the time of my 1924 experiment in Los Angeles and my next contact with William Gibbs McAdoo. This time, then a United States Senator from California, McAdoo called me from Los Angeles. Following an exchange of greetings, the senator asked me if a Malaysian and Caucasian could be legally married in New Mexico. I told him that it had always been my understanding that no impediment to such a marriage existed in our state. He then said, "Well, a couple with such a racial background cannot be legally married in California." I then told Senator McAdoo that in order to make certain I would check the state constitution and laws of New Mexico and telephone him my opinion. Within a few moments I telephoned the senator confirming the previous opinion. He then told me of his difficulty.

"Our nineteen year old daughter, Ellen, is determined to marry a man born in the Philippine Islands. Although his parents were Spaniards, he and my daughter cannot be married in California. Ellen's mother and I have done everything possible to discourage her from this marriage, but apparently she has inherited an inflexible will from her grandfather Woodrow Wilson." Before the conversation ended, McAdoo and I arranged that he would send his daughter on a TAT (forerunner of TWA) plane to Albuquerque that night. His daughter was to be accompanied by her fiance, Rafael Lopez de Oñate, referred to the next day by a Los Angeles newspaper as a "Hollywood film actor, known in the screen world as Ralph Navarro."

Mrs. Keleher and I met Ellen McAdoo and de Oñate at the TAT airfield on the west mesa, and we took Ellen to our home where she was our guest until after the marriage. We had made arrangements for de Oñate to stop at the Alvarado Hotel, the same hotel in which Harriett McAdoo, Ellen's half-sister, had been a guest on the eve of her marriage in Albuquerque twenty-two years before. The county clerk was kind enough to bring the marriage license book to our home and issue the license without asking any unnecessary questions. The marriage ceremony was performed on November 10, 1934, in our home by Rev. George J. Weber, pastor of the First Congregational Church in Albuquerque, a long-time personal friend of mine, later pastor of the Congregational Church in Salt Lake City, Utah. Mrs. Keleher and I were the attending witnesses.

Ellen McAdoo seemed very childlike, standing beside her intended husband, who looked older than thirty-one years. We took the newlyweds to the Santa Fe Railway station, and helped them aboard an eastbound train. By a peculiar twist of fate, the Pullman car in which they had reservations bore the name "Oñate."

On November 12, 1934, William G. McAdoo, who was probably a busy man at the time because of the criticism following his rather recent divorce from Eleanor Wilson

McAdoo, and the difficulties resulting from his daughter's marriage against his wishes, found time nevertheless to write us the following letter expressing his thanks and appreciation.

> In addition to the telegram I sent you Saturday, I want to send you over my own signature, a line of appreciation for your and Mrs. Keleher's very great kindness to my daughter, Ellen. No friend could have been more considerate and helpful in a matter of such great importance to Mrs. McAdoo and to myself. I think things were handled splendidly at your end of the line. I think the publicity was all right. My hope now is that the couple may not be pursued further by reporters, although I see by this morning's paper that there is no indication yet that the publicity siege is over. However, they will have to take care of the rest of it themselves.
>
> My very warmest regards and gratitude to you and Mrs. Keleher always.
>
> > Cordially yours,
> > WILLIAM G. MCADOO

Time and events have almost engulfed the name and fame of William Gibbs McAdoo, told in the story of his life in *Crowded Years*, published in 1931. He gave me an autographed copy of the book. Although interesting enough, I was a bit disappointed to learn sometime later that a "ghost writer" was the author of the book.

CHAPTER FIVE

Trying to Become a Lawyer

As TIME went on it became apparent that it might be possible for me to realize a long cherished wish to attend law school. Years before I had left grade school, confident that I would return in the not distant future. So I decided in 1913 to quit my $30.00 a week job as a reporter and city editor on the *Albuquerque Herald* and go back to school. The decision to study law had not been arrived at without considerable thought. I was not in any sense of the words a "burning bush" candidate for the bar. However, I had a feeling that perhaps destiny was guiding me in the direction of the courtroom. While employed six years as a reporter, I had covered the County Court House every business day, had talked to people in many walks of life, and had observed people of many occupations. In the beginning of my quest to be a lawyer it had seemed possible for me to try to become one by studying in a lawyer's office. Most lawyers practicing in Albuquerque at the time had entered the profession through the "study in office" gate. Only a comparatively few lawyers then practicing in Albuquerque had gone to law school. I began to study for the bar in the office of Judge Benjamin Franklin Adams, who had resigned as a district judge in

Texas and came to New Mexico in 1896. He began to practice at once, and apparently had a thriving general practice with a good clientele in the business field. I had observed Judge Adams in several trials and had been impressed by his ability and sincerity.

Judge Adams was a recluse type of bachelor and I knew that he found comfort and solace at times through drink. The Judge was a man of fixed habits. He lived pretty much according to the calendar. He was a huge man physically, built on the dimensions of William Jennings Bryan, whom Adams greatly admired. Judge Adams wore tailor-made clothes, always cut from the same pattern. In the fall and winter he wore a black broadcloth outfit, consisting of wide pantaloons, a clerical looking vest and a statesmanlike Prince Albert coat. On June 1 of each year regardless of the temperature, he changed over to a similar suit of starched white linen.

I first came to know Judge Adams while working for the Western Union as a telegraph operator. On occasion he was a good Western Union patron. He had a habit, particularly when on a drinking bout, of searching the daily papers for odds and ends of news items which he would use as a basis for sending telegrams to conform to his mood, invariably signing "Uncle Pollock" to the telegrams and always sending them "collect."

An Associated Press story with a Princeton, New Jersey date line, published in the Albuquerque afternoon paper caught the Judge's eye. The story stated that former President Grover Cleveland, then lecturing at Princeton University, had declined to be interviewed on a public question by a newspaper reporter. Having meditated on the Grover Cleveland story, Judge Adams walked a short distance from his office in the Cromwell building to the

Western Union office across the street and handed me a telegram, requesting that it be sent at once, charges "collect." The hastily scribbled message read as follows:

> Hon. Grover Cleveland, Princeton, New Jersey.
> Congratulations that you have at last realized that the American people do not desire your opinion on any subject.
> Uncle Pollock

I told Adams that Mr. Cleveland would probably refuse to pay for the telegram, but he insisted that it be sent promptly, charges collect. The Western Union office in Princeton reported "payment refused," and Judge Adams cheerfully paid for his little joke.

Several months later, Adams sent a collect telegram to the Governor of Washington. The newspapers of the day were publishing stories about one Tracy, an outlaw on the loose in the Northwest. Adams, again in the Western Union office, handed me a telegram and asked that it be sent at once. The telegram read:

> At a mass meeting of citizens of Albuquerque tonight it was unanimously decided that you employ Nick Carter the world-famous detective to help capture Tracy.
> Uncle Pollock

This time the telegraph tolls were paid on the other end.

Judge Adams had several eccentricities, some of them no doubt disconcerting to his stenographer. When dictating to her, it was the Judge's habit to walk up and down in his office, shoes creaking and squeaking, all the while chewing gum vigorously, cracking it exasperatingly. It was the Judge's habit also to always supply the stenographer when dictating, with punctuation marks, generous with periods, commas, colons, semi-colons, dots, dashes, question marks and exclamation points.

Fellow lawyers rated Judge Adams as "well grounded in the law," particularly capable in the preparation of pleadings and business agreements. The Judge was well able to take care of himself in trials before court or jury. On one occasion he returned to his office, and tossing several law books on a table, remarked that he had just given a named fellow lawyer "a damned good licking" in the trial of a lawsuit, adding that the case he had won was not one to be tried by "a school-teacher lawyer," thus taking a dig at some Albuquerque lawyers who had taught school before practicing law.

After the Judge had allowed me to "read law" in his office, he took the job seriously. He referred to himself as my *praeceptor,* and assigned for each day's reading several pages of Blackstone's *Commentaries.* The assignment appeared to me dull, monotonous, even exasperating reading, discouraging to anyone trying to become a lawyer. Following the Judge's instruction, I read in Blackstone, day after day, about "Nature of Laws in General," "Rights of Persons," "The King's Duties," "The King's Prerogatives," and "The King's Revenues." I did not seem to be making much progress toward my goal.

Before starting to study law in Judge Adams' office, I had tried with little success to complete a correspondence school course, which, according to the school's advertisements virtually guaranteed admission to the bar. I can presently recall only a few of the definitions salvaged from the correspondence course. One of them: "Law is a rule of action." Another: "Equity is the correction of that which, wherein the law because of its universality, is deficient."

During my comparatively brief association with Judge Adams, I seldom saw him reading a law book or, in fact, a book of any kind. When retained in litigation, however, he would make prompt and diligent preparation, study the reported decisions, and dictate a trial brief to the accompaniment of much gum chewing. Judge Adams was a good salesman of his legal ability, and successful in handling clients, advising them with skill and diplomacy. On several occasions I listened to his conversations as he sought to impress clients with the scope and extent of his knowledge of the law, using the case of Pennoyer vs. Neff, 95 U.S. 714, as an example. Although that case had been decided in 1879, Adams always talked about the decision as if it had been rendered the day before, and would, by apt illustration, apply it to any case in which the client might be interested at the time. Pennoyer vs. Neff, although it seldom had even a remote connection with the client's case, frequently afforded the Judge an opportunity to tell about a case he had in Texas years before which began in a county Justice of the Peace Court as a replevin suit for the recovery of a span of mules, and wound up in the Supreme Court of the United States as an ejectment suit over a section of land. Pennoyer vs. Neff probably had nothing whatever to do with the client's legal troubles, or so it seemed to me, but he cited the case frequently to demonstrate that he was abreast of the law, and I never heard a client object to his somewhat involved explanations.

Dissatisfied with the progress I was making in my studies in the office of Judge Adams, I arranged to study in the office of Frank W. Clancy, at the time District Attorney of the Second Judicial District. Frank Clancy, as I later learned, was a New Englander, born in Dover, New Hampshire in 1852, who came to New Mexico in 1879. Although living in New Mexico for many years, it seemed to me he lived and died a New Englander, not a New Mexican.

The first recollection I had of Mr. Clancy was in 1894. Shortly after noon one day in the fall of that year, on my way home from school, at the northeast corner of Fifth Street and Railroad Avenue, I saw Mr. Clancy, five foot seven or eight, chubby and paunchy, attack Alonzo B. McMillen, a slim six footer, another Albuquerque lawyer. When I first noticed McMillen, he was walking west on the north side of Railroad Avenue, approaching Fifth Street, apparently attending to his own business. Before the battle between the two men had become of championship calibre, it was stopped by bystanders. Spectators said that Clancy and McMillen had continued on the street a quarrel that had begun the day before in the courthouse.

Fifty years later, while traveling on a day-long train trip from Roswell to Albuquerque, McMillen told me some of the background of his life; that he was born and reared on a farm in Van Wert County, Ohio, had received a law degree from the University of Michigan in 1886. After practicing several years in Paulding, Ohio, he went to Los Gatos, near San Jose, California, in 1891. Failing to find the success he hoped for in California, McMillen wrote to several people in the Southwest, among them Rev. John Menaul, pastor of the First Presbyterian Church in Albuquerque, asking about the opportunity for a lawyer in their community. Preacher Menaul showed the letter to Joshua S. Raynolds, a member of his church, at the time president of the First National Bank of Albuquerque. Raynolds told the minister how to answer McMillen's letter: "Write and ask him just one question: 'Would he be willing to sue another lawyer and get judgment against him on a promissory note?' " Raynolds, it appeared, had been exasperated by the excuse of "professional courtesy" in dealing with lawyers. He could not collect the bank's money on notes which lawyers had signed and had about reached the conclusion that Albuquerque lawyers had entered into a conspiracy not to sue each other.

McMillen's answer to the minister he told me, was as follows: "If the debt is just, I can see no reason why I should not sue other lawyers and collect the money on a court judgment." Raynolds told Rev. Menaul: "Tell that man McMillen to come on to Albuquerque at once. I will see that he is appointed lawyer for the bank." McMillen said that he had left San Jose at once and arrived in Albuquerque on January 31, 1893. Subsequently, he specialized in perfecting the rights of owners of Spanish and Mexican land grants. He was assisted in the work by Amado Chaves, of San Mateo, Valencia County, New Mexico, an expert in genealogy.

Changing from the Adams office to the Clancy office proved of little help in increasing my prospects for a legal education. I completed Clancy's first assignment, the reading and re-reading of Smith's *Elementary Law,* and then discovered to my disappointment that Clancy, too, was a disciple of Blackstone, perhaps more dedicated to the *Commentaries* than Judge Adams had been. Clancy encouraged me to study particularly the chapters in Blackstone on "Private Wrongs," and "Public Wrongs." To me they appeared to have but little relevancy to the practice of law in New Mexico.

Within a few weeks I concluded that "Clancy School of Law" like the Adams school, was somewhat disenchanting. I left Mr. Clancy's office with my thanks and gratitude to him, conscious of the fact that I would be obliged to look for other avenues of approach to the bar. On a vacation trip to Los Angeles I explored the opportunities there. I hoped that I might effect some arrangement to study law, supporting myself by newspaper work. William Dawson Hoffman, a good friend, at the time an editorial writer on the *Los Angeles Tribune,* offered to introduce me at both the *Los Angeles Examiner* and *Los Angeles*

Times. However, things were dull in the business world in Los Angeles at that time and the prospects for employment did not seem encouraging. I looked over the University of Southern California Law School, at the time located on upper floors of the Tajo Building on Broadway. For no apparent reason, I decided rather abruptly while visiting one of the classrooms there, that it would not be wise for me to attempt to go to law school and to work either day or night, that such an arrangement would literally "take too much out of my hide." As a result, I returned to Albuquerque, and went east to study law, as told later in this book.

What became of Judge Benjamin Franklin Adams? The details are lacking, but I learned later that Judge Adams had been paid a fee of $30,000 for defending several men who had been indicted on a cattle stealing charge in Apache County, Arizona. Judge Adams devoted almost his entire time and effort for many months to the work of defending his clients. As a young man, he had lived on Texas ranches and knew much about cattle, cattle brands, and the ways of the cowboy. While defending his clients, Adams closed his Albuquerque office and lived for months at a time at the hotel in St. Johns, county seat of Apache County, spending spare time playing chess and checkers with the men of the countryside. By such means, he got to know many men who served on the jury panel, became well acquainted with some of the men who were key witnesses for the prosecution in the trials in which his clients were defendants. Juries returned "not guilty" verdicts for every man Adams defended.

Judge Adams returned to Albuquerque at the conclusion of the Arizona trials, remained only a few days, then turned the key in the lock in his Cromwell Building office, as it turned out, for the last time. Adams went to New

York City, registered at the Waldorf Astoria Hotel of that day; and the story found its way back to Albuquerque that he planned to remain in New York until the $30,000 fee he had received for defending the cattle theft case had been exhausted. Month after month Adams paid his office rent, writing to the landlord's agent several times that he "expected to be back in Albuquerque before long." Then news came from New York that Judge Adams, still a guest at the Waldorf, had been retained at a substantial sum, by a British Mission stopping at the same hotel, to give legal advice on munition and war materiel purchase contracts. Then a telegram came to Albuquerque saying that Judge Adams had died suddenly in his hotel room following a heart attack. Later, when office rent went unpaid, the landlord had the Judge's office furniture and law books stored in a warehouse. They were finally sold at public auction in a suit to foreclose the landlord's lien.

After trying for several years to obtain a legal education, studying in the offices of Judge Adams and District Attorney Clancy, and by such other means as were available, I decided that a law school course would be the proper way for me to become a lawyer. As a result, on September 13, 1913, I enrolled as a special student in the Law School at Washington and Lee University in Lexington, Virginia. I was twenty-seven years old at the time and had been out of school for more than thirteen years. Several things influenced me in applying for admission to Washington and Lee, among them the favorable reputation of its Law School in the south and west. New Mexico friends had encouraged me to attend Washington and Lee, saying that faculty members were friendly and sincerely interested in the welfare of the individual student. Friends told me of the attitude of Washington and Lee students, all of whom courteously spoke to each other on the campus, regardless of formal introduction.

From Albuquerque, I telegraphed Martin P. Burks, Dean of the Law School, outlining my limited qualifications and asking permission to enroll as a special student. Dean Burks telegraphed his consent and within a few days I was in his office in Lexington. I had traveled to Chicago on the Santa Fe Railroad, to Cincinnati on the Chesapeake and Ohio, and to Lexington on the Baltimore and Ohio, by way of Balcony Falls, Buena Vista and other Blue Ridge Mountain towns, a long distance from New Mexico, it seemed to me.

In enrolling me as a special student, Dean Burks was carrying on a tradition established during post Civil War years by General Robert E. Lee, President of Washington College, who had encouraged many Civil War veterans and other young men kept out of school by the war, regardless of age to continue their studies after the fighting had ceased. At the time of my enrollment in 1913 Washington and Lee was a two-year law school, with an enrollment of 150. High school graduates were accepted as candidates for a degree of Bachelor of Laws. Subsequently, it became a three-year school and still later students were obliged to have a Bachelor of Arts degree before entering.

The day of my arrival in Lexington had been declared a day of mourning as a mark of respect following the death the previous day of Professor Abram Penn Staples, for many years a member of the law school faculty, affectionately known, I learned later, as "Sunny Jim" Staples. The body of Professor Staples was escorted from Lee Chapel on the campus to the railroad station. I joined in the procession, marking my first participation in University events.

Dean Burks had taken me at my word when I told him

that I could attend law school only one year and that I hoped to learn as much law as I could during the year, in order to take the New Mexico bar examinations. The Dean made out a schedule of classes for me and I bought the text books: Torts, Contracts, Constitutional Law, Corporations, Equity, Negotiable Instruments, Pleading and Practice, Real Property and Evidence. While handing me a study list and class assignments, Dean Burks remarked, "Keleher, that's about all you will be able to say grace over." My schedule called for lectures on five days a week, from 8:30 a.m. to 4:00 p.m., with a noon hour recess.

I read the cases assigned by the professors and worked in the library almost every weekday evening until the lights were turned off at 11 o'clock. In order to keep up with my classes, it was necessary not only to study every school day, but also to study in the library almost every Saturday and Sunday. As a result I failed to attend several important Saturday football games and other athletic events, which in retrospect it appears I should have seen.

Most of the men in my classes were much younger. Several were members of Phi Beta Kappa. I did not fully appreciate or understand the significance of a Phi Beta Kappa key at the time. Some forty years later, on April 13, 1953, Gamma of Virginia, at Washington and Lee, elected me to membership in Phi Beta Kappa fraternity, an honor which made me proud and happy, and for which I was and am truly grateful. I went to Lexington for the initiation. Earlier memberships in fraternities had come my way while in school at Washington and Lee. On January 10, 1914, I was made a member of Zeta Chapter of the Sigma Chi fraternity, and on January 28, 1915, became a member of Tucker Chapter of Phi Delta Phi, a legal fraternity. Many years later the University of New Mexico conferred on me an honorary Master of Arts degree on June 24, 1946, and an honorary LL.D. on April 20, 1968, and the College of St. Joseph on the Rio Grande (University of Albuquerque) an honorary LL.D. on May 29, 1960.

The Lexington I knew during my student days, to a great extent, is comparable with the Lexington of today, a distinctly southern town of a few thousand people, beautifully situated in the Blue Ridge Mountains. The atmosphere of the genuine hospitality of the old South permeates even to this day. White-columned stately mansions of ante-bellum days dominate Lexington's residential section, truly a charming, picturesque area. With House Mountain as a backdrop, the North River flowing silently nearby, a wealth of bluegrass in season, great patches of dogwood and laurel in early May, strangers, especially those from the Southwest, cannot fail to be impressed by the beauty of the countryside. Lexington is unique among American towns, differing from other southern college towns, such as Oxford, Mississippi, home of the late famed William Faulkner, because Lexington is the final resting place of two great southern heroes, Robert E. Lee, who died there on October 12, 1870 and is buried in Lee Chapel on the campus; and Thomas Jonathan ("Stonewall") Jackson, who died in Chancellorville, Virginia, on May 10, 1862, and is buried in Lexington. During the years 1851 and 1861, General Jackson lived in Lexington, and taught philosophy and artillery tactics at Virginia Military Institute, adjoining the Washington and Lee campus.

When June 1914 arrived, and the grades had been posted on the bulletin board at Tucker Hall, my name was among those who had made passing grades. I was sorry to learn, however, that I had failed Dean Burks' course on "Pleading and Practice," a subject he taught from his own textbook. I told my friends and classmates goodbye, never expecting to return to Lexington. Friends in Albuquerque, however, made it possible for me to get summer work as a newspaper reporter. My mother, my brother Ralph, and my sisters Julia and Katherine, all stood by loyally and helped me financially and I was able to return to finish the law course. Paul M. Penick, Treasurer of the University, took my note for $125.00 as part payment of my second year tuition, a debt which I paid within a year after graduation.

Returning to Lexington in September, 1914, I found I would have considerable spare time available. I had already passed the examinations in the most important law courses and believed I could pass without difficulty the examination in several remaining courses, which included Carriers, Divorce, Partnership, Criminal Law and Roman Law. Roman Law was at the time a required subject because of conditions attached to a gift made by T. S. Woolsey, of Yale University, when establishing the chair of Roman Law at Washington and Lee. Only a short distance from the law school in Tucker Hall, were the stately red brick, white-columned buildings in which the liberal arts departments were located. Anxious to do such college work as might be possible, I received permission from several teachers in the academic department to attend their classes, among them Dr. Edgar F. Shannon, Sr. (father of Dr. Edgar F. Shannon, Jr., now president of the University of Virginia), Dr. James Robert Howerton, a retired clergyman, one-time moderator of the general Presbyterian Assembly, and Dr. Franklin L. Riley. Dr. Shannon taught English literary courses. Dr. Howerton lectured on the Bible, taught psychology and philosophy, and Dr. Riley taught American history.

On June 16, 1915, Washington and Lee University conferred on me the degree of Bachelor of Laws. The commencement exercises were held in Lee Chapel. I mailed my diploma promptly to my family in Albuquerque and on the same day left for Washington. In the nation's capital, then still a comparatively quiet town, I called on Aristieus A. Jones, First Assistant Secretary of the Interior under Secretary Franklin K. Lane. I had known Mr. Jones for some years, and had written in advance for an appointment to discuss possible employment. Mr. Jones told me on the occasion of my visit that he could promise me a job in the General Land Office. He advised me, however, to look about town for a day or two, and see if I thought it best to remain in Washington as a government employee instead of returning to New Mexico and starting to practice law. Acting on Mr. Jones's recommendation, I walked about Washington, watched hundreds of men and women entering public buildings in the morning, most of them carrying a lunch. I observed them leave the buildings in the evening. Watching the government employees go to and from work, the meaning of the message Mr. Jones sought to convey to me needed little interpretation.

Returning to the Department of the Interior next day, I told Mr. Jones of my gratitude to him for the offer of a position, but said that I had decided to return to New Mexico. Then he said, "Will, since you have reached that decision yourself, I want to tell you that in my opinion it is the correct one." He then told me of his experiences when beginning to practice law in Las Vegas, New Mexico; that in the first year of his practice he had "taken in" only $300.00, in the second year, $600.00, and in the third year, $900.00. The rest of the story was well known to me because Mr. Jones had the reputation throughout New Mexico of being a very successful lawyer. On November 7, 1917, Mr. Jones was elected to the United States Senate from New Mexico. (I helped in a small way in his campaign, and he reciprocated by having me appointed in 1917 to the post of New Mexico attorney for a half dozen counties in the state. I was to represent the recently organized Federal Land Bank of Wichita, Kansas.)

In a few days after my interview with Mr. Jones in Washington, I was back in Albuquerque, my own home town, in which I have practiced law for more than fifty years.

Across the fifty-odd intervening years since my graduation from Washington and Lee in 1915, it seems appropriate to pay tribute to the professors of the law school, particularly to the names and memories of Dean Martin Park Burks, Prof. W. H. Moreland, and Prof. Joseph Raglan Long; and to Dr. Shannon, Dr. Howerton and Dr. Riley, in the academic department, for their kindness, consideration and courtesy to me; and I would like to express my gratitude and appreciation to the memory of Peter F. McCanna (April 15, 1865–January 10, 1922) for many acts of friendship and kindness during the time I was in law school, and in the early years of my law practice.

CHAPTER SIX

Detour to El Paso

WHILE WORKING as a small-town reporter, it had been important and necessary for me to rush out of the office to cover a fire, hurry down to the police station to learn about an arrest, or get an interview from some celebrity pausing briefly in our community. I was only vaguely aware of the code of ethics which prohibited professional men from directly or indirectly soliciting business. It was not until after I had tried to practice law for a few months, however, that I felt the impact of the difference between the hustling, aggressive, active life of a newspaper reporter and the hum-drum, day-to-day life of an embryo lawyer. Apparently a lawyer was by tradition expected to sit in his office endlessly reading a book or newspaper, or just twiddling his thumbs.

Sitting in my chair in my 12 x 14 office in the Cromwell Building in Albuquerque day after day, occasionally reading a bit of law, staring out of the window, hopefully waiting for clients who never came, proved boring and depressing. On several occasions I caught myself listening to footsteps in the hall-space of the second floor of my building, hoping that a kind fate might guide a client to my office. Always, or so it seemed, the destination of the prospect was some other lawyer's office. Following serious

99

reflection and perhaps an indulgence in self-pity, I concluded that a newspaper reporter's life, hurrying after items of news, pounding out on the typewriter exciting stories about people and events seemed greatly to be preferred to the drablike existence of a struggling young lawyer.

Having reached such a conclusion and discouraged over the prospects and outlook for professional success, it seemed to me realistic to execute an about-face, retrace my steps and resume my former occupation as a newspaper reporter. Convinced of this, I wrote, on December 10, 1915, to James S. Black, my old boss on Albuquerque newspapers, then managing editor of the *El Paso Times,* El Paso, Texas, explaining my situation and asked him for a job. A few days later Mr. Black telegraphed me: "Come at once, City Editor, $30.00 a week."

Telling only a few people of my plans, I theoretically took down my shingle one evening, locked the door to my office, and took the night train for El Paso.

Ten years before, in 1906, I had worked in El Paso as an operator for the Western Union Telegraph Company, located at that time at 109 South Oregon Street. Because of my prior residence there, I was fairly well acquainted with El Paso, a frontierlike town in 1916 of some 30,000. It was not important in the economy of Texas, being isolated, situated hundreds of miles from Austin, the capital, and some seven hundred miles from Texarkana, Texas, straddling the Texas-Arkansas border. Although comparatively unimportant to most of Texas, El Paso, because of its banks and commercial establishments, was of considerable importance to Mexico, particularly to the States of Chihuahua and Durango and parts of Sonora.

Juarez, just across the Rio Grande from El Paso, was the rail gateway to Chihuahua, Durango, and Mexico

City. In many respects El Paso was the Arizona-New Mexico hubs of the mining and livestock trade in the Southwest. In 1912 and for several years thereafter, El Paso was enmeshed in the throes of Mexican revolutions. It was for many years an ideal sanctuary for Mexican refugees, offering safety to person and property, in many cases entire immunity from arrest. Names of revolutionary leaders, among them Pancho Villa, Huerta, Orozco and Zapata, were well known in El Paso and nearby border towns.

My first important assignment on the El Paso *Times,* after my arrival there in the early part of January 1916, handed to me by Managing Editor Black, was to maintain a death watch on General Victoriano Huerta, long-time story petrol of the Mexican political and military world. The General was at the time living in El Paso in exile, one of President Woodrow Wilson's more important casualties, a victim of Wilson's calculated determination to smash Huerta's political power in Mexico. Following a severe illness which had lasted many weeks, Victoriana Huerta died in El Paso on January 13, 1916. I covered the story for the *Times,* and supplemented it by an interview with General Ygnacio Bravo, from whom I had learned a great deal about Huerta's public life. On Friday, January 14, 1916, on page one, there was published in the *Times* the last story I ever wrote for compensation on a newspaper.

The top headline on the Huerta story was in 48 point type: "General Huerta Passes Away With Prayer Upon Lips." The details of the General's death were told in lower decks, in ten and twelve point type: "Exiled dictator of Mexico, fortified with last rites of his church, announces forgiveness of enemies and sinks into sleep that knows no waking." "Dies surrounded by family and friends." On the day of the publication of the story, I was perhaps a bit proud of the first two or three paragraphs. On re-reading the story some fifty years later, I must confess that the writing was worse than mediocre. The first and second paragraphs were as follows:

> Exiled from the land of his birth, the land that he had fought for in the days of his power and might, until recently a closely guarded prisoner in the country of his adoption in times of stress, with a benediction on his lips and in his heart for all mankind, at peace with God and the world, General Victoriano Huerta, 73 years old, former provisional president of Mexico, and one of the most notable figures in Mexican affairs since the beginning of the revolution, passed out of this life at his home at 415 West Boulevard at 8:35 o'clock last night.
> The general died fortified with the last rites of the Catholic Church, which had been administered several hours before, when in full possession of his faculties, and surrounded by members of his family and most of his close personal friends, most of whom were members of his staff in the days of former glory.

The Huerta story was continued in the *Times* from page 1 to page 3. On page 3 there also was printed a related story I had written, telling of Huerta's life and career as it had been narrated to me by General Bravo.

It seemed to me on the morning of January 15, 1916, that I had done a fairly competent job of getting the facts together about General Huerta and had written a passable story. However, upon returning to the Huerta residence the afternoon of that day to get details about the funeral arrangements, I encountered a chilly, hostile atmosphere. Although admitted to the residence with proverbial Mexican courtesy and politeness, I quickly found out that I was not a welcome visitor. General Bravo spoke for the family, saying, "We thought we treated you courteously, but you have forfeited entrance to this home. You have abused our hospitality. We ask you to please go and not to return." As he spoke, General Bravo was surrounded by fellow officers and friends of the deceased. Realizing they shared his sentiments, I left the house at once.

I returned to the *Times* office and told Mr. Black about my experience at the Huerta home. He quickly explained what appeared to me to be a puzzle. The El Paso *Times*, Jim Black told me, printed two separate and independent newspapers, one entirely in English, the other entirely in Spanish. The Spanish edition had a large circulation in Northern Mexico. Each publication, Black pointed out, had its own staff of reporters and editors; each had its own printers and pressmen. It had so happened in the Huerta case that the writers on the Spanish edition of the *Times* had taken from my story, published in the English edition, only a few facts about the General's death. The story in the Spanish edition had been written by staff members so composed as to blacken the General's memory. It was immaterial whether the story expressed individual beliefs of the writer or whether the writing followed instructions of political superiors directing the paper's policy. Huerta was described in the Spanish story of the *Times* as "a low down dog." In other places in the story there was ample evidence of hatred and hostility against the deceased political leader. General Bravo and other friends of Huerto, having read the Spanish edition of the *Times*, assumed that I had written the article as it appeared in Spanish, and held me responsible.

Having learned through the Huerta episode that payment could be enacted in exchange for the excitement in the newspaper world, I was convinced that perhaps a lawyer's life after all might have compensations. As a result, I returned to Albuquerque, unlocked the door to my office and resumed the practice of the legal profession.

Among the few letters which the mail carrier had tossed over the transom of my office during my absence was one from T. K. D. Maddison, Clerk of the Second Judicial District Court, notifying me that Judge Herbert F. Raynolds had appointed me to defend José Medina, Angelo Rodriguez, Anastacio Jiminez and Guadalupe Roches, Mexican Nationals, on a charge of first degree murder. I soon began to investigate facts in the case. The four men, all from Santiago Valley, State of Guanajuato, Mexico, were in the United States on temporary work permits, and had been in New Mexico only a few months. They had recently been indicted for the murder on January 10, 1916 of Frank Chavez, a well known business man of San José, Precinct No. 1, Bernalillo County, situated in the southeast section of Albuquerque.

Defending the accused men was perhaps a bit beyond my ability. My previous experience in the law had been limited to the trial of a few cases, one or two of them before a jury, in Justice of the Peace Courts. I was fairly familiar, however, with the technique of trying civil and criminal cases before a jury in the District Court as the result of having attended the trial of many cases while covering the courthouse for six years as a newspaper reporter.

Because all four men were destitute, a poverty affidavit was filed on their behalf, and a court order was obtained granting free process. I then filed a petition asking the Court for a writ of *habeas corpus*. The petition alleged that the defendants were being imprisoned and restrained of their liberty by Sheriff Jesus Romero, in the county jail; that they were not being detained by the final judgment of any order of any competent tribunal, but were being unlawfully detained and unjustly deprived of their liberty.

The writ was granted as a matter of course, and Judge Raynolds heard the testimony. At the hearing, the prosecution introduced a statement signed by Medina which the court admitted in evidence over my objection. In the statement Medina admitted his own guilt and implicated the three other men. The court discharged the writ and remanded the defendants to jail.

The trial of the case before a jury of twelve men, a majority of whom were of Spanish-American ancestry, continued for six days. All testimony, all proceedings, arguments of counsel, the rulings by the trial judge were translated from English into Spanish, from Spanish into English. Medina's signed confession, admitted into evidence at the trial was of major importance. The testimony submitted by the prosecution was to the effect that Medina had been courting a sixteen-year-old girl, a native of Mexico, who was produced as an adverse witness by the State. She admitted that she knew Medina, and had been acquainted with Frank Chavez, but testified to little else.

The State proved by other witnesses that Frank Chavez, some ten or fifteen years older than Medina, owner of a grocery store in San José, had attempted to interfere with a romance between Medina and the young Mexican girl. Angered by the alleged interference, Medina had planned revenge. Angelo Rodriguez, perhaps bringing into play some of the romantic intrigues in which he had engaged in Mexico, apparently had masterminded the conspiracy which resulted in the murder of Frank Chavez.

Rodriguez had apparently taken Guadalupe Roches into the conspiracy. A man of talent and artistic bent, Roches had learned in Mexico to be a *florista*, a maker of artificial flowers, and had established a small scale flower business in Albuquerque, furnishing wreaths and floral pieces for funerals, weddings, and other occasions.

Anastacio Jiminez, introduced by Rodriguez as the fourth accomplice in the venture, was a man of unusual strength and courage. Rodriguez had recruited him perhaps as a sort of second for Medina in the drama in which he was to participate with Frank Chavez. From the testimony introduced at the trial, it appeared that Guadalupe Roches had been cast to act the part of a Judas goat in the real-life play that was to be enacted. Posing as his friend, Rodriguez went to the Chavez grocery store at an appointed time on the night fixed for the commission of the crime, and whispered a few important words: "Follow me, *Señor Chavez*, and I will take you to a young lady in whom you have shown an interest. She is expecting you and most anxiously waiting your presence. She told me to give you this flower as a token of her devotion."

Following the script to the letter, Roches handed to Frank Chavez, at the appointed time and place, a choice artificial rose, delicately scented. Guadalupe Roches then led Chavez to the place where presumably the Mexican girl would be waiting for him. The place, according to the State's testimony, was a dark alley on the edge of San José, adjacent to a long since abandoned brick plant. There Roches had said to Frank Chavez, *"Buenas noches, Señor,"* and walked away into the night. Instead of finding the young lady waiting for him, Chavez was suddenly confronted by José Medina, no doubt half crazed from jealousy. Seizing the opportunity for long-anticipated revenge, Medina, from all indications, had attacked Chavez with an iron bar. The testimony at the trial showed that Chavez's assailant struck him repeated blows on the head with the iron bar, which sent him reeling to the ground. The autopsy, according to the physician who performed it, showed that Chavez had suffered a fractured skull, many contusions, lacerations and wounds, almost any one of which would have caused death.

Persuaded, no doubt, by Medina's signed confession and other damaging testimony admitted into evidence over my repeated objections, the jury, at dusk on the sixth day, found him guilty of murder in the first degree. To the surprise of many, the jury found Rodriguez, Jiminez and Roches not guilty. Medina appeared to accept the verdict with indifference.

I filed the customary motion for a new trial which was overruled by Judge Raynolds. The motion included the following grounds:

> Because Medina had been without counsel until after he had plead guilty upon arraignment in a justice of the peace court; because he had not been properly warned that any statement he might make would be used against him in his trial; because he had never been advised that he had a constitutional right not to incriminate himself; because after the severance of the indictment against Medina, the court refused to allow the motion of counsel for Medina to have the codefendants, Angelo Rodriguez, Anastacio Jiminez and Guadalupe Roches, tried first; because the court permitted Deputy Sheriff Mosais Saavedra, Policeman Pablo Lujan, and City Marshal Thomas McMillin, witnesses for the prosecution, to testify over the objections of Medina's counsel to a confession alleged to have been made by Medina to Saavedra, Lujan and McMillin, and which confession was produced and induced by fear, misapprehension, persuasion and ignorance; because the court permitted Saavedra to testify as to the alleged confession on the part of the defendant Medina, said confession having been induced by threats being made by Saavedra.

Today, more than fifty years after Medina's conviction, Judge Raynolds would have been compelled, under decision of the Supreme Court of the United States, to refuse to allow Medina's confession to be introduced in evidence, and if admitted, would have been obliged to grant him a new trial, under the holdings in the case of Miranda vs. United States, the decision in the Escobedo case, and in other landmark cases of recent years, among them Vigera vs. New York, Westover vs. United States, California vs. Stewart and Schmerber vs. California. After having overruled the motion for a new trial, Judge Raynolds sentenced Medina to be "hanged by the neck until dead" on Friday, June 2, 1916.

During Medina's trial, he had grown pale to a much greater extent than could have been accounted for by ordinary imprisonment producing pallor. In the days following his conviction he lost a great deal of weight and soon appeared to be only a shadow of his former self. The county physician examined Medina and said he was suffering from "galloping consumption."

Being of the opinion that the record contained reversible error, I filed a petition asking for free process on appeal. Judge Raynolds denied the motion. With the execution set for June 2, I took an appeal to the Supreme Court, which automatically acted as a stay of execution.

While employed as a newspaper reporter, I had become fairly well acquainted with Governor William C. McDonald, of Lincoln County, a strong character, a non-political type minded-man, who had been elected New Mexico's first governor. I talked to the governor about the Medina case soon after Medina had been convicted, and wrote to him on May 29, 1916, explaining the case somewhat in detail. Among other things, I asked the governor to make available to me $100.00 out of his contingent fund to pay for a transcript of the record on appeal, asking him in the alternative to exercise executive clemency by commuting Medina's sentence to life imprisonment.

In reply to my letter of May 29, Governor McDonald wrote on June 1, saying that inasmuch as I had appealed Medina's case to the Supreme Court, he saw no particular hurry about "looking into it." He promised to consider my request for paying the cost of the transcript and said he would visit Medina at the penitentiary to observe personally his physical condition, and might even talk to him about some phases of the case. The governor's letter concluded: "In case of an appeal to the Supreme Court, I have always refused to consider any case until it has been determined there. I will talk the matter over with you later, and we can decide just what can be done."

Confident that Governor McDonald would not allow José Medina to be hanged, regardless of what the Supreme Court might say, I decided not to ask the court reporter to begin work on the transcript of the record on the contemplated appeal. I was satisfied to keep myself informed about Medina's physical condition. I had no regrets when I learned that my client's condition was deteriorating each day. On May 30, 1916, Medina was taken to the State Penitentiary in Santa Fe, under the provisions of a statute in the case of a defendant sentenced to death who had taken an appeal to the Supreme Court. A long time acquaintance of mine, John B. McManus (father of Judge John B. McManus, Jr., of the District Court of Bernalillo County) was at the time warden of the penitentiary. On June 23, 1916, Warden McManus telephoned me that Medina had died that day in the prison hospital, and asked for instructions. I told the warden that Medina was from a remote place in Mexico, had no relatives in the United States, and recommended burial in the prison cemetery, which was done.

With Medina dead, there seemed no reason for his countrymen, Rodriguez, Jiminez and Roches to continue to remain in the United States. The three men called on me at my office to tell me goodbye, and thank me once more for the services I had rendered them in their time of trouble. On this occasion of farewell, the three men were resplendent in the color and dignity of their native dress, costumes ordinarily worn on *fiesta* days in Guanajuato, center of the hot country in Mexico, loose fitting cotton pantaloons and shirt, embroidered cloth belt, thonged sandals, the ensemble of each being accentuated by a high-crowned straw sombrero, balanced and held in place on the head by an elastic chin strap; all of them wore gaily-colored cotton zarapes thrown about their shoulders.

Angelo Rodriguez, as usual, was the spokesman: "*Señor,* we are going home to Mexico; we are going for always. We will never return to this country now that José Medina is dead. We have settled all of our debts and obligations with everybody. At last we come to settle with you." I had told Rodriguez more than once that I had been appointed by the court to defend them, that I could not accept any compensation; that they owed me nothing. I again told my callers there was no charge. Then Rodriguez said, "But, *Señor,* it will make us feel so much better to pay you for what you have done. It will help make it possible to return to Mexico out of debt to everybody." Placed on this basis, I had no alternative but to accept. So I said, "*Amigos,* if you insist, let it be as you wish." Pleased that I agreed, the three men held a conference in a corner of my small office, apparently talking about the amount to be paid as a fee. The conference over, Rodriguez produced a cotton tobacco sack. Poking a forefinger and thumb into the sack, Rodriguez carefully withdrew, counted and gave me three American silver dollars. All three men gathered about my desk, beaming and happy. In the best Spanish at my command I thanked them sincerely and with appreciation, realizing that the payment represented a gift straight from the heart. Shaking hands with each, telling them a last *adios,* my friends from Santiago Valley walked quietly out of my office, closing the door politely and gently behind them. I never saw or heard from any one of them again.

CHAPTER SEVEN

Municipal Government

FOR MANY years following the establishment of Albuquerque's town government in 1885, and the city government in 1891, there was acute rivalry, if not hostility, between Republicans and Democrats striving for political preferment. Under territorial statutes New Mexico cities and towns elected a mayor and aldermen every two years. Under both town and city government Albuquerque was partitioned into four wards. One alderman was elected every two years from each ward, so that the people of a ward were always certain of representation by one alderman under any administration. Although for many years the Republicans controlled Bernalillo County because most of the voters in the outlying precincts were of Spanish-American ancestry, having inherited their political faith from Civil War days, the voters in Albuquerque, nearly all Anglos, were about equally divided between Republican and Democrat in party allegiance. The town government had no regular meeting place, but held council meetings at convenient places, most of the time in the office of whoever might then be town attorney. As of 1892 I recall wandering into the then official seat of government in Albuquerque, at 214 South Second Street, and looking with interest at the iron bars fastened across the windows on the north side of the building, facing the east and west alley, and on the east side, facing a north and south alley. On July 18, 1894, the city government moved to more commodious quarters on the north side of Tijeras Road, between First and Second Streets, and occupied a building owned at the time by Perfecto Armijo, later owned by Filomena Otero, wife of Mariano S. Otero. The city later was named as a defendant in a lawsuit over the condition in which it allegedly had left the property when vacated. The case went to the Supreme Court, but was not decided until June 27, 1916, the case being reported as City of Albuquerque vs. Otero, 22 N.M. 128.

When the Perfecto Armijo-Otero building was vacated by the city, old-timer Jacob Korber, a blacksmith, hardware merchant, and extensive owner of real estate, was prevailed upon to remodel and lease to the city several storerooms he owned on the east side of North Second Street between Copper Avenue and Tijeras Road. The city government was moved into the new quarters in 1907, installed in the facilities the fire department, consisting of two fine fire horses and one fire wagon, the fire chief's horse and buggy; partitioned off space for a jail, equipped with heavy steel bars guaranteed to hold the most hardened criminal, and built quarters for the town marshal and the police force of eight men. Rooms were provided on the second floor of the Korber property for the City Clerk, and for use as a meeting place for the city council. The steel bars in the jail were installed as a result of the hue and cry that had followed the arrest of two men accused of robbing Simpson's pawnshop (209 South Second Street) of several valuable diamonds, and the thieves subsequent sensational escape from the jail on the recently abandoned Armijo-Otero property. The police were either unable or unwilling to satisfactorily explain the circumstances surrounding the escape of the suspects. They had simply disappeared over night, while awaiting trial, apparently dropping through the jail floor. They were never seen or heard from again. Henry Simpson, the pawnbroker victim of the robbery, had been humiliated by the loss to such an extent that he had soon returned to England, from whence he had emigrated to America. Simpson's pawnshop had been considered a model place, a reliable and trustworthy establishment, especially by the gambling fraternity of Albuquerque, the members of which with perfect confidence had left their precious stones with Simpson, as security for loans when at the gaming tables the dice had rolled in a wrong direction, or unfortunately an unwanted card had turned face up. Some citizens became disillusioned when it became public knowledge that Pawnbroker Simpson's license required the posting of only a $500 security bond.

Following the Simpson robbery and jail escape, citizens generally expressed the belief that Albuquerque should now be considered a place of permanent habitation and the voters at the next general election authorized the sale of a $30,000 bond issue to be used to buy land and to construct a city building. The council bought the lots for the city hall site at the southwest corner of Second Street and Tijeras Road. City Engineer James N. Gladding prepared the plans and specifications for a new city hall, and it was built and occupied in 1912, and used for many years thereafter as Albuquerque's first permanent municipal home.

The rivalry between the Republicans and Democrats became so intense that for some years mayors were elected or defeated by a margin of only a few votes. In 1912 Felix H. Lester, Democrat, was declared elected mayor by one vote over David H. Boatright, Republican. The Supreme Court decided, however, that Boatright had really

MUNICIPAL GOVERNMENT 115

won the election, and Lester was obliged in the final weeks of his administration to turn the gavel over to Boatright.

Leaders of remnants of a badly shattered Albuquerque democratic political machine held a meeting on January 30, 1916 and decided to attempt to recapture the city hall. Frank Butt, late of Alabama, owner of drug stores in Albuquerque and Santa Fe, already ambitious to be governor of New Mexico, was elected chairman of the executive committee, and I was elected secretary. The convention nominated Henry Westerfeld, a cigar maker, for mayor, and he was elected, with strong backing by labor unions, on April 4, 1916, by a majority of six votes. Warren Graham was elected City Treasurer by a majority of 131 votes. Clyde Tingley, Democrat, a newcomer to Albuquerque, was elected alderman from the Second Ward. Tingley had been nominated largely through the influence of Dr. Solomon L. Burton, a strong advocate of municipal ownership of the water supply company. Democrat W. F. Switzer, owner of an elite barber shop, was elected an alderman from the Fourth Ward. All other elective offices went to Republicans. Westerfield's chief bid for political preferment had been based on the firm foundation, so it was claimed, that he was the maker of the "Affidavit" cigar, a pure Havana product, which had found favor with the voters. Those who were well acquainted with Mayor Westerfield and his ways advised all those preparing to call on the mayor to discuss business or professional matters, to approach his honor puffing away at an Affidavit cigar, and to be sure and address him as "Mr. Mayor."

On April 17, 1916, Mayor-elect Westerfield announced his choice of men to fill the top offices during his administration. The announcement followed several caucuses with political leaders. All the appointees were Democrats; all had helped win the election. The mayor placed in nomination, and the council confirmed, the following men: J. R. Galusha, Chief of Police; Pat O'Grady, Police Captain; N. M. Miller, Police Sergeant; W. A. Keleher, City Attorney; J. W. Burnett, Fire Chief; E. M. Clayton, City Physician; John Tandberg, Sanitary Officer; Edmund Ross, City Engineer; and William Wallace McClellan, Police Judge.

J. R. Galusha, the newly appointed chief of police, was one of the last of the colorful frontier peace officers of his day. Although born in Palmyra, Missouri, and technically a Missourian by birth, Galusha's father was a Texan and had for many years served in that state as a peace officer. Galusha apparently had no fear when the chips were down. In attempting to arrest law violators he was an exceptionally brave and courageous man, or so it always seemed to me.

Pat O'Grady, appointed police captain, was born in Dublin, Ireland, March 17 and thus a true son of St. Patrick. O'Grady told me that his first job in America after landing in 1906, was that of chasing hoboes from the Chicago and Northwestern Railroad yards in Chicago. Eventually O'Grady succeeded Galusha as chief of police in Albuquerque. O'Grady had great pride in his police department. A strict disciplinarian, Pat O'Grady would arrest his own grandmother and put her in jail if he believed it was his duty to do so.

Edmund G. Ross, the newly-appointed city engineer, was a grandson and namesake of Edmund Gibson Ross, for decades a distinguished, colorful figure on the national political scene in America. Ed Ross's grandfather's fame rested in part from the fact that as a United States Senator from Kansas, on May 16, 1868, he had voted "no"

MUNICIPAL GOVERNMENT 117

on the roll call in the Senate on the bill to impeach Andrew Johnson, President of the United States. Because of his "no" vote, it was claimed that Ross had been ostracized and forced to leave Kansas. He came to Albuquerque in 1882, and worked at a printer's case on the *Albuquerque Journal*. On May 28, 1885, President Grover Cleveland nominated Ross, a Republican in politics, to be Governor of the Territory of New Mexico. Ross served as Governor throughout Cleveland's first administration.

I had talked on several occasions with Edmund G. Ross about his grandfather's career. I also had talked to his father, Pitt Ross, and Pitt's sister, Eddie Ross Cobb, who had worked as secretary to Governor Ross. I had known Governor Ross by sight since 1893, on a day in that year when my mother called to me to look at Ross, slowly walking past our home at 303 Baca (now Santa Fe) Avenue in Albuquerque. Mother told me that she wanted me to see Governor Ross; that he had cast the deciding vote against the impeachment of President Johnson, about which I did not understand at the time, but studied in detail in later years. Mother knew Ross by sight in Albuquerque because she had lived in Lawrence, Kansas, Ross's home town for several years and had seen him there many times. Edmund Gibson Ross died in Albuquerque on May 8, 1907, and was buried in Fairview Cemetery in Albuquerque.

Mayor Westerfeld had appointed me as city attorney in 1916 as a reward for services rendered in the campaign which had elected him. The $100 a month salary appeared to me to be a princely sum. Subsequent events, however, demonstrated that the prestige of the office was even more important to me because it gave me an opportunity to meet new people and to learn considerable about municipal government. All too soon I found myself pitched headlong into representing the city as its attorney in important litigation, an experience which proved of value in later years. Being city attorney, however attractive as it seemed to be, had its drawbacks. On July 6, 1914, Mayor David Boatright, a Republican, had appointed Thomas N. Wilkerson, an ex-alderman and loyal Republican, as city attorney. When Mayor Westerfeld appointed me as city attorney, Wilkerson refused to concede the legality of the appointment. "Nothing personal about it, you understand," Wilkerson told me on several occasions. At every regular weekly meeting of the council for several months after my appointment, Tom Wilkerson was present, and at some stage in the proceedings, arose and addressed the mayor and council, politely and with due deference, stating for the record, asking that his statement be inserted in the minutes of the meeting, that he was present in person, and was the duly appointed, qualified and acting city attorney of the city of Albuquerque; that he was ready, able and willing to serve the city; and that Westerfeld's appointment of me was an act of usurpation, and therefore null and void.

After being rebuffed several times by the city council, Wilkerson filed a suit in the District Court of Bernalillo County, asking judgment against the city for the amount claimed to be then due as salary as city attorney, and for future salary. He asked for a decree declaring him to be entitled to the office of city attorney. I filed an answer to Wilkerson's complaint for the city, alleging that on April 17, 1916, it had employed me as city attorney, and ever since had rightfully paid me the salary provided by ordinance; denied that anything was due Wilkerson and asking that I be declared city attorney. Judge Herbert F. Raynolds disqualified himself and Judge Reed Holloman, of Santa Fe, was designated by the Supreme Court to try the case.

During a recess on the day of trial Judge Holloman told me that because Judge Raynolds had ruled against me on several law points before he had taken over the case, that he felt obliged to hold that Wilkerson was the *de jure* city attorney and entitled to judgment against the city. Holloman told me that the fact that Wilkerson was a Republican, and I was a Democrat, had nothing to do with his legal view of the case. A bit sorrowfully, I thought, Holloman told me that when a young man "back in Indiana," he had been a Democrat, but had become a Republican during the Bryan-McKinley campaign of 1896.

The city appealed Holloman's decision and on October 21, 1919, the Supreme Court reversed the case, much to my satisfaction, because if it had been affirmed I would probably have been asked to repay the city the salary paid me as city attorney, which I was poorly prepared to do at that particular time. In its opinion in the case of City of Albuquerque vs. Wilkerson, 23 N.M. 368, 174 Pac. 217, the Supreme Court, among other things, held:

> Where a city has paid to a *de facto* officer holding under color of title, salary for the time actually spent in the performance of his duties, such payment is a complete defense to a suit for the salary by the *de jure* officer. The remedy of the *de jure* officer is to secure an adjudication of his title to the office, and then sue the *de facto* officer for the salary which he has collected.

As most lawyers recognize, lawyers are reluctant to sue each other; and as most lawyers know, lawyers as a class are not too anxious to do a lot of work in or out of court unless assured of success or unless a cherished principle of law is at stake. Consequently, it did not surprise me greatly when Wilkerson vs. City of Albuquerque became a closed file in the city attorney's office and in my life.

Clyde Tingley, sworn in as an alderman from the Second Ward at the Council's meeting on April 17, 1916, had been nominated for the office because Thomas Isherwood, a Republican, part owner of the Albuquerque Foundry and Machine Company, twice elected alderman from that ward, had declined to run again. At the time of his election Tingley was almost a stranger to the political bosses of the town, and to most people in the Second Ward. Helping in the campaign, it was part of my job at headquarters to see that the candidates spent as much time as possible on the highways and in the byways canvassing votes. Campaign leaders recognized that the Democrats had an uphill fight, but Tingley was consistently optimistic. He never doubted but that he would be elected. When prodded by me and others to go into the streets and alleys in the South Highlands of the Second Ward, to ring bells and knock on doors, Tingley claimed that such campaigning would accomplish nothing. He claimed that the voters had made up their minds; that he was sure he knew how they were going to vote in the 1916 election. Tingley defeated H. S. Lithgow, a bookbinder, by a vote of 287 to 229, marking the commencement of a career in public life which saw him a candidate for city commissioner many times, and which finally won for him the governorship of the state of New Mexico.

Subsequent to the 1916 city election, I learned something additional of Tingley's background. He was born in Madison County, near London, Ohio, on January 5, 1881. Tingley attended country schools in Ohio; was never much of a student. He preferred tinkering with machinery; worked briefly as a mechanic for Wright Brothers in their early-day airplane experiments, later worked for the National Cash Register Company in Dayton. After learning the machinist's trade, Tingley became a pattern-maker and tool-dresser. From all accounts, Clyde Tingley was not much of a reader, probably never read a book completely on any subject. He read newspapers occasionally, most of the time only scanning page one headlines. If an editorial commended or flattered him, Tingley would read it with interest. If a newspaper criticized or scolded him, Tingley would quickly toss it into the nearest wastebasket. Not insensitive to the influence of the press, Tingley was always anxious to know "which way the wind was blowing." He left behind him when he died several scrap books as evidence of his continued interest in public affairs in New Mexico during his political career.

While working in Bowling Green, Ohio, Tingley made the acquaintance of Carrie Wooster, daughter of Connecticut-born George Clark Wooster and Helen Reed, a native of Bowling Green. Carrie Wooster was advised by her physician to go to the Southwest for the arrest of incipient pulmonary tuberculosis. Accompanied by her mother, Carrie Wooster started from Bowling Green, intending to go to Phoenix, Arizona, became ill enroute and with her mother left the train at Albuquerque. Clyde Tingley soon followed Carrie Wooster to Albuquerque. They were married in Albuquerque on April 21, 1911 in the Congregational Church. In Ohio, Tingley had been a Dunkard. However, there were few Dunkards in New Mexico and Tingley accepted his wife's religion. The Tingleys and her mother lived for several years after their marriage in a rented home, a modest health-seeker's cottage at 717 East Iron Avenue.

Clyde Tingley enjoyed participating in political campaigns. He was a candidate for office many times, mostly for the office of city commission in the City of Albuquerque. When elected to the commission, Tingley nearly always managed to get himself elected Chairman of the Commission, which carried with it the title "ex-officio Mayor of Albuquerque," in order to comply with state law. The experience Tingley gained in municipal government in Albuquerque proved beneficial during his four years as governor. Tingley liked to hire and fire employees. Nothing gave him more pleasure than to give a deserving politician a job. Few things gave him more satisfaction than firing a man he considered disloyal to him personally or politically. In addition to being financially independent, because of his wife's inheritance, Tingley had another asset of great value in his political life, that of possessing exceptional physical strength and endurance. On one occasion, at Domingo railroad station, looking down the Santa Fe main line tracks there, Tingley told me, "See those railroad tracks? Well, I'm as strong and tough in my way as that track is in its way."

Above all, Tingley in official life in Albuquerque and in Santa Fe was an honest man. He fired instantly any employee thought to be guilty of stealing money or property; would tolerate no dishonesty.

Although not much on book learning, Tingley shrewdly recognized that an education for every child was important, and that it was good politics to vote for, work for, and publicly support school and educational-purpose bond issues.

CHAPTER EIGHT

City Water Works

THE MOST important legal business to come before the city council during my first two years as city attorney (1916–1918) revolved around the legal right of the City of Albuquerque to "buy or build a water supply." The voters had authorized the issuance of $400,000 in bonds on April 4, 1916. The water plant, built in 1882 by Angus A. Grant, a Canadian contractor who had built parts of the Atlantic and Pacific and Santa Fe Railroads into Albuquerque, passed into other hands after Grant's death. The Water Supply Company, a New Mexico corporation, owned it for many years prior to 1916. Alonzo Bertram McMillen, attorney for the First National Bank of Albuquerque, and Frank A. Hubbell, successful sheep and cattle raiser, owned the control stock of the corporation, its assets including wells and pumping stations in the valley, most of them located on a large tract of land situated at Broadway and Tijeras Road. The Water Supply Company rigidly clung to a policy of refusing to extend service lines unless, in its opinion, cost of the extension could be justified, the company insisting on a net annual return of 8%. Many consumers claimed the policy to be shortsighted, contending that it retarded the growth and expansion of the city.

The men who managed the Water Company business apparently had no concern with establishing and maintaining good relations with the consumers, seemingly going out of their way to antagonize citizens. Customer complaints, so it was contended, were brushed off with scant courtesy, and little attempt made to conciliate the complainant. Some of those antagonized pointed to the Henry Lee Ensign fountain case as an example of the alleged indifferent attitude. The Ensign fountain had been erected in 1908 at the intersection of Second Street and Railroad Avenue and then moved to Broadway and Railroad Avenue, dedicated to public use, largely through the efforts of Attorney R. W. D. Bryan. The drinking fountain, a humanitarian project, was primarily for the use of thirsty dogs, horses and other animals. Acting under what it conceived to be its franchise rights, the City of Albuquerque requested the Water Company to furnish free water for the fountain. The company disputed the city's interpretation of the franchise, and sent the city a bill for every gallon of water used at the fountain, insisted upon prompt payment, threatened to turn off the water. The city went to court. The plea for free water for the animals was upheld by the Supreme Court in Water Supply Co. vs. City of Albuquerque, 17 N.M. 326, decided on November 7, 1912.

The company's main reservoir had been built on land adjacent to today's northeast corner of Yale and Central Avenue. The original reservoir has been replaced on the same site by a reservoir of much greater capacity, much to the distress and disappointment of officials of the University of New Mexico. The construction of one replacement reservoir was the subject of a quarrel in 1923 between Dr. David Spence Hill, President of the University of New Mexico, and Edwin B. Swope, Chairman of the

City Commission and ex-officio mayor of the City of Albuquerque. The men met at the reservoir site by prearrangement to discuss, ostensibly in a friendly manner, the most direct method of "getting rid of the reservoir." The meeting between Hill and Swope started off pleasantly enough, but soon degenerated into a name calling contest. After having exchanged harsh words, neither man was willing to yield an inch of ground. As a result the old reservoir was razed and another one built in the same location to take its place on land that should been acquired by the University. The controversy testified to the stubbornness of two men, ordinarily anxious to accomplish something worthwhile for the public good.

The voters of the city, having voted $400,000 to "buy or build a plant," had placed a strong bargaining-club in the hands of the men making up the city administration. McMillen, a shrewd and capable lawyer and businessman, knew that his sole course of action was to try and make a deal by which the water property would be sold to the city. He realized that it would be dangerous to permit the water company to be manuevered into a position which would justify the city in building a competing plant. The buy or build phrase of the business passed into the negotiating stages and bitterness developed between and among the negotiators, delaying progress. An entirely new factor was injected into the situation when the voters of Albuquerque, at a special election held on September 25, 1917, adopted a city charter establishing the city manager commission form of government, with December 4, 1917, as the mandatory effective date.

The recently organized Albuquerque Rotary Club, looking about for a timely public project it could wholeheartedly support, with no political overtones, decided to throw the weight and prestige of its membership behind a new form of government for Albuquerque. The Rotarians contended that the city had outgrown the aldermanic form of government, under which it had been governed since 1891, and campaigned vigorously and with surprising effect, in favor of modern type of municipal organization. The Rotarians, most of them tyros in politics, managed to have the state legislature enact an enabling act in 1917. William P. Metcalf, a real estate and fire insurance broker, who had graduated many years previously from Brown University, and to the surprise of many fellow citizens, spoke French fluently and read French novels voraciously, volunteered to write a proposed charter, which was to be submitted to the voters for adoption or rejection.

"Mecky" as he was known to friend and foe alike, was considered to be a red-hot socialist, steeped in the doctrine and political philosophy of Eugene V. Debs. In several Territorial elections, Metcalf had been the Socialist candidate for delegate in Congress. In some elections he polled several hundred votes, most of them, his enemies claimed, being cast by those anxious to get him to reside in Washington, D.C., instead of in Albuquerque. At a non-intermission "sitting" in an afternoon, as observers later reported, Metcalf managed to peck out on an old-fashioned typewriter, Albuquerque's first city charter, providing for a commissioner-city manager form of government, which contained machinery for the initiative, referendum, recall, at the time considered dangerous, Socialistic, almost Communistic. To the astonishment of politicians, Democrat and Republican, the charter was adopted by the voters of Albuquerque as submitted, and although amended from time to time over the intervening years, remained the basic law under which Albuquerque is governed.

Soon after Mayor Westerfield had taken office, the council authorized the execution of a buy and sell agreement between the city and water company. Among other things, the agreement provided for arbitration as to price. Assuming the arbitrators fixed a price of more than $400,000, the city would have the right to refuse to buy. The city named Black and Veatch, Kansas City engineers, as its arbitrators. James N. Gladding, one-time Albuquerque city engineer, was designated to act for the Water Supply Company. The arbitrators fixed $453,591 as the reasonable value of the property. The city refused to buy. Mayor Westerfield, on behalf of the city, announced in a newspaper interview that the city would promptly begin to build an entirely new, modern plant.

Well aware of the powers of the city to build an entirely new plant, together with distribution lines, and recognizing that its own franchise to sell water in Albuquerque would expire in a few months, the Water Supply owners decided to throw in their chips. The city of Albuquerque had won in the biggest poker game then in town. A new contract was executed, by which the city agreed to pay and the company agreed to accept $400,000 in bonds, par value, plus accrued interest, for the water property.

John C. Thompson, New York bond attorney, acting for the water company, rendered an opinion pointing out several defects in the bond proceedings. Mr. Thompson required a decision by the New Mexico Supreme Court before he would certify the bonds as valid and binding on the municipality. The water company filed a complaint against the City of Albuquerque, alleging that $400,000 in bonds had been voted, reciting the several agreements in regard to sale and purchase, and alleged certain various defects in the proceedings. On July 10, 1918, the Supreme Court of New Mexico validated the bonds in a fifty-six page opinion, City of Albuquerque vs. Water Supply Company, 24 N.M. 368, which held, among other things that the city had acted within the law in submitting a "buy or build" ballot at the April 4, 1916 election; and holding that there was no illegality in the transaction, notwithstanding it had been initiated under the aldermanic form of government, completed under a city-manager-commission form of government. Nothing now remained except the mechanics of delivering the bonds in exchange for deeds of conveyance, a bill of sale and assurance of title. At an appointed time, City Treasurer Warren Graham and I met A. B. McMillen in the County Clerk's office in the Courthouse in Old Town to close the deal. McMillen was to hand to Graham, for the city, a warranty deed and bill of sale, duly signed and sealed, conveying the real and personal property to the city, together with a release of a deed of trust securing a bond issue on the property, signed by The Harris Trust Company of Chicago, Trustee. Warren Graham was thereupon to hand McMillen a package containing the bonds.

At the last moment, it was discovered that the deed of conveyance did not have attached to it the necessary United States revenue stamps. Graham balked at closing the deal unless revenue stamps were provided. Driving a new automobile, with Graham and Keleher in the back seat, McMillen left the Courthouse en route to the new town. Near a cluster of *adobe* houses known at the time as *Rancho Seco*, a small boy suddenly darted across the road, right in the path of the oncoming automobile. With the day of the four-wheel brake years in the future, McMillen relied on the emergency brake, veering to a stop when the car struck a large cottonwood tree on the north side of the road. The small boy escaped unhurt.

Although badly shaken, McMillen continued his quest

for revenue stamps, the search ending in the office of Carl A. Hatch, at the time Collector of U.S. Internal Revenue for New Mexico, near Third Street and Gold Avenue. Collector Carl Hatch was destined to become, some years later, United States Senator from New Mexico, and then United States District Judge for New Mexico. At the time, however, Hatch, together with one clerk and one bookkeeper-cashier, made up the entire staff of the New Mexico Collector's office.

CHAPTER NINE

Political Destinies

FOR YEARS before and after 1930, David Chavez, Jr., a Santa Fe lawyer, was the acknowledged leader of the Democratic party in the northern New Mexico counties of Santa Fe, San Miguel, Sandoval, Rio Arriba, Taos, and Mora. Born in Albuquerque on November 12, 1898, Chavez attended Albuquerque schools and the University of New Mexico. He joined the Army in 1918, and after finishing his military service as an artillery officer, studied law at Georgetown University in Washington. After graduation from Georgetown with an LL.B. in 1922, Chavez moved from Albuquerque, his home town, to Santa Fe in 1923. He began to practice law there and soon became a successful lawyer and a political leader. It would be difficult to say just how much of his political strength was bestowed on him because he was a brother of Congressman, later Senator Dennis Chavez, but it is quite certain that even without the prestige that came to him as the result of such relationship, David Chavez would on his own have become an important political power in his part of the state.

David Chavez was only casually interested in Albuquerque politics. He was fairly well acquainted with Clyde Tingley, but had never considered him seriously as a prospective candidate for state office. I was aware that Tingley, deep down in his secretive soul, harbored political ambitions; that he had nourished political leadership plans as far back as the Arthur T. Hannett administration of 1923 and 1924, during which Tingley blossomed out for the first time as a figure in state politics. Hannett had made him a District Highway Engineer, with jurisdiction over eleven counties in central and eastern New Mexico. Within a few months Hannett decided that Tingley was spending too much time talking politics and not enough time in building highways. Hannett clipped Tingley's wings by reducing his territory to four counties: Bernalillo, Sandoval, Torrance and Valencia. Tingley was smart enough not to express resentment or attempt to retaliate.

In 1931 I learned that Tingley was not only interested in becoming the Democratic party's candidate for governor at the coming state convention, but was already making plans to further his chances. Not long afterward, I talked to David Chavez, Jr., about Tingley's situation. My viewpoint was that, with his power in northern counties, Chavez could form an alliance with Tingley in Bernalillo County, and that combined they could muster enough delegate strength in the state convention to dictate a ticket. At the time, David Chavez was ambitious to be mayor of Santa Fe, but told me frankly that the Democrats there lacked the "sinews of war" to wage a winning campaign. At my request, Chavez prepared a tentative budget for an imaginary campaign in Santa Fe. The list contained a memorandum of so many dollars for helpers to ring door bells in Santa Fe; and so many dollars for workers to go from house to house spreading the good news that at long last Dave Chavez had been persuaded to run for mayor; a modest number of dollars for radio and newspaper advertising; small sums for placards and signs, and for payment of workers and challengers at polling places. Expenditures itemized for automobiles and paid drivers, oil and gasoline for volunteer workers with cars of their own brought the Chavez-Santa Fe budget up to a staggering total of $1,900.

Clyde Tingley promptly agreed to underwrite the budget, which in the language of the politician meant that Tingley or someone for him would put up the money. I asked Dave Chavez to drive from Santa Fe and to meet Tingley the next day at Santo Domingo, an Indian Pueblo located half way between the two towns. "I will have Tingley there at 10 o'clock tomorrow morning," I told Chavez. "He will travel alone, but will be accompanied by a small suitcase." Chavez was at the threshold of a distinguished career, which eventually placed him as a United States District Judge in Puerto Rico, and the Chief Judgeship of the Supreme Court of New Mexico. Dave Chavez met Tingley at the appointed rendezvous.

As a partial result of Tingley's timely assistance, the Santa Fe campaign got off to a running start. Chavez was elected mayor of Santa Fe on April 5, 1932, after a hard-hitting campaign, defeating P. C. Berardinelli 3,040 to 2,136, a majority of 904, a decisive victory in a town long considered a Republican stronghold. Recognizing that in David Chavez they had a winning candidate, the Democrats elected him district attorney on November 8, 1932, after he had served some months during an interim appointment to that office. In cooperating with David Chavez in the Santa Fe campaign, Tingley took a giant stride toward being governor of New Mexico. Democratic political leaders in Santa Fe, Rio Arriba and other northern counties quickly got the word that Tingley had helped

POLITICAL DESTINIES 133

Dave Chavez become mayor of Santa Fe, and that he might run for governor.

The time came on January 1, 1935, when Clyde Tingley was sworn in as governor of the State of New Mexico, claimed by many politicians to be a high honor, by many others looked upon only as a political graveyard.

When he became governor, Tingley succeeded Andrew William Hockenhull, lawyer, banker, farmer, of Clovis, Curry County, a former Missourian, who had been catapulted into the governor's chair following Governor Arthur Seligman's death on September 25, 1933. Hockenhull did not presume to be a politician. He ran the Governor's office on a business basis. Because he would not play politics their way, some important party leaders decided not to renominate him and threw their strength to Clyde Tingley.

At his request I wrote Tingley's inaugural address for him, which was delivered on Tuesday, January 1, 1935. The full text of the address was published in the *Santa Fe New Mexican* on the same day. The speech was based entirely on my ideas. Neither Tingley nor any other person offered any suggestions as to content. I believed I was aware of the sentiment of the people of New Mexico generally, and knew what Tingley should say. I wrote also at Tingley's request, the governor's first message to the legislature. In the first paragraph of the inaugural address, some things were said that would perhaps bear repeating today:

> The government of the United States in 1848 found here the descendants of those Spanish conquerors, far removed from the seat of Mexican government at Mexico City, estranged and isolated, working out with great courage, their own destiny, many thousands of miles from the mother land

of Spain, sympathetic in the main with the idea of becoming loyal American citizens. But the government of the United States, with a stupidity unbelievable today, left the people of New Mexico, recent nationals of another country, speaking another language, almost as it found them, making no provision for education in the English language, for the teaching of the history of the United States, or for any forward looking enterprise on their behalf. Any contribution that the government of the United States can make today to right the wrong done New Mexico and her people will only be a feeble gestures of restoration and restitution, the payment of a debt long past due.

In an editorial published in the *Santa Fe New Mexican* on January 2, 1935, Dana Johnson appraised the Tingley speech:

Having some lingering doubts as to the frequency with which it will have opportunities to agree with Clyde Tingley, the new governor of New Mexico, the *New Mexican* hastens to approve three items in his inaugural address, which were about the only three definite statements of his speech yesterday. They are as follows: To reduce the costs of government in every department down to the smallest school district. Intelligent development and settlement of New Mexico in a manner to retain its distinctive atmosphere and tradition, as against the present loudly ballyhooed movement of the "tourist development league," and other individuals to bring millions upon millions of people here, so long as they are people, by spending highway funds for advertising. Mr. Tingley's promise to be governor of all the people, not merely governor of Tingley Democrats, a fraction of the population.

For the rest, Mr. Tingley's speech revealed a mastery of poetical and musical diction and polished English, a deep emotional feeling for state traditions and the Spanish culture and a familiarity with state history, which proved most surprising and delightful. As to the cooperation of all the people of New Mexico, the new governor, to whom we extend best wishes, will get it in exactly the proportion in which he proves an inclination to cooperate with all the people of New Mexico.

Arthur Seligman had appointed me as a member of the State Board of Finance soon after his inauguration on January 1, 1933. Upon Seligman's death, Governor Hockenhull, his successor, asked me to remain on the board during the rest of his term. The Board of Finance, composed of the governor, state auditor and three citizens, was perhaps the most powerful and influential board or commission participating in state government at the time. Politicians dubbed the board "the little legislature," and in some respects the appellation was appropriate. During the two-year intervals between sessions of the legislature, the Board of Finance had sufficient legal authority to keep the financial affairs of the state in motion. As originally constituted under the Act of January 1, 1917, the board was composed of the governor, the state auditor and the state treasurer. The 1917 Statutes were amended by the Legislature of 1923 to provide for a finance board made up of the governor, state auditor and three additional members, not more than two of whom should belong to the same political party.

In my time of service on the board, the members had the authority, among other things: to supervise the sale of state bonds and highway debentures; to supervise the investment of public funds by the state treasurer; to supervise the acts of the state fiscal agency; and in time of emergency and urgent public need, to make funds available for a public purpose by selling to the State Treasurer casual certificates of indebtedness in an amount not exceeding $200,000. We were authorized to decrease legislative appropriations to the extent of not more than ten per cent and to subsequently restore any decrease.

The power to interfere with the disbursement of money appropriated by the legislature made it possible for a governor or board wishing to play politics to punish some institutions and reward others. However, it was my experience, extending over a period of sixteen consecutive years, under Governors Seligman, Hockenhull, Tingley, Miles, Dempsey and Mabry, that political motives were not permitted to influence important decisions, or determine policy.

Membership on the State Board of Finance made it possible for me to know and understand financial and other major problems of the various state institutions of higher learning, hospitals, the reform school, the penitentiary and other state facilities; to study the budgets of the State Highway Department, Department of Public Welfare and other like departments, and to become acquainted with the executive officers of the various institutions and departments. Most of these officers were purposeful, dedicated, well-qualified men and women interested in doing a good job for the public rather than in playing politics.

Of the six governors under whom I served on the State Board of Finance, Seligman, Hockenhull, Tingley, Miles, Dempsey and Mabry, it is my belief that Tingley was the best qualified man for the job. Seligman was better educated than Tingley, much more astute, quite brilliant, and mentally resourceful in many avenues of approach. Tingley was plain and plodding, independent financially because Mrs. Tingley was a comparatively wealthy woman, and he had nothing to do but be governor, hunt and fish. He yelled when he was hurt politically, listened too much to the "hangers-on." He never learned, as Arthur T. Hannett had, to "lick sore paws and say nothing." Hockenhull was a fine governor in many respects; he thought in terms of banking and business, and had great respect for the value of the dollar.

The outdoor sportsman's life was a serious avocation with Clyde Tingley. He enjoyed roughing it in the mountains and plains of New Mexico. He was a good shot with rifle or shotgun, and a tireless hunter, whether shooting at prairie chickens, ducks or geese, or on the trail of predatory animals. When he became governor of New Mexico Tingley moved into the upper echelon of hunters and fishermen. He had a boat on Elephant Butte Lake, hunted elk and other big game on the Vermejo in Colfax County, which became his favorite hunting ground. While Governor, Tingley invited friends to hunt, and as they hunted de luxe they were almost certain to be successful. During the 1936 elk season Tingley had Douglas Fairbanks as his guest on the Vermejo and saw to it that Fairbanks shot a good-sized animal. When Tingley became a candidate to succeed himself as governor at the November 3, 1936 election, Douglas Fairbanks, then living in Hollywood and quite a popular motion picture actor, offered to come to New Mexico and make a speech on Tingley's behalf. Tingley accepted the offer and asked me to write a speech for Fairbanks, to be delivered at a rally in the Armory in Albuquerque a few days before the election. The speech was to be short, typed on one sheet of paper. I had the speech ready for Douglas Fairbanks on his arrival in Albuquerque by airplane from Los Angeles. He accompanied me to the Armory, where he was to speak, so that he could appraise the situation, took the one page speech I handed him, studied it for a moment or two, as if photographing it in his memory, then crumpled it in his hands, making a ball of the paper, and tossed it into the air. When the time came to deliver the speech, Fairbanks delivered it almost verbatim.

It is doubtful if the speech Douglas Fairbanks made in

the Albuquerque Armory influenced many voters, but Tingley was elected over his opponent Jaffa Miller by a vote of 98,089 to 72,511.

It may be appropriate here to say that Governor William C. McDonald, the first elected governor after statehood, was in my estimation, the nearest approach to an ideal governor during my time of personal acquaintance with governors, extending over a period of more than fifty years. Arthur T. Hannett, elected governor for a two-year term, by a margin of 199 votes over Manuel B. Otero, on November 4, 1924, endeavored to follow in McDonald's footsteps, and made an excellent governor. Hannett was disastrously defeated by Richard C. Dillon when he ran for a second term in 1926, largely through the instrumentality of Bronson Cutting, who backed Dillon heavily. Cutting, although a Republican, had supported Hannett when he ran for governor in 1924, and was entitled to ask Hannett to be remembered in the distribution of patronage. Upon the death of Justiniano Baca, recently elected Commissioner of Public Lands, Cutting had asked Hannett to name Jesus Baca to succeed him. Hannett refused on the ground that in his opinion Jesus Baca was not qualified to hold the office. Cutting then asked Hannett to appoint any Spanish-American of his own selection as Justiniano Baca's successor. Hannett again refused and appointed Edwin B. Swope as commissioner. Some time after the Swope appointment, I asked Hannett why he had appointed Swope; why he had not acceded to Cutting's request, suggesting that it would not have been difficult to appoint Jesus Baca as commissioner upon condition that a qualified professional supervise the work of the office. Hannett admitted that his refusal to comply with Cutting's request had been a major political mistake, but said that Swope wanted the appointment, that he was entitled to it and that he, Hannett, had no alternative but to name him for the place.

Tingley was not an original idea man, but once he realized the significance and vote-getting potential in an idea offered by someone else, he was quick to adopt it, and capable in furthering its objective. During the 1935 Legislature, while Tingley was serving his first term as governor, he was greatly disturbed by the financial crisis pending in educational finance in the common schools and higher educational institutions. Tax collections had plummeted to an all-time record low. Salaries of teachers went unpaid in some school districts for month after month. No funds were in sight to keep the school doors open. Parents, teachers and others interested in the schools, became desperate, bitter and disillusioned. School officials became alarmed. Tingley called a special meeting of his Board of Finance. Julian O. Seth, anchor man on the Finance Board, and I urged Tingley to send a special message to the Legislature, asking the enactment of a sales tax, at the time a comparatively new concept of taxation, but commonplace today.

Tingley was reluctant to support such a tax, fearing possible political retaliation on election day. The governor fiinally agreed to the proposed tax when it was pointed out to him that he could assure the voters that the tax law might possibly prove to be only a temporary measure, and emphasizing that its purpose was to save the common schools. When Tingley finally agreed, Seth and I sat up most of one night drawing a bill for submission to the Legislature the next day. We had as legal guide posts only the Constitution of New Mexico, and the recently enacted Mississippi sales tax law. The bill, introduced in the Legislature with the title "Temporary Emergency School Sales Tax," was passed with a "a whoop and a holler," as Tingley later described it. The Sales Tax Statute withstood a number of attacks in court. Instead of an "emergency tax," however, the sales tax law became a permanent fixture of the taxation and revenue procedure in New Mexico, still on the law books some thirty-five years after its enactment. The tax made it possible for the common schools of the state to survive and prosper beyond the expectations of the most enthusiastic advocates of better education.

Drastic and far-reaching national recovery statutes, enacted by the National Congress during the early part of Franklin D. Roosevelt's "New Deal" administration proved a most welcome diversion to Governor Clyde Tingley. As he saw it, Washington was at long last appropriating money for projects which Tingley could understand: making money available to put men back to work; and putting to practical use the upper echelon philosophy of bulk vote getting. Plans, specifications, blue prints, as Tingley well knew, could be quickly transformed into payrolls and cash flow for industry through P.W.A. and W.P.A. projects. Knowing that the money-trees in Washington would not bloom indefinitely, Tingley worked feverishly to garner public project funds while they were available. Tingley made twenty-three railway round-trips from Santa Fe to Washington. Incidental to such visits, he got promises of money help for many New Mexico projects, and as a by-product became well acquainted with President Roosevelt. In 1936 Tingley was asked to be the President's guest on a special train-swing around the circle of seven western states, much to Tingley's delight and elation.

While going in and out of the White House to talk to the President's aides about projects for New Mexico, Tingley was promised help from the President in person for a hospital Tingley proposed to build on an already selected site at Hot Springs (Truth or Consequences) in Sierra County, New Mexico, for the treatment of crippled children. Although Tingley was enthusiastic about the proposed hospital project, the credit for the establishment of such an institution really belonged to the Governor's wife who had been a frequent visitor at St. Anthony's Hospital in Las Vegas, New Mexico, a pioneer in the treatment of infantile paralysis. Impressed with the need for such facilities in New Mexico, Mrs. Tingley persuaded the Governor to ask for help in Washington. President Roosevelt promised Tingley that not only would he help him obtain funds for a such a project, but would get for him without cost the services of the architects who had designed the hospital at the Georgia Warm Springs Foundation where the President had been a patient, and had established his "little White House."

With the promise of federal funds and other assistance from Washington, Tingley took the first train from Washington to Chicago, talked to President E. J. Engel, of the Santa Fe Railroad and received from him a promise to at once publish new tariffs for freight shipments from all points on the Santa Fe system to Engle, the nearest railway point to the hospital site. Returning to Santa Fe, Tingley promptly called a special meeting of the Board of Penitentiary Commissioners and the board adopted a resolution authorizing and directing the State Penitentiary Warden to deliver free at the hospital site all brick and tile from the penitentiary kilns in Santa Fe required for the construction of the hospital.

Prohibited by the New Mexico Constitution from serving more than two consecutive terms, Governor Tingley in 1937 became obsessed with the idea that he ought to run for a third term. During his second term he became convinced that the people of New Mexico wanted him for at least two additional years, apparently considering the Constitutional prohibition against a third term as merely an obstacle to be overcome. Encouraged by several close political advisors, Tingley succeeded in having the 1937 Legislature adopt House Joint Resolution No. 25, which was approved on March 5, 1937, the title to which read as follows: "A Joint Resolution proposing to amend section one of article five of the Constitution of the State of New Mexico, relating to state officers, term, ineligibility and residence."

The proposed amendment deleted all words prohibiting a governor serving more than two successive terms. The Secretary of State issued the required proclamation calling an election to be held on September 21, 1937. Some days after the proclamation had been published for the first time, I asked Governor Tingley to tell me something about his plans for carrying the election. He told me of the many thousands of votes he could count on receiving in several counties. He told about the majorities he could expect through the work of various organizations and of the important support he could rely on by the State Highway Department. I remarked: "Governor Tingley, unless you have more support than you have told me about, I am afraid it won't be possible for you to win." The governor pressed me for my reasons and I told him that he had not accounted for three men: United States Senator Dennis Chavez, former Governor A. T. Hannett and John E. Miles, long time chairman of the State Central Committee. Each man had been for years an individual political powerhouse in his own right. All three of them were weatherbeaten, tough, seasoned veterans of the political wars, in no sense whatever party hacks. It seemed to me

POLITICAL DESTINIES 143

vital that their combined support would be essential for Tingley's success at the polls.

Ever a man of action, Tingley said, "All right, Bill Keleher, if things seem that way to you, better get those men together in your office in Albuquerque at 4:00 o'clock tomorrow afternoon. I'll be there and talk to them."

I got the three men together as the governor had requested. Promptly at 4:00 o'clock, Tingley walked into my office, shook hands politely with Chavez, Hannett and Miles. I sensed at once that the prevailing atmosphere was not one conducive to a successful meeting. After the amenities of the occasion had been observed, Tingley got down to business. He told the men somewhat in detail of his plans to run for reelection; said he was confident that the voters would back the proposed constitutional amendment and asked them for their support and influence. The silence that followed Tingley's statement was significant and embarrassing. Finally Chavez spoke: "Governor, we have all been a good deal surprised and perplexed by your attitude in this matter. You didn't ask our advice. Certainly you didn't consult me about your intention to ask the Legislature to submit this constitutional amendment to the people." Tingley instantly replied, "Senator, neither did I consult anybody when I decided to appoint you to the United States Senate."

To this perhaps unexpected reply, Chavez, somewhat disconcerted, made no immediate comment. The talk drifted in the direction of generalities and finally ceased altogether. No promises, no assurances, no pledge of friendship came from Hannett, Chavez or Miles.

There being no further need for discussion, the conference was abruptly terminated. Tingley arose, maintaining as much poise and dignity as possible under the circumstances. He said by way of farewell, "Good afternoon, gentlemen," and stalked out of the office. Chavez, Hannett and Miles remained behind for only a few moments, saying nothing of importance, then left, taking with them a secret well-guarded for many weeks thereafter. They had already agreed, among themselves, it became evident later, not only to knife Tingley's proposed constitutional amendment, but to nominate and elect John E. Miles as New Mexico's next governor.

The Carrie Tingley Memorial Hospital, built at Hot Springs, in the heart of the Caballo Mountains, was completed, ready for occupancy by September 1, 1937, a magnificent group of buildings, equipped with the latest facilities for the treatment of crippled and deformed children. The dedication, originally scheduled for May 29, but postponed from time to time at the Governor's request, was finally fixed for September 19, 1937. From the practical standpoint, this date conflicted to quite an extent with the special election scheduled for September 21, 1937. The results of that election would tell whether Clyde Tingley was to be the undisputed leader of the democratic organization in New Mexico, or a political "has been."

After Chavez, Hannett and Miles openly declared their united opposition to the proposed third term announcement, Congressmen John J. Dempsey joined them in the rebellion against Tingley. By September 19, 1937, the day set for the dedication to the public of the Carrie Tingley Hospital for Crippled Children, Governor Tingley well knew that he was fighting a desperate back-to-the-wall battle for political survival. Confidential reports poured in to his headquarters from field commanders telling of desertions from Tingley's side. Senator Chavez and Congressman Dempsey, with much federal patronage to dispense or withhold, had knocked out many party workers who ordinarily would have been identified with Tingley's cause.

Realizing the situation, Tingley was in a belligerent mood as he walked up the steps of the platform erected for the program in front of the hospital in Hot Springs on the day of the dedication, an unhappy participant. Under-Secretary Charles West, of the Department of the Interior, had come from Washington to represent the federal government, to bring with him a personal message of congratulations and good will from President Rosevelt, addressed to Governor Tingley, and through him to the people of New Mexico. The band played bravely, and the crowd of several hundred cheered as Governor Tingley rose to speak. He touched brieflly on the hospital, saying among other things that he and Mrs. Tingley had worked hard to make a reality of their dream of a hospital for unfortunate children. He said he had made fifty-nine round trips between Santa Fe and Hot Springs, "many of them by driving late at night and early in the morning." Tossing away his prepared speech, the governor began a blistering personal attack on Senator Chavez, Congressman Dempsey, former Governor Hannett and political chieftain John E. Miles. Fortunately, just as Tingley began his attack on the politicians, something went wrong with the broadcasting mechanism and communication with the radio station in Albuquerque was cut off, depriving the voters of the Tingley speech.

The Chavez-Hannett-Dempsey-Miles wing of the Democratic party beat Tingley in the special election by a vote of 56,749 to 34,826, or a majority of 21,923. Tingley bowed to the inevitable. At a succeeding primary election, he was elated when Congressman Jack Dempsey filed as a candidate for the United States Senate against Dennis

Chavez, causing Chavez no end of trouble. Tingley smiled, too, with satisfaction, two years later when he learned that his successor, Governor John E. Miles, had induced the Interstate Streams Commission, at a special meeting in Carlsbad, to send a telegram to A. T. Hannett notifying him in a surprise move that he had lost his thousand dollar a month job as attorney for the commission.

Carrie Tingley Hospital for Crippled Children at Truth or Consequences, New Mexico, stands today as an enduring achievement of the Clyde Tingley administration, a lasting monument to his public life and to the splendid work of his wife, Carrie Wooster Tingley, the inspiration for the institution. Since the hospital was dedicated on September 19, 1937, and through December 31, 1968, a total of 13,921 children have been treated as out-patients; 5,877 children have been treated as in-patients; more than 4,775 children have received orthopedic surgery at the hospital. Thousands of New Mexicans, parents, fathers and mothers of its young patients, have been recipients of joy and happiness, as intangible results of the establishment and maintenance of the hospital.

John Miles was elected governor in his first campaign over Albert K. Mitchell, an able, highly-respected, widely-known Republican, in a tough race, by a vote of 82,344 to 75,017. The outgoing governor, Clyde Tingley was a reluctant witness to the Miles inaugural ceremonies in 1939. He had been prevailed upon, at almost the last moment, to ride to the ceremonies in an automobile with the governor-elect. He gave lip-service only to the events of the day. Tingley listened with scant interest to the new governor's address; he joined the audience on occasion in a mild burst of applause.

As the echoes of the sixteen-gun salute faded away announcing the end of the old administration and the beginning of the new one, Tingley quietly slipped away from the platform and joined Mrs. Tingley, who was waiting for him on the outskirts of the crowd. Together they walked the short distance to the Governor's mansion, a three-story Territorial style buff brick building. By their attitude and demeanor it was apparent they had come to say good bye to a place which had been their home for four consecutive years; here they had lived as Governor and First Lady of their adopted state of New Mexico. Suddenly, as if on impulse, Tingley excused himself, explaining to Mrs. Tingley that he wanted to take a last look at the mansion. Their furniture had been already removed from the mansion and shipped to Albuquerque. Returning to Mrs. Tingley's side after a few moments, the former governor, secretive as always, neglected to tell Mrs. Tingley that while on the farewell tour he had locked and bolted every window and door, leaving the incoming governor to enter the mansion as best he could. Tingley had carried away all the keys, and kept them for many years as souvenirs.

It was difficult for Clyde Tingley to accept the fact that he was no longer governor of New Mexico. Not long after he had moved back to Albuquerque from Santa Fe, Tingley complained about some of the appointments being made by John Miles, his successor, firing Tingley's appointees, making his own appointments. I told Tingley: "Governor, you will find it necessary to face this kind of thing. The King is dead, long live the King." To this remark Tingley had a ready answer: "Who in the hell said anything about a king being dead?"

Whether or not he had even heard of John Quincy Adams, sixth president of the United States, who had served many years in the Congress after he had been president, nevertheless, Clyde Tingley decided to pursue a like course. Instead of champing at the bit after he was no longer governor of New Mexico, Tingley became once again a candidate for the City Commission, was elected and re-elected, rendering valuable service in his old position as Chairman of the Commission and ex-officio Mayor of Albuquerque.

John Esten Miles, born in Murfreesboro, Tennessee on July 28, 1884, one of the political trio, Chavez, Hannett and Miles, which had conspired to defeat Tingley's bid for a third term, became Governor of New Mexico on January 1, 1939. "A poor boy from the country" if there ever was one, Miles went from Tennessee to Oklahoma, then emigrated to San Jon, Quay County, New Mexico in 1906, beginning his political career in that country in 1908 as a deputy county assessor. John Miles made a very good governor, in my opinion, despite the constant pressure of old political cronies to whom he tried his best to be loyal. He was re-elected for a second term in 1940.

John Miles, who succeeded Tingley as governor, had more down-to-earth, close, personal friends than Tingley. Miles made life-long friends where Tingley's friendships were mostly based on expedient political alliance. Dempsey thought twice as fast as Tingley, but lacked the common touch. He could not command or hold, as Tingley could, the affection and friendship of the ordinary mine-run politician. The years of the Dempsey administration were clouded by the governor's dream of a rock asphalt empire. Thomas J. Mabry worked hard at being governor. He was always anxious to accomplish as much as possible for the state and its people. Almost every Sunday, Governor and Mrs. Mabry attended religious services in Santa Fe or elsewhere in the state and then went on a long motor ride to off-the-beaten-path places, associating with people of different beliefs and customs, nearly always in Indian pueblos and ancient Spanish-American villages.

During the waning months of the Mabry administration persistent rumors were in circulation throughout the state that wide-open gambling was not only permitted and tolerated, but that games of chance were being welcomed in several border counties. Men close to the situation in Santa Fe claimed that although the State Police had knowledge of the gambling violations, they ignored them, and refused to cooperate with citizens willing to sign affidavits which would justify prosecution. Illegal gambling appeared to be particularly flagrant in Dona Ana County. A committee of prominent Las Cruces lawyers, composed of Wayne C. Whatley, Judge Edwin Mechem and Rufus C. Garland, having despaired of receiving assistance from local officials, went to Santa Fe and submitted their grievances to Clarence R. Brice, Chief Justice of the Supreme Court of New Mexico. Alarmed by the recital of the Las Cruces lawyers, Judge Brice promptly placed the complaints before Governor Mabry and received assurance from him of prompt investigation. Before Messrs. Whatley, Mechem and Garland returned to Las Cruces, they filed a petition in the Supreme Court asking that Judge James B. McGhee of the Fifth Judicial District, of Roswell, be designated to have exclusive jurisdiction in a specified area over all grand jury proceedings and prosecutions relating to alleged gambling violations. Based on the petition Chief Justice Brice caused a sweeping Supreme Court order to be entered, and within a few days Judge McGhee swung into action. He spent several days investigating on his own, learned about plans for a complete take-over by the gambling syndicate; was convinced that from the standpoint of the gambling fraternity "there was gold to be found in them thar hills." Locations were being eagerly sought after in areas adjacent to Texas and Oklahoma, accessible to places where the big gamblers and high rollers had their habitat. Anapra, Dona Ana County, New Mexico, not far from El Paso, and Ruidoso, in Lea County, were already on an agreed upon "pay" basis of $4,500 per month. Eagle Nest, Colfax County, accessible to Oklahoma, and only a short distance from a New Mexico race track, was also in the $4,500 category. Some local authorities in Hot Springs, Sierra County, approached the matter of revenue from a practical viewpoint. According to testimony given under oath in a Sierra County grand jury investigation, the "pay off" due Hot Springs went direct, without any deduction, to a Hot Springs street improvement fund. The same witness, before the same grand jury, given immunity from prosecution, testified as to the scale of payment on slot machines throughout several counties: Forty percent went to the owner of the location in which the machine was installed, forty percent to the owner of the machine, and twenty percent to politicians.

Although there was never any outward manifestation of concurrence or understanding as to objectives, there was little doubt but that Judge Brice and Judge McGhee had the same idea in mind: "Save Tom Mabry's administration from any manipulation by gamblers." It was apparent that the two judges had decided to take such steps as might be required to either ignore or erase at least for the time being, the thin line of demarcation established in New Mexico between the executive and judicial branches of government, or at least it so appeared to astonished observers of their maneuvering.

In the Supreme Court Chief Justice Brice, with a profound knowledge of the Constitution of New Mexico, because he had helped frame it as a member of the Constitutional Convention from Eddy County in 1910, had seen to it that the order designating Judge McGhee to act was sufficiently broad to give him almost a free hand in undertaking and carrying out his plans for a reformation of the gambling world. The order of designation had authorized him to "forwith empanel a grand jury in all named counties," and to "issue and have served without delay all necessary orders of the court in the interest of justice." Judge McGhee, almost sixty years old at the time, wearing the same style Stetson semi-cowboy pork-pie hat he had worn in young manhood in his native Vernon, Texas, was the ideal jurist to collaborate with Judge Brice in such an enterprise, which for holy daring had no parallel in the legal or political history of New Mexico. One wag in Hot Springs claimed that Judge McGhee in person himself looked like an old-time gambler, and in fact had been mistaken several times for one of the brethren. Seasoned politicians watched with amazement as the two jurists, under statutory authority and inherent power of the court, virtually kidnapped the executive branch of state government of New Mexico. When Judge McGhee announced that he expected to hold court in Las Cruces on a certain day, the gambler contingent there was reported to have defied him, sending word to him in Roswell "to refrain from doing so," threatened that if he showed up at the courthouse in Las Cruces, he might never leave it alive. Judge McGhee telephoned at once to Frank Young, of Roswell, a long-time personal friend, a fearless peace officer, asked him to accompany him to Las Cruces. Frank Young, known all over the state as a man who would not tolerate any nonsense or foolishness when in the discharge of his official duties, was sworn in as a special deputy, went to Las Cruces with McGhee, prepared for a quick draw and a "shoot 'em dead" battle. Judge McGhee was not molested. He completed his work in Las Cruces, then went to Hot Springs, accompanied by Frank Young as a bodyguard.

The Brice-McGhee plan for subjugation and eradication proved to be a complete success. Frightened or bluffed out by the unexpected turn of events, realizing the certainty of ultimately encountering a tough minded trial judge who would refuse to be intimidated, the gamblers cleared out, scrambled to get back their poker chips, slot machines, roulette wheels and other games of chance paraphernalia out of the jurisdiction of New Mexico courts. A tough minded judge, grand juries composed of good citizens, indictments followed by trial by a petit jury of right-thinking men, were things they had not anticipated or bargained for. Small wonder that Governor John Burroughs, when announcing Judge McGhee's retirement from the State Supreme Court on July 1, 1960, paid him this tribute:

> There are few words I can find to express the great debt owed to Judge James B. McGhee by the citizens of New Mexico for his devotion to our state. I know I speak for his many friends in wishing him many happy years to come in a retirement richly deserved for his 27 years of dedicated service in the higher courts of New Mexico.

CHAPTER TEN

About Elfego Baca

ALTHOUGH I had known Elfego Baca by sight for several years, beginning in 1908, my acquaintance with him began when we were formally introduced to each other by Sheriff Perfecto Armijo in the Bernalillo County jail yard on May 16, 1913. The occasion was the scheduled hanging on that day of Demecio Delgadillo, a twenty-eight year old native of Chihuahua, Mexico, who had been convicted of the murder on September 22, 1912, of Soledad Sarracino de Pino, in her home near Fourteenth Street and Mountain Road in Albuquerque. The murder weapon, according to testimony presented by the prosecution, was a snub-nosed .38 revolver. I attended the hanging as a reporter for the Albuquerque *Journal*. Nearly two years before, I had written the running story of the murder trial for the Albuquerque *Herald*. Up to the very last moment of his life Delgadillo had maintained his innocence of the crime. Shortly before the trap was sprung, Sheriff Armijo asked Delgadillo in Spanish if he had anything to say. He replied in Spanish, "I am not guilty. I did not kill that woman."

Elfego Baca, a veteran witness to hangings, had been invited by Sheriff Armijo to help his chief deputy, Dick Lewis and Jailor Querino Coulter, to make the arrangements for the execution. Incident to that work, Baca had supervised the erection of the scaffold and had conducted preliminary tests, using sand bags of proper weight in the simulated hanging. Baca served as the *bastonero* for the occasion. The seldom used word *bastonero* is the Spanish equivalent for a master of ceremonies in English. A *bastonero* is responsible for supervising all arrangements down to the most minute detail, for banquets, *fiestas,* weddings, funerals, and other affairs requiring expert knowledge of technique and protocol.

The trap having been sprung as scheduled for the Delgadillo execution, Elfego Baca stationed himself near the attending physician, busily engaged at the time counting the murmurs and pulsations of Delgadillo's heart beat. The physician whispered the result of his findings to Elfego, who then announced: "Gentlemen, the official time is three minutes and sixteen seconds," speaking grimly through clenched teeth. He continued, "Gentlemen, this is one of the nicest hangings I have ever seen. Everything went off beautifully." The *Journal,* by prearrangement, waiting word from me, was holding up going to press. I hurried to a telephone in the jail office and notified the paper that Delgadillo had been hanged and had officially been pronounced dead. Returning to the jail yard, I noticed that Elfego Baca was talking to Father A. M. Gentile, the Jesuit priest, who had accompanied Delgadillo to the scaffold, and offered him final religious consolation. As I neared the two men, I overheard the Father ask Baca this question: "Mr. Baca, how long has it been since you approached the sacraments?" Apparently taken unawares, Baca made his way through the remaining knot of spectators, not answering Father Gentile.

On several occasions over a period of several years,

Elfego Baca consulted me informally concerning personal ethical problems which had been bothering him. Anxious to observe the niceties of the legal profession, Baca, a headstrong, determined man, was nevertheless willing at times to seek a bit of guidance. One day he asked my opinion as a friend, not in a professional capacity, on a problem then concerning him. The question was as to what he could properly do in presenting and offering evidence under circumstances he outlined to me. The facts submitted were somewhat complicated. I told Elfego that the scheme he had in mind was too close to the borderline for comfort; that a reputable lawyer should not undertake a project such as he proposed. Then he asked me another question: "Could a private detective under the same circumstances do what he had proposed to do as a lawyer?" The answer: "Yes, under the circumstances outlined a private detective might do what an attorney could not do."

Quite elated, Baca then said, "I felt sure some way could be found to solve this problem. You must remember that I am not only a lawyer, but also a private detective." Baca then handed me his professional card. On one side these words were printed: "Elfego Baca, Attorney-at-Law, Licensed to practice in all courts from Justice of the Peace in New Mexico to the United States Supreme Court. Fees moderate." On the other side of the card, printed in red ink, were the words: "Elfego Baca, Private Detective: Discreet Shadowing Done: Civil and Criminal Investigations; Divorce Investigations our Specialty." I said to him, "Elfego, it appears from what you tell me that in trying this case you would be acting in a dual capacity. You should not try to serve as the trial lawyer and testify as a detective in the case." I reminded him of an illustration given by George W. Armijo, a mutual friend: "A man cannot ring the bell in the church steeple and walk in the procession on the ground at the same time."

In 1927, Elfego Baca asked me if I would write a book on his life. Unable to undertake the work at the time, I told him I would recommend Kyle Crichton to do the work if agreeable to him. I arranged a meeting between the two men and they agreed to work together on the book. All went well for some weeks. Then Crichton, no doubt a bit frightened, talked to me confidentially and threatened to abandon the project at once, saying, "This man Elfego Baca scares the hell out of me. Here we are only about half way through the story of his life and he has already told me about killing seven men. I am afraid he will go on a rampage some fine day and murder me if I make him out in the book as a bad character, and that's all I can see ahead, that he is a bad man." I reassured Kyle Crichton somewhat by telling him that Elfego Baca would be disappointed if, in his writing, he failed to hold him out to the public as a first class gunman, and a more than typical bad man of the Southwest. Persuaded that Baca would not be offended by what he proposed to write, Crichton completed the book. It was published in 1928 under the title *Law and Order, Ltd., the Rousing Life of Elfego Baca of New Mexico,* by Kyle Crichton. Published by the Santa Fe New Mexican Printing Corporation, Santa Fe, perhaps with some of the expense borne by Bronson Cutting, the Crichton book soon became a classic on Southwest bookshelves.

In the story of the gunfight in the 80's on the Frisco river in Socorro (now Catron) County in southwestern New Mexico, Baca, as related in the Baca-Crichton book, fought eighty Texas cowboys to a standstill, firing from a *jacal,* "killing four, wounding eight, and coming through unscathed himself." In the *jacal* during all the fight,

Mi Señora Santa Ana and Elfego Baca, 73 years old, survivors of gun fight on Frisco river in southwestern Socorro County, New Mexico, in 1884.

Baca's sole companion had been a *santo* or wooden image of a saint, later described by Baca as *Mi Señora Santa Ana*. Some years after the publication of Crichton's book, while in Socorro waiting my turn to begin a jury trial, Elfego Baca asked me to drive him in my car to Magdalena, forty-eight miles to the west, on important business. Judge Harry P. Owen told me to go ahead and drive Baca to Magdalena, that the case under way would not go to the jury until late the next day. On the way from Socorro to Magdalena, Elfego told me about the important business he had in hand. It seemed that only recently he had learned the whereabouts of his long lost *Santa Ana*, and the name and address of the owner. Baca's mission to Magdalena was to buy the statue and take it with him on a lecture tour throughout New Mexico.

A few miles from Magdalena I said to Baca, "Elfego, several times you have told me about all the men you have killed in your life, but when I go to the county courthouses to check up on the information you have given me, I cannot verify your statements from the records. I would like to have you give me some details about them. I can only find official confirmation of two killings. You were charged with killing William Hearne in that cowboy fight on the Frisco river. You were tried for that killing in Bernalillo County on a change of venue from Socorro County, and the jury found you not guilty. About January 31, 1915, you are supposed to have killed Celestino Otero in El Paso, Texas. You told me one time that you were tried for the Otero killing before a jury in the 34th Texas District Court in El Paso and acquitted after the jury of Texans deliberated only twelve minutes. Now, I would like to have you give me the names and dates of any other men you killed."

No doubt thinking that I was presuming too much and treading dangerously close to strictly personal affairs, Elfego Baca looked far off toward the Mountain of Our Lady of Magdalena on the horizon, glowered a bit, then spoke glumly, "Why do you ask? What do you want to know for?" I answered, "I was wondering, I was just curious, that's all." On that note our conversation ended and I never referred to the subject again.

Upon reaching Magdalena, Elfego started out at once to find Town Marshal Bob Lewis, a noted character, widely known in the old days of Socorro and Grant Counties. Baca soon located Lewis and thanked him for giving him the tip and the name of the man who owned the *santo*. Lewis told Baca where to find the man, pointing out how to get there. For forty years and more, Bob Lewis had held a deputy sheriff's commission in Socorro County. No posse ever started on the trail of a dangerous outlaw in Socorro County without first inviting Bob Lewis to go along.

In Magdalena that day, Elfego Baca and Bob Lewis reminisced until noon on the corner of the one and only street in Magdalena. Then, Bob Lewis took a look at the open-faced silver watch he carried in his vest pocket and announced, "Elfego, it's noon time, time for dinner." Presumably Lewis proposed to be the host for the occasion and extend hospitality to Elfego and me, and we went to the only restaurant in town. I was most interested in the conversation of the two men. Having consulted the menu card, both ordered large steaks and the trimmings, helped themselves generously to catsup and Worcestershire sauce, drank plentifully of the coffee. For dessert Lewis and Baca ordered out-of-season strawberries.

Having dined expansively and somewhat expensively,

both men experienced a mildly embarrassing moment. Bob Lewis spoke first. "Elfego, I just now find that I haven't got a dollar on me." Elfego Baca grinned and said, "Bob, I'm in the same fix." Both men looked inquiringly at me. Seeing that I was elected to be the involuntary host, I paid the check for the meal. During the dinner hour Bob Lewis told several stories. One story was as follows:

Bob was riding a horse on Duck Creek one day in the early 80's with several ranchers, on the lookout for a roving band of Apache Indians. Geronimo, himself, was reported to be in the country. Not sighting any Apaches, Lewis and the ranchers returned to their homes. Many years later Lewis, at the time a deputy marshal, was in El Reno, Oklahoma, on official business for United States Marshal Creighton M. Foraker of Albuquerque.

A brother El Reno officer asked Lewis if he could do anything for him. Lewis replied, "Yes, I would like to see Geronimo." The El Reno officer said, "Geronimo is a part-time parolee. He goes and comes from the fort almost as he wishes. Every evening about 5:00 o'clock he goes to the railroad depot and watches the passenger train pass through town. Go to the depot this afternoon and you will see Geronimo there."

Before train time, Bob Lewis was at the El Reno depot, saw Geronimo and talked to him about old times. Geronimo said, "Bob, the last time I saw you was on Duck Creek near Alma. You rode a roan horse with white stockings on the forelegs and a star in the forehead. You were so close I could have killed you." Lewis said, "Geronimo, why didn't you kill me that day? You knew we were out looking for you and would have shot you on sight." Geronimo said, "Well, Bob, I didn't kill you when I had that chance because I knew that the Cavalry were in that country looking for Apaches. If I shot at you, the soldiers would have heard the shot. In a few minutes they would have found your body. Before long they would have killed me and the other Apaches with me. So I held my fire and let you ride on."

In Magdalena Lewis also told of the time he was riding with a posse on the trail of an outlaw:

> I became separated from the posse and wandered about for a long time in a country that was strange to me. It started to snow heavily. Darkness closed in on me very fast. Luckily, I found a deserted shanty. The place looked as if it had been abandoned in a hurry. I found a kerosene lamp in the kitchen, lighted it, and made a meal out of some canned goods left in a lean-to. With the lamp burning brightly I sat in a chair in the living room of the shack and began to read an old newspaper. A bullet crashed through the front window, shattering the lamp. All of a sudden everything was dark. I took my 30/30 rifle, poked it through the broken window pane and pulled the trigger, firing blindly.
>
> As soon as it was daylight I went outside and saw bloody footprints in the snow. I followed the footprints and saw where a body had been dragged in the snow by two or three men. I followed the bloody trail and saw where earth from a newly dug grave had been piled into a mound. I suppose I should have reported the whole thing to the sheriff in Socorro but somehow it didn't seem important to me at the time. I never told anybody about it for years. I kept thinking somebody might be reported missing and I would then volunteer my information, but nothing ever came of it.

Bob Lewis and Elfego Baca bade each other an affectionate farewell on a street corner in Magdalena. Elfego carried on with the business of the day, but made little progress. Elfego seemed to know everybody in Magdalena, and shook hands with everybody. Several friends volunteered to accompany him to the home of the *santo* owner. In the beginning this man was not willing to even talk about nor consider a sale of the statue. However, Baca was a persistent and persuasive talker. Bit by bit he overcame the owner's resistance. Finally a price of $500.00 was agreed upon. Then followed the most delicate and diplomatic part of the bargaining. Baca explained that he had no cash at the time, but planned to take the *santo* with him to Albuquerque, leave soon on a lecture tour, and in a few days would have the purchase price. Pending payment in full, and by way of security, Baca offered to give the owner a promissory note for the $500.00, payable in one year, with ten per cent interest payable every thirty days. The owner refused to sell on Baca's terms, demanded spot payment or there would be no sale. Finally, the situation appearing hopeless, Baca arose from his chair, motioned to me to follow him, and we started on the return trip to Socorro. A disappointed man, Baca had little to say on the way home. Some months later Elfego Baca gave me a framed photograph bearing the typewritten inscription: *"Mi Señora Santana.* Statue over 500 years old and Elfego Baca at 73."

Elfego Baca came to my office in Albuquerque several months after our trip to Magdalena and asked me if I knew Charles F. Wilson, a fire insurance adjuster. I said, "Yes, I know him." Elfego then asked: "Is he a friend of yours?" I replied, "No, not a personal friend, only a business acquaintance. Why?" Elfego Baca said, "Well, if he was your personal friend, I might try to help save his life, but as it is, I guess he will have to die." Elfego then explained somewhat in detail.

He had gone to El Paso the previous Saturday night, had spent Sunday on business in Juarez, Mexico, across the Rio Grande. Monday morning he had received a telegram telling him that his Albuquerque printing establishment, in which Elfego's paper, *La Opinion Publica*, was published once a week, had been badly damaged by fire. Elfego had taken the first train home, found the newsplant a shambles. He then made a claim for the loss, showing the insurance policies, all premiums paid, to the company agents. Charles F. Wilson arrived from Denver to adjust the claim, determined it to be $600, and offered to pay this money to Baca in exchange for a full release. Baca had indignantly brushed aside the offer, insisting that Wilson pay him double the amount, $1,200. Wilson had declared in a final, heated interview, according to Baca, that he would see him in hell before he would pay a cent more than $600, for him "to take it or leave it."

Elfego asked me to talk to Charles F. Wilson at once, placing him on notice that Baca was looking for him, and had asked me to tell him as a favor that unless he paid Baca $1,200 before noon of that very day, that he would find himself dead in the middle of Central Avenue. It was already 10:00 o'clock when Baca delivered the ultimatum, and if Baca were to be believed, Wilson had only two hours to live.

I got Wilson on the telephone at once at the Alvarado Hotel and gave him Baca's message. Wilson's instant emphatic reply was: "Tell Elfego Baca to go straight to hell." I promptly relayed the message to Baca, at the time in his office. At 11:50 a.m. I received a call from Wilson. A rather weak voice said over the telephone: "Keleher, this is Charley Wilson. Can you get hold of Elfego Baca at once?" My answer was, "I don't know, Mr. Wilson, but I will surely try." Wilson said, "Well, be sure and get him before noon. You will have to act quickly. Tell him to go to Guy Rogers at the First National Bank and draw on me for $1,200. Mr. Rogers has had all the necessary instructions."

When I called Elfego Baca once again, he answered the telephone personally. I gave him Wilson's message. Baca grunted, asked me to telephone Guy Rogers and tell him that Elfego Baca was on his way to the bank and that he should wait until he got there. Baca went to the bank, signed a draft for $1,200.00, Rogers credited the amount to Baca's checking account, and Wilson lived, going on his way, adjusting other fire losses.

CHAPTER ELEVEN

Bronson Cutting and Elfego Baca

IN ALL the vast sweep of mountain and plain country embracing some 122,000 square miles of territory designated on the map as New Mexico, it would be difficult to find two more disparate personalities than Bronson Cutting, United States Senator from New Mexico at the time of his death, and Elfego Baca, described in headlines in New Mexico newspapers at the time of his death as an "old frontier-link, gun-fighting hero."

Born in Oakdale, Long Island, New York, on January 28, 1888, of wealthy parents, Bronson Cutting attended famed preparatory schools, was graduated from Harvard in 1910 at the age of twenty-two. Soon after graduation he came to live in Santa Fe, New Mexico, hopeful of preventing further progress of incipient pulmonary tuberculosis. Cutting was good looking, over six feet in height, and of commanding presence; he was as well equipped as any young man in the America of his day to follow a career in business, finance, diplomacy, politics or in any other walk of life in which family background, substantial wealth, education, and social prestige would be considered valuable assets. Soon after becoming a resident of New Mexico, Cutting began the study of Spanish, and within a few months had mastered the language. To speak fluent Spanish in New Mexico at the time was a valuable possession, even as it is today, in Santa Fe, Sandoval, Rio Arriba, Taos, San Miguel, Mora, Valencia and Socorro counties.

When he arrived in Santa Fe, Cutting presented letters of introduction to several Santa Fe men, including Miguel A. Otero, an Independent Republican who had served as governor of the territory for nine years from 1897 to 1906. Cutting also had a letter to Arthur Seligman, veteran Democratic leader, destined to be governor of New Mexico in 1930. By inheritance and conviction, Bronson Cutting was an Independent Republican in politics at the time of his arrival in New Mexico, much inclined to think along the lines of the LaFollette-Norris school of political thought. Former Governor Otero and Arthur Seligman, both political veterans, volunteered to tutor Bronson Cutting in New Mexico politics during the early years of his residence. With Governor Otero, Independent Republican, telling him one thing, and Arthur Seligman, Old Guard Democrat, telling him another, it may well be that Cutting had a somewhat difficult time becoming adjusted to the New Mexico political scene, and perhaps decided to mark out his own political pathway.

Both Otero and Seligman wisely advised him to buy the *Santa Fe New Mexican,* which he did, in 1912, for a comparatively small sum, contrasted with the price paid later when Jesus M. Baca, who inherited the paper from Cutting, sold it in 1940 to Frank C. Rand, Jr.; and when compared with the much greater price Frank Rand received nine years later when he sold the newspaper to Robert McKinney.

Following Governor Otero's death, Arthur Seligman became Cutting's principal political guide and mentor. Seligman volunteered the information to me in 1932 that

Bronson Murray Cutting, from a photograph taken shortly after he became a United States Senator from New Mexico in 1927.

in his opinion, Bronson Cutting, then United States Senator from New Mexico, would support Franklin D. Roosevelt in the approaching presidential campaign. Seligman also told me in the same conversation that Cutting, since becoming a resident of New Mexico, had spent not less than $25,000 each year in politics, and that Cutting had always allowed him to use his own judgment in placing the money "where it would do the most good for Bronson."

Seligman's prediction that Cutting would support Roosevelt proved correct. He came out for Roosevelt in 1932, soon after the president announced his intention to again be a candidate. Observers in New Mexico and perhaps other states watched with interest to see whether Franklin D. Roosevelt, a long-time personal friend of Cutting's would reciprocate by supporting Cutting, Republican, when he ran for the Senate against Dennis Chavez, Democrat, in 1934. Apparently following party policy routine, Roosevelt failed to lift a finger to help Cutting in his race.

My personal contacts with Bronson Cutting were formal and limited in scope. I had been acquainted with him since his arrival in New Mexico in 1910, but our acquaintance had never progressed to a point of what might be termed personal friendship. I was a dinner guest at his home on one occasion, the evening of the day I was admitted to the bar in New Mexico on August 17, 1915, but this was because of my acquaintance with Miguel A. Otero, a law school classmate, admitted to the bar the same day. He was an intimate friend of Bronson Cutting's. On occasional meetings with Cutting, he greeted me as "Bill" and I called him Bronson. Our relationship over the years might be described as one of mutual respect.

There came a time, however, in 1932, when I served as an intermediary in a matter which, if it had taken a dif-

BRONSON CUTTING AND ELFEGO BACA 169

ferent turn, might have altered entirely the course of Cutting's career. In 1932 he was junior United States Senator from New Mexico. He had been appointed to the Senate on December 29, 1927 by Governor Richard C. Dillon, and had been elected to the senate in his own right as the Republican candidate on November 6, 1928, defeating Jethro S. Vaught by a vote of 68,070 to 49,913. The political wheel of fortune had spun and spun again in New Mexico in the 30's bringing new faces to the fore as leaders in the Democratic party. In 1932, Andrew W. Hockenhull, of Curry County, was governor of New Mexico and Sam Gilbert Bratton of the same county, was senior United States Senator from New Mexico. With Hockenhull in the governor's chair, many Democratic party leaders chafed at the bit because Bronson Cutting was in the United States Senate, an honor which they felt rightfully belonged to a deserving Democrat. These party leaders were anxious to have Cutting out of the senate and exiled from New Mexico. Many meetings were held; whispered confidences exchanged. As a result, a plan was designed, and once designed some leaders at least were anxious to see it executed. Most of the whispered conversations revolved around the alleged assurance that President Franklin D. Roosevelt had given to some zealots that he would appoint Bronson Cutting ambassador to Mexico if he could be induced to resign from the senate. I knew nothing of the plan, however, until one day in November, 1932, out of the blue sky of New Mexico, certain members of the high command of the Democratic party, notified me that I had the honor of having been selected to approach Senator Cutting and sound him out on a proposition revolving around the Mexican Embassy.

In retrospect it appears that I should have refused, pointblank, to have any part in the negotiations. However, after discussing the contemplated project with Brian Boru Dunn, of Santa Fe, at the time Cutting's personal secretary, and having heard him express the opinion to me that the Senator might possibly be interested, I took the problem directly to Bronson Cutting. Senator Cutting was gracious, and not hostile. He did not seem to be affronted as he might well have been, and accuse me of stupidity and overstepping the bounds of propriety. I was well aware, in approaching the senator, that he would be justified in angrily denouncing the plan as an awkwardly conceived scheme to eliminate him from the New Mexico political scene, and permit Governor Hockenhull to appoint perhaps a political enemy as his successor. Insofar as I ever learned, Bronson Cutting considered the proposition as tendered in good faith. He promised to advise me promptly of his decision. The senator wrote me a letter from Santa Fe on November 19, 1932, which read:

> Honorable W. A. Keleher
> First National Bank Bldg.
> Albuquerque, New Mexico
>
> My dear Bill:
> Many thanks for your very kind letter of November 16th.
> I appreciate your thinking of me in connection with the Mexican Embassy. Under ordinary circumstances I must confess there is no job which I would rather tackle. It seems to me, however, that I am under an obligation to the people of the State to serve out the term in the Senate to which they elected me, and I do not feel that I could consider any other position at the present time, even in the remote chance of my being eligible for one.
> With warmest personal regards, believe me always
> Sincerely yours,
> BRONSON CUTTING

No question but that Bronson Cutting was the most erudite man of wealth from out-of-state to become a per-

BRONSON CUTTING AND ELFEGO BACA 171

manent resident of New Mexico. In time he broke loose from his native inherent dignity which had been a political handicap to him, and made friends with the mine-run of people of the state, establishing and maintaining many permanent, cherished friendships, particularly among the Spanish-American population. Becoming increasingly involved in New Mexico politics, Bronson Cutting developed a willingness to play marbles for keeps with important New Mexico old guard politicians of the Republican faith, among them an occasional erstwhile Democrat. Cutting, on more than one occasion, crossed swords with some of the topnotch political leaders of the day. He led the Independent Republican troops to battle in the state senate in 1928 over the Labor Commission bill, showing for the first time a willingness to use brass knucks if necessary in knock-down and drag-out, rough and tumble political jousting.

Senator Cutting, forty-seven years old, outstanding as a national liberal, progressive Republican, was at the zenith of his career, considered by most of his colleagues and by many political advisors as a potential candidate for the presidency of the United States, at the time of his death in an airplane crash on May 6, 1935, while flying over Missouri on his return to Washington from Santa Fe. The senator had been in New Mexico conferring with associates, mapping out strategy contemplated to be used in the then-pending contest for his senate seat. The contest was an outgrowth of the election held on November 6, 1934, in which Congressman Dennis Chavez had sought to defeat Cutting. On the face of the returns Cutting had been elected by a vote of 76,228, a majority of 1,284. Chavez received 74,944 votes.

Funeral services for Senator Cutting were held in New York City on Friday, May 10, 1935, in St. James Protestant Episcopal Church, Madison Avenue and Seventy-first Street. His body had been brought on the previous Wednesday night from Atlantic, Missouri, a small town near where he had met his tragic death, to the New York City home of his mother, Mrs. W. Bayard Cutting, at 24 East Seventy-second Street. The Rev. Dr. Barney T. Phillips, Chaplain of the Senate, and rector of the Episcopal Church of the Epiphany, in Washington, conducted the funeral services, assisted by Rev. Horace W. B. Donegan, rector of the St. James Church. Burial was in Greenwood Cemetery, Brooklyn, N.Y. Members of the House and Senate attended the funeral services as honorary pallbearers. From the House: Charles A. Plumley, John J. Dempsey, Melvin J. Maas, Mathew J. Merritt. From the Senate: Robert LaFollette, Carl A. Hatch, Hiram W. Johnson, Edward T. Costigan, George W. Norris, Burton K. Wheeler, William E. Borah, Joseph P. Robinson, Gerald T. Nye, Robert F. Wagner. Honorary pallbearers from New Mexico: A. C. McConvery, Dana Johnson, Maurice Miera, Herman Baca, Jesus Baca, Edgar Puryear, Clifford McCarthy, T. M. Pepperday, Brian Boru Dunn, H. H. Dorman, Cyrus McCormick, Severino Trujillo, William Barnes, M. A. Otero, Jr., Mrs. M. A. Otero, Jr.

Countless editorials, published in metropolitan and county weekly newspapers throughout the nation, testified to Senator Cutting's stature. The *New York Times,* in an editorial entitled, "A Loss to the Senate," published the day following the senator's death, accused James A. Farley, at the time Chairman of the National Democratic Committee, with engaging in vindictive retaliatory tactics:

> Senator Cutting's tragic death yesterday takes from the Senate an able and independent member. Going to New Mexico years ago for reasons of health, he soon established himself in newspaper work there. From this he seemed to gain a flair for

BRONSON CUTTING AND ELFEGO BACA 173

politics, for which he soon displayed a marked talent. It was not long before he became dominant in the State of his adoption, and his election to the Senate naturally followed. There he promptly showed his resolve to be his own man. Partly from native bent, and partly, perhaps, because he had to fear no rival in New Mexico, he set out to exercise a free and independent judgment on measures and parties and men. Known as a Liberal, or Progressive, he was numbered among the group that President Roosevelt cultivated in 1932. Afterward their paths separated. Last year Senator Cutting came out against the New Deal. As a result he was opposed for the re-election by the Democratic organization and Chairman Farley, but won by a substantial majority.

Mr. Cutting, however, was pursued by Farley, so that his election was contested on the ground that he had spent more money to regain his seat in the Senate than was allowed by the state laws. Chairman Farley could not bear the thought of spending money to carry an election. The case was still pending in the Senate. Now it will be dropped, and probably the Governor of New Mexico, who is a Democrat, will appoint to the vacancy temporarily the man who contested Senator Cutting's election. But it will be long before New Mexico, or any other state, sends to the Senate a man of Mr. Cutting's intellectual quality, personal weight and political integrity. The Senate is made poorer by the lamentable accident which ended his life.

On May 6, 1939, the fourth anniversary of Senator Cutting's death, Hon. Sam G. Bratton, United States Circuit Judge, was the speaker of the day at the dedication of a statue, erected in Bronson Cutting's memory, on the capitol grounds in Santa Fe, with funds provided by friends and admirers of the late senator. Judge Bratton had served in the senate, as senior senator from New Mexico, during the service of Senator Cutting as junior senator. Judge Bratton delivered a beautiful and moving eulogy, published in full in the Congressional Record on May 8, 1939, upon motion of Senator Carl A. Hatch of

New Mexico. In the course of his eulogy, Judge Bratton touched briefly on the Cutting wealth, but continued:

> Senator Cutting's material inheritance was important, but . . . more important was the intellectual inheritance; a profound sense of his obligation to society; and implicit assumption that wealth was not a personal possession, but a trust and a social responsibility; a lively sensitiveness to the misfortunes and deprivations of the underprivileged; and a passionate, though never intemperate desire to contribute to the creation of an economy which should provide opportunities for all, a society which should protect those who were unfitted for the struggle of competition.

Of Senator Cutting's death itself, Judge Bratton said in the peroration: "Senator Cutting's death was an irreparable loss. Men and women throughout New Mexico and in all parts of the nation mourn his departure. We miss him tremendously. His like will not soon pass this way again."

Senator Cutting's death, an event of first importance in New Mexico, of particular interest to many politicians, Democrat and Republican alike, meant many things to many men. There was much speculation about the fate of his newspaper, the *Santa Fe New Mexican.* Under Cutting's will, executed on December 20, 1934, several months before his death, E. Dana Johnson, for some twenty-five years editor of the *New Mexican,* was bequeathed $25,000. Jesus M. Baca, a long-time personal friend and political associate, was bequeathed $150,000 and Cutting's entire interest in the Santa Fe New Mexican Publishing Corporation, which published the *Santa Fe New Mexican.* Johnson was a disappointed man when he learned of the provision for him in the Cutting will. He felt particularly aggrieved because the "boss" had preferred Jesus Baca over him to such a considerable extent. Dana Johnson talked to me briefly about the situation some days after he had resigned as an editor of the *New Mexican*. At the time he was enroute from Santa Fe to Pasadena, California. Johnson told me that "this Cutting business has been very hard for me to accept. I edited the *New Mexican* for Bronson Cutting for twenty-five years. I did everything I could for him. I wrote hundreds and hundreds of editorials and news stories to further his interests. I just can't understand it." Dana Johnson died in California on December 15, 1937.

To Dennis Chavez, who had risked his seat in the congress to which he was certain of re-election, in order to run for the senate against Cutting, the untimely death of Senator Cutting meant the termination of the then-pending Chavez-Cutting election contest which had been filed by Chavez. The proceedings were becoming expensive and burdensome for Chavez and his friends and supporters, some of whom were concerned because of alleged foot-dragging by three Democratic members of the committee on elections in Washington, who, it was claimed, had shown signs of being a bit too lenient towards Cutting's side of the controversy.

Senator Cutting's death made it necessary for Governor Clyde Tingley to appoint a successor to serve until the next general election. Dennis Chavez, having made the race against Cutting, was the logical choice. He could rightfully contend that he had tried to oust Cutting in part through loyalty to the Democratic party; that he could have played it safe and have been re-elected to the House.

By all the rules of the game it appeared that Dennis Chavez was entitled to the appointment, but complications developed. Governor Tingley, it appeared, was obligated to many people as the result of his successful campaign for the governorship. Some of these people were knocking at Tingley's door, demanding that he honor their political I.O.U.'s. When the time came for Tingley to fish or cut bait, he found himself in a most serious predicament. Ruth Hanna McCormick Simms, daughter of famed Mark Hanna, of Cleveland, who had been instrumental in electing William McKinley president in 1896, and her husband Albert G. Simms, had not only openly supported Tingley for governor, but had also supported Dennis Chavez in his race for the senate against Cutting, contributing generously to the organization in many parts of New Mexico. With Cutting dead, Albert and Ruth Simms strongly urged Tingley to appoint as his successor to the senate Judge John Field Simms, Albert's brother, an able lawyer, formerly Justice of the Supreme Court and a long-time distinguished and influential Democratic party leader in New Mexico.

Subsequent to one important meeting in Santa Fe, attended by Albert and Ruth Simms on the one side, and Tingley and two close advisors on the other, word leaked out from the governor's office and spread quickly throughout the capitol, that Tingley had promised that he would, on the next day, appoint Judge Simms to fill the vacancy. Those in Tingley's confidence placed considerable credence in the report. When the rumor reached the ears of Judge David Chavez, brother of Dennis Chavez, he became very much disturbed. He immediately conferred with Arthur T. Hannett, former governor of New Mexico, chief legal counsel for Dennis Chavez throughout his political career. Hannett hurried to Santa Fe from Albuquerque and went with Judge Chavez in all haste to see Governor Tingley.

Listeners who had stationed themselves discreetly outside the doors of the Governor's inner office were horrified at some of the intemperate language which seeped through the door and over the transom; aghast at the threats and counter-threats of retaliation, astonished at the cajoling and wheedling on one side or the other. Finally the smoke and roar of battle cleared away and Governor Tingley emerged from his office, arm in arm with Hannett and Chavez. Spectator friends of Dennis Chavez observed: "It's all over. Tingley is going to appoint Dennis." On May 11, 1935, five days after Cutting's death, Tingley appointed Dennis Chavez to the United States Senate to fill the vacancy, thus ending suspense and speculation. Chavez was elected on November 3, 1936, to fill Cutting's unexpired term, ending January 3, 1941, and was thereafter re-elected to succeed himself, term after term, until death on November 18, 1962, ended his colorful career in public office.

It is gratifying to me to be numbered among those who recognized the stature and ability of Senator Chavez while he was still alive and active. In December, 1961, Will Harrison, of Santa Fe, who published a widely read column in the *Santa Fe New Mexican,* the *Albuquerque Tribune,* and other papers in New Mexico, conducted a symposium for the purpose of determining the name of the greatest native born New Mexican living or dead. Judge Charles R. Brice, of Roswell, among others, nominated Senator Chavez for the honor, and I promptly seconded the nomination. On December 20, 1961, Columnist Harrison published my nominating letter, which read as follows:

> Please add my name to those who are seconding the nomination of Senator Chavez as the candidate for honors as New Mexico's greatest native born son. It appears to me that he is entitled to the accolade on many counts.
> In his boyhood he manfully brushed aside a host of difficulties

in order to obtain an education. As a young man he overcame many obstacles and eventually achieved for himself a place in New Mexico's history which will become more important and significant with the passing of time. Dennis Chavez and many others of his day and generation were caught in the backwash of the American Occupation. Spanish, his mother tongue, proved both an asset and a liability.

Growing up at a time when most young people in New Mexico left school at the eighth grade, Dennis Chavez became gainfully employed at an early age, and pressed on educationally to finally receive an LL.B. from an accredited law school and became a capable lawyer.

He won his Ph.D. in politics where the race is not only to the swift and strong, but can be won only by those who have stamina to survive in an arena of constant warfare. In my opinion Senator Chavez's enduring place in New Mexico history will rest on this firm foundation.

He furnished constructive leadership for his people; he showed them the way to the promised land of educational opportunity and achievement, taught them to participate in the affairs of their own native state, and to become leaders in business and professional life in their own communities.

Moses failed to reach the Promised Land although the Lord permitted him to point it out to his people. Chavez not only pointed out the Promised Land but entered it himself. Dennis Chavez, in my opinion, deserves the award.

Will Harrison declared Senator Chavez the winner in the survey he had conducted. On January 9, 1962, Senator Chavez, a friend of mine as boy and man, wrote me from Washington:

Dear Bill:
Thank you for nominating me. It is a great honor. Bill, I am making progress in my recovery. Will be at the opening session tomorrow.

Although Bronson Cutting was born with the proverbial silver spoon in his mouth, Elfego Baca was born not only on "the other side of the tracks," but on the other side of the world, it might be said, of humble parents, Francisco and Juanita Baca, in Socorro County, New Mexico, on February 27, 1865. He was reared in the backwash of the Civil War, receiving scanty schooling in the lower grades. He lived dangerously as a frontier law officer. He was admitted to practice law while serving as a Socorro County deputy sheriff, by District Judge A. A. Freeman in the atmosphere of a friendly court in the heart of the "Billy the Kid" country at Lincoln, after having read Smith's *Elementary Law,* and a few chapters of Blackstone's *Commentaries,* assuredly a scant preparation for the bar. Among his other qualifications for the bar, Baca spoke excellent English, without any trace of a Spanish accent.

In 1910, when Bronson Cutting became a resident of Santa Fe, Elfego Baca was forty-five years old, Cutting twenty-two. Bronson Cutting was considered a wealthy man; Elfego Baca was casting about at the time to find ways and means of making a living for himself, his wife and five children. In 1910 Baca moved to Albuquerque from Socorro, his home town, determined to make his way at the bar, as a private detective, or in any other honorable and legitimate way open to him. Mrs. Baca, the former Francisquita Pohmer, born in Old Albuquerque on September 13, 1869, was the daughter of Joseph Pohmer, and Dolores Chavez Pohmer. Elfego Baca told me about the romance which led to their marriage. He had been in Albuquerque for a few days "attending court," long years before he had been admitted to the bar.

Elfego was attending court because he was the defendant in the case of the Territory of New Mexico vs. Elfego Baca, charged with the murder of William Hearne, brought into Bernalillo County on a change of venue from Socorro County. The case was tried before a jury on May 7th, 8th, and 9th, 1885. While going to the courthouse one day, Elfego Baca made the acquaintance of pretty sixteen-year-old Francisquita Pohmer as she was on the way to Sister Blandina's Convent School on the plaza. When Baca proposed marriage after only a few meetings, Francisquita promised to marry him if the jury acquitted him of the murder charge. The jury found Baca not guilty. Despite the protests of Joseph Pohmer, a sturdy German emigrant who owned the best meat market in Old Albuquerque, Francisquita and Elfego were married, and although they did not exactly live happily ever afterward, nevertheless, they lived together as husband and wife until his death on August 27, 1945.

Fifteen years before his death, Elfego Baca erected a modern combination office and residential building on the northeast corner of Sixth Street and Gold Avenue. Some things about the building did not work out as Elfego had planned. Over the years of joint use of the property with Mrs. Baca, Elfego saw many objections to such an arrangement. He claimed that the joint use made it possible for Mrs. Baca to leave at any moment the rooms set aside for residential purposes and enter the quarters set aside for his office use, barging in, as Elfego contended, most unexpectedly. She never knocked on the door marked "Private," before entering, he claimed, much to Elfego's embarrassment, particularly when counselling with lady clients.

One day Elfego called on me to complain about Mrs. Baca's inconsiderate conduct, asking me to prepare a complaint for him to sign, detailing his grievances, which he wanted to have filed that very day, asking the court for an injunction restraining Mrs. Baca from molesting or interfering with him or his business affairs, particularly in connection with sudden and unexpected entrance into his office. Reluctant to be identified with the proposed family quarrel, I argued with Elfego Baca, discouraging him from believing that the court might enjoin Mrs. Baca from carrying on her usual pursuits in the home-office quarters. My advice to him was about as follows: "Elfego, it will be embarrassing and humiliating for you to ask the court to enjoin Mrs. Baca in a matter of this kind. All the world knows that you are a gunman, a fighter, that you have killed several men, and many people will be unable to understand how it comes that you are unable to handle Mrs. Baca. It seems to me that if you file a complaint against her, you will be confessing your inability to control your own wife." With the hard look in his eyes always present when backed into a corner Elfego replied, "You just don't know Mrs. Baca," and walked quickly out of my office.

In Albuquerque, on October 18, 1932, Elfego Baca wrote a businesslike letter in Spanish on office stationery, addressed to his wife, Mrs. Francisquita Pohmer de Baca, 1010 Sixteenth Street, Apt. 3, San Diego, California. He marked "Personal" on the envelope and sent it by registered mail, "Return Receipt Requested." The contents of the letter were as follows:

> As of this date I made my testament and placed in my *Safety Deposit Box* in the *First National Bank of Albuquerque, N.M.* I send you herewith the key to No. 116 in case of my death. Only you and the lawyer, W. A. Keleher have the right to open the box. He has his office in the same National Bank and is a good laywer, very honorable and very Catholic, so that he can see that no one takes advantage of you after I die. Greetings to all those who remember me.
>
> Your spouse
> ELFEGO BACA

It is somewhat difficult to say when Bronson Cutting and Elfego Baca became political associates. Baca's name was mentioned from time to time in Cutting's newspaper, the *Santa Fe New Mexican* in the early '20's as a potential candidate for governor. At about the same time, Cutting began to take a very active interest in organizing American Legion Posts in the predominantly Spanish-speaking counties, sending Herman Baca and his cousin Jesus M. Baca into those counties as ambassadors-at-large. During this period Elfego Baca (not related to either Herman Baca or Jesus M. Baca) began to organize "independent progressive Republican clubs," demonstrating for Cutting's benefit what could be accomplished. Elfego Baca was an experienced politician, an efficient organizer, and a capable moulder of public opinion. Baca had wide experience in running for office on his own. Being a candidate for public office was almost an occupational disease with Elfego Baca. Since reaching his majority, with two or three exceptions, he had run for office in almost every election. He was elected county clerk of Socorro County in 1893 and again in 1895; he was elected Superintendent of Schools of Socorro County in 1900 and 1901; he was elected sheriff of Socorro County at two year intervals, serving intermittently from 1919 to 1929.

Notwithstanding the political alliance which had been formed between Cutting and Baca, they were never on intimate terms of friendship. Neither man entirely trusted the other. As a result, Elfego Baca was never taken into the Cutting inner circle. Baca appraised Cutting as being perhaps smarter, politically and otherwise than the general public thought him to be. Baca was never invited to be a guest at the Cutting residence in Santa Fe or to attend an impromptu concert to hear Cutting play Bach or Beethoven on the grand piano.

The inventory of Cutting's assets filed in his estate some months after his death was conclusive evidence that Bronson Cutting had been a wealthy man. Many people in New Mexico and elsewhere were interested in the details of the Senator's will. Old political friends and associates found it necessary to abide by a formula used in taking care of political associates under a testamentary device. Cutting had been an efficient bookkeeper. He had carefully noted the amounts of money borrowed from him from time to time over the years and the amounts advanced to his friends and political co-workers. In and about making the loans, Cutting had been quite businesslike, requiring each borrower to sign a promissory note, payable on demand.

In his will, the senator bequeathed to each note-maker a sum of money equivalent to the maker's debt to him. The formula adopted made it possible for the executors to offset bequest by the use of each individual's promissory note. Credit against debit. Such an arrangement afforded a neat legal method of balancing the equities. The plan used by the testator disappointed some political followers who had no doubt hoped and even expected that the senator would "remember them" with no strings attached.

To a considerable extent, Senator Cutting's death further complicated Elfego Baca's rather involved political and financial affairs, which had been deteriorating for some time. Beginning with 1923, Elfego Baca's prosperous years appeared to belong to past history. Future years looked anything but bright. Never one to regret the past, Baca, however, referred on several occasions to his inability to recognize some important opportunities in his past life. He recalled in particular the fee he had failed to receive, as the result of slow thinking, in the General José Ynez Salazar case. The General, an important military leader in the Mexican Revolution of 1914, had been indicted in the federal court in New Mexico on a charge of violating United States neutrality laws. Arrested in El Paso and detained by the Army at Ft. Bliss, Salazar asked Elfego Baca to represent him, instructed him to go to Washington and interview named persons. Elfego Baca went to Washington at once and was escorted to the Riggs National Bank, where officers asked him to name his fee for defending Salazar. Recalling the incident years later, Baca told me that his mind failed to function properly at a very important and critical moment in his life. Desperately in need of money at the time, Baca hesitated to name a fee which the bank officers might consider exorbitant. He remembered several murder cases he had tried in New Mexico, some of them lasting for many days, and receiving a fee of only a few hundred dollars. When asked to name his fee, Baca took a deep breath, anticipating hard bargaining and suggested $30,000, the largest amount he could think of at that moment. The banker soon gave Elfego a cashier's check for $30,000, saying, "Mr. Baca, here is your money. It might be of interest for you to know that we had been authorized to pay your fee in any amount up to $100,000." Playing poker with the banker, Baca managed to grin a bit sheepishly, then said, "Mr. Banker, I thank you for this check. It might be of interest to you, also, sir, to know that I was prepared to accept a much smaller fee than the amount you have just paid me."

Several weeks after Bronson Cutting's death, Olivia Cutting, Bronson Cutting's sister, and Jesus M. Baca, a friend and political associate, were appointed executors under Cutting's will, by the Probate Court of Santa Fe County. Later the estate proceedings were removed from the Probate to the District Court of Santa Fe County. On September 14, 1935, Reed Holloman, of Santa Fe, attorney for the estate, wrote a letter to Elfego Baca demanding the surrender to the estate of the property known as

BRONSON CUTTING AND ELFEGO BACA 185

Lots 23 and 24 in Block Numbered 19 of New Mexico Townsite Addition to the City of Albuquerque, on which Baca some years before had built a one-story cement block building measuring fifty feet on Gold Avenue and 142 feet on Sixth Street. The building had been partitioned to provide living quarters, law offices, and a storeroom housing a printing plant. Always prompt in business affairs, Baca answered on September 18th Holloman's letter of the 14th saying:

> Dear Judge:
> I heard you were looking for me lately and I thought you wanted to talk politics as you and I always do. Now, coming down to the contents of your letter, the building that you speak about, is my building, but in the name of Bronson M. Cutting. I think you had better proceed in the proper court and I will get out of the building whenever proper order is issued and by the proper court. Thanking you for your kind invitation, believe me to be, as I have always been, your friend,
> ELFEGO BACA

The Holloman-Baca letter marked the beginning of much correspondence and prolonged negotiations, which brought to light a hitherto unsuspected personal and confidential relationship between the deceased senator and Elfego Baca.

On November 13, 1935, Reed Holloman, Claude S. Mann and Allen M. Tonkin, attorneys for the Cutting estate, filed an ejectment suit in the District Court of Bernalillo County, seeking to have the sheriff oust Elfego Baca from possession of the disputed property. Baca was not particularly pleased that the Cutting estate had sued him, and threatened to use a six-shooter in defense of his rights, but after thinking for a day or two, decided to fight the case in court instead of with a gun.

Baca brought the complaint to our office and A. H.

McLeod, Robert J. Nordhaus and I began to prepare the defense. Elfego Baca was an ideal client in many respects, admitting that he was pretty much a stranger to civil litigation, saying that most of his practice had been in criminal law.

We filed an answer for Baca, denying all excepting the formal allegations in the complaint and alleged by way of defense, that the deed purporting to vest title in Bronson Cutting had been intended to be a mortgage; and in a cross-complaint, asked for the return of the real estate and for judgment against the Cutting estate for $44,000, claimed to be due Baca on account of detective services rendered to Cutting in his lifetime. We also filed for Baca a claim for $44,000 against the executors under the Cutting will in the District Court of Santa Fe County, alleging performance of detective work by Baca at Cutting's request for which he had not been paid.

Elfego Baca's narration of his political and business relations with Bronson Cutting sounded a bit naive now and then, but appeared to hold together. The transaction with Cutting, Baca explained, had been a business-like one undertaken and accomplished while he was trying to save himself from what he described as "financial ruin." Baca had filed a petition in the Federal Court in Santa Fe, admitting insolvency. He was adjudged bankrupt on March 15, 1924. The bankruptcy petition disclosed that Baca's most valuable asset was the real estate he owned at Sixth and Gold in Albuquerque, previously mortgaged to an Albuquerque bank to secure a debt of $5,645.41. This property was appraised in the bankruptcy court at $6,500.00. Baca told Bronson Cutting of his predicament, and Cutting promised to help him. Cutting arranged with George C. Taylor, Referee in Bankruptcy, to buy the real estate from the Trustee in Bankruptcy, clear of all encumbrances, for $7,000.

According to Baca, Cutting urged him to take the title in his own name as soon as seemed practical after being discharged from bankruptcy. However, Baca asked Cutting to keep the title as an accommodation to him because he was having trouble with his wife and feared if he took title in his name, Mrs. Baca's attorney would ask the court to set it aside for her in the proceedings incident to a pending divorce case. Baca's apprehension in this direction proved groundless. The Bacas eventually patched up their differences, mostly brought on by his excessive drinking, and they lived together as husband and wife until the marriage was terminated by Baca's death.

The defense developed for Baca by Archibald McLeod and Robert Nordhaus, was one in which they offered to prove that Cutting had held the title to the disputed property as trustee for Baca, and that the estate was bound by Cutting's alleged promise to allow Baca to redeem the property at any time upon payment of the sum of money advanced by Cutting for the deed of conveyance, plus interest, taxes, fire insurance premiums and maintenance costs. Baca offered to stipulate that no written agreement had ever been executed concerning the property and that both and he and Cutting had always considered the deal a "gentlemen's agreement." The defense submitted on Baca's behalf failed to make any particular impression on Reed Holloman, who took the position that Baca was trying to defeat a legitimate claim.

Fortunately Elfego Baca had kept a detailed record of time spent on the "detective work" he claimed to have done for Cutting. Baca had also kept carbon copies of the numerous letters and reports he had mailed to Cutting, in

Santa Fe and Washington, containing detailed information on political affairs in New Mexico, some of which contained verbatim quotations extracted from conversations, some of them remarks, about Bronson Cutting.

Robert Nordhaus was pleased when Judge Holloman filed a motion in the lawsuit demanding that the defendant be required to file a Bill of Particulars. When the court granted Holloman's motion, Nordhaus filed a rather comprehensive Bill of Particulars specifying the dates on which Baca had rendered detective service for Cutting, and submitted other detailed information. Within a few days thereafter, Holloman came to Albuquerque "to talk things over about Elfego Baca's case," a call probably the result of word Holloman had received from New York that Mrs. Cutting, Bronson Cutting's mother, did not look with favor on the litigation. Mrs. Cutting's attorney, Otis T. Bradley of Davis, Polk, Wardwell, Gardner and Reed (formerly Stetson, Jennings & Russell) 15 Broad Street, New York, Baca learned later, had written to Holloman telling him that it was Mrs. Cutting's wish that "Elfego Baca be treated fairly and justly."

Talking in Albuquerque about the Response to the Bill of Particulars, Holloman asked Robert Nordhaus many questions about Baca's detective work and asked if Baca expected to offer many exhibits in the case. Nordhaus pointed to stacks of letters and copies of letters on his desk selected at random from Elfego's files, and said that many of them might be exhibits. Glancing at the piles of correspondence Holloman asked, "Mind if I sample a few of these?" Nordhaus answered, "Not at all, Judge, help yourself. In fact, here is a copy of a letter written by Baca to Bronson Cutting in which he tells about an interview he had with you, on a certain date in which Baca claimed that you had spoken disparagingly of Cutting's political machine."

Holloman frowned as he read the copy of Baca's letter, in which his name was mentioned, read bits of copies of other letters and reports. Then Holloman said, "Well, I'll be damned!" After a brief silence, Holloman spoke again. "Gentlemen, it looks to me as if this case is one that should be settled out of court." Nordhaus didn't seem to be particularly happy over the prospect of an out-of-court settlement, recalling perhaps, the many cases he had read and the work he had done in preparing a trial brief. McLeod, frequently at odds on a friendly basis in and out of court with Allen Tonkin of Holloman's co-counsel, wrote out the proposed settlement. Nordhaus concurred, as Elfego Baca standing by, nodded his head in approval.

Counsel for the Cutting estate and the defendant all agreed on the wording of a stipulation, dated November 23, 1936, signed by Claude S. Mann, Allen Tonkin, J. D. Atwood and Reed Holloman for the estate, and by W. A. Keleher, A. H. McLeod and Robert J. Nordhaus, for Baca and by Elfego Baca, "attorney *pro se*." The stipulation disposing of the litigation, signed two days before the date set for commencement of the trial before a jury, ended the litigation.

Among other things the stipulation provided for the dismissal by the court with prejudice of the pending complaint and cross-complaint in the ejectment suit and provided that Elfego Baca's claim against the Cutting estate should be disapproved "with no right on the part of the claimant to take an appeal to the Supreme Court of New Mexico, or any other court or forum or to file any suit or file any claim in any court based on said claim."

The stipulation also provided that the residuary legatees

and devisees under the Cutting will should "as soon as practicable, after the date of the stipulation, but prior to the dismissal of the ejectment suit and complaint, and the disallowance of the claim against the estate, execute and hold for delivery, a quitclaim deed, vesting title in Elfego Baca to Lots Numbered 23 and 24, Block Numbered 19 of the New Mexico Town Company's Original Townsite of the City of Albuquerque." Justine Ward and Iris Margaret Oriego, devisees under the Cutting will, executed a quitclaim deed to the real estate naming Elfego Baca as grantee. Baca filed the deed for record in the County Clerk's office of Bernalillo County on January 6, 1937, and it was recorded in Book 144, page 377, Records of the County.

Thirteen years having elapsed between the date of the deed to Cutting from the Bankruptcy Court and the end of the litigation, Elfego Baca was once more the owner of the fee simple title to his property at Sixth and Gold in Albuquerque. All during the intervening years, Baca had received the benefits of ownership. He had used the premises for business and residential purposes; he had published *La Opinion Publica* in the building, a Spanish newspaper which had praised Bronson Cutting on many occasions as an astute politician and a great statesman. During all of the time of Baca's occupancy of the property, Bronson Cutting had paid the taxes and fire insurance premiums and through agents had paid for all required repairs. The arrangement had been ideal for Elfego Baca. The transaction, however, had not been one sided. During all of the intervening years Elfego Baca had been Bronson Cutting's true friend and staunch political supporter; had interviewed many politicians, and by letter and report he had no doubt kept Cutting informed on an ever-changing political situation.

Several months after Elfego Baca regained title to the property, two smart-looking, well-dressed men called on him at his office on Gold Avenue, introduced themselves as being federal agents from Washington, and said they had been sent to Albuquerque to talk to him about either buying his property, or filing a suit to condemn it as a future site for a federal building. Remembering, perhaps, the recent ordeal concerning title to the property and wishing to be left in peace, Baca without a word wheeled around in his swivel chair, grabbed from his desk two six-shooters. Holding a gun in each hand, Elfego told them in a commanding voice, "Gentlemen, get the hell out of my office." The visitors left Elfego Baca's office promptly and soon returned to Washington, for further instructions from their chief. Today, long years after Elfego Baca had chased the men out of his office, a multi-storied federal building extending on Gold Avenue from Fifth to Sixth Street, occupies a part of the lots once owned by Elfego Baca. Unfortunately, at a time when he was pressed for funds Elfego sold his property at a price much lower than the federal government would have paid him.

CHAPTER TWELVE

National Bank Failure

THE FIRST NATIONAL BANK of Albuquerque, at the time perhaps the most important and influential financial institution in New Mexico, doubtless insolvent, closed its doors on April 15, 1933. Two days later, on April 17, 1933, F. F. Awalt, Acting Comptroller of the Currency in Washington, appointed me by telegraph as Conservator of the bank. My appointment was made on recommendation of Frank A. Rees of Kansas City, Chief Deputy National Bank Examiner for the Tenth Federal Reserve District, who had recently completed a report of the bank's condition. The appointment of a conservator for national banks by the Comptroller had been authorized some two weeks before by the Act of Congress of March 3, 1933, a measure enacted at the request of President Roosevelt, entitled "An Act to Provide Relief in the Existing National Emergency in Banking and for Other Purposes." Prior to the enactment of the new law, federal courts had exclusive jurisdiction to appoint receivers in connection with the liquidation of insolvent national banks.

In 1924, ten years prior to my appointment, I had served as one of two attorneys for Francis A. Chapman, Receiver of the insolvent State National Bank of Albuquerque. It was my experience that a conservator, acting

NATIONAL BANK FAILURE 193

directly under the Comptroller of the Currency, and not a receiver, acting under a federal court, was in a better position to serve the needs of an insolvent financial institution promptly and efficiently. The crash of the First National Bank of Albuquerque, like the falling of a huge tree in a forest, had caused widespread repercussions in business and financial circles in Albuquerque, in central New Mexico, and in northern Arizona. The panic conditions prevailing generally throughout the United States in the spring and summer of 1933, paralyzed business in Albuquerque as elsewhere.

The failure of the First National Bank of Albuquerque had not been entirely unexpected. The Raynolds banking dynasty, established in New Mexico fifty years before by Jefferson and Joshua Raynolds, brothers, had begun to crumble when, on September 7, 1931, the First National Bank of El Paso, Texas, a Raynolds bank, closed its doors forever, despite the heroic efforts at rehabilitation by James Graham McNary, a Joshua Raynolds son-in-law, and other members of the Raynolds family.

The First National Bank of Albuquerque had a long history of successful banking, a background of honesty and integrity. On December 24, 1881, the Comptroller of the Currency had granted a charter for the bank to Mariano S. Otero, Nicolas T. Armijo, Daniel Geary, Felipe Chavez, Justo R. Armijo, Thomas C. Gutierrez, Louis Huning, Elias S. Stover, José Leandro Perea and Cristobal Armijo, all prominent and highly respected citizens of Bernalillo County, most of whom were wealthy. In 1876, three brothers from Canton, Ohio, Frederick, Jefferson and Joshua Raynolds, all of them well and personally acquainted with William McKinley, then a resident of Canton, later to be president of the United States, moved to Las Vegas, New Mexico, from Central City, Colorado, where they had been in the banking business. In Las Vegas, Jefferson and Joshua Raynolds in 1878 obtained a charter from the Territory of New Mexico for "The Central Bank" and in 1883 established a bank and began business under that name in Old Albuquerque. In 1883 the Raynolds brothers began to build, at a cost of $16,000, a two-story brick building in New Albuquerque, on the northwest corner of Second Street and Gold Avenue, to house The Central Bank, contemplating removal from Old to New Albuquerque, when the building had been completed. The iron step at the entrance door had the words "Central Bank" stamped in the metal, and the same words had been stamped in a grating above the entrance. At the time when it appeared that the new town of Albuquerque would be the business and commercial center because of the proximity of the Santa Fe and Atlantic and Pacific Railroad tracks, the owners of the control stock of the First National Bank of Albuquerque sold it on December 19, 1884 to the Raynolds Brothers, and the First National located in the Old Town at the intersection of Romero Avenue and the Plaza, was abandoned. In the merger effected between Central Bank and First National Bank of Albuquerque, the latter name was retained as the surviving corporation. The furniture and equipment of both banks were moved to Second and Gold in the new town. Business was continued in that location from 1884 until 1924, when a new eight-story bank building was erected on the northeast corner of Third Street and Central Avenue, at a cost of $580,000 on a site 100 x 142 feet, purchased for $100,000.

It is only fair and just to record here that in my work as Conservator of the First National Bank of Albuquerque there was no indication of the slightest incident of manipulation, fraud or dishonesty in connection with the business of the bank. John M. Raynolds, the bank's president, was a man of great integrity and outstanding honesty. Fate decreed that he would be obliged to stand by and helplessly witness the bank's failure. As it appeared to me, Raynolds had placed too much faith and confidence in the advice of Eastern bankers, who had recommended to him that he invest substantial funds in Joint Stock Land Bank bonds, which he bought at $100.00, plus accrued interest. He watched as they went down to $32.00 on the hundred. Raynolds had invested heavily in United States bonds, bought at $100.00, saw the market decline to $82.00. These and similar investments appeared to have contributed largely to the bank's insolvency.

The failure of the First Savings Bank & Trust Co., of Albuquerque, an affiliate of the First National Bank of Albuquerque, closely followed by the failure of the First National itself, resulted in the stagnation of business in Albuquerque and adjacent territory. The closing of the First National brought out the best and the worst in people. Some depositors, threatened with financial ruin, seemed to accept the situation calmly and worked for rehabilitation of the bank; others, facing a comparatively insignificant loss, excitedly threatened the bank officials with every form of reprisal. Soon after the collapse of the First National, depositors organized committees, elected chairmen and vice-chairmen, adopted resolutions, endorsing or opposing reorganization plans. Four weeks after the bank closed, charges were made of malfeasance and misfeasance on the part of men who had been in active charge of the bank. The Bernalillo County Grand Jury was summoned in special session, many witnesses testified, but no indictments were returned. During this period the bank's Conservator occupied a particularly unenviable position. He was at times the target of inflammatory accusations made by over-zealous and excited citizens, some of whom, it later developed, were neither depositors nor stockholders, but anxious only to participate in any kind of public clamor.

Many plans were submitted by individuals and groups looking toward rehabilitation of the bank. Most plans were based on the assumption that the federal government would extend financial assistance. Some of the plans deserved careful study. Others appeared to be purposely designed to gain control of the bank's assets, at bargain prices, with a view to disposing of them later at a substantial profit. Whenever in doubt about a suggested plan, I would go to Santa Fe and ask Levi A. Hughes, President of the First National Bank of Santa Fe, upon whose advice I knew I could rely, for a recommendation. By letter and long distance telephone, extensive negotiations were carried on with a number of people, among them Walter B. Bimson, at the time President of Valley Bank & Trust Co., of Phoenix, Arizona, and Charles Q. Chandler, at the time Chairman of the Board of the First National Bank of Wichita, Kansas.

During most of the month of June, 1933, Mr. Bimson appeared to be a most likely prospect to take over the bank. However, on June 26, Mr. Bimson telephoned me from Phoenix and told me that he had too much to do in his own back yard in Arizona to consider entering into banking in New Mexico. A courteously worded telegram confirmed his telephone message.

With Mr. Bimson eliminated as a prospect, I began serious negotiations with Mr. Chandler, who had previously told me in a long distance telephone conversation that his son, Charles J. Chandler, might be willing to serve as president of a newly organized bank in Albuquerque, to be capitalized by friends and business associates. Mr. Chandler came to Albuquerque from Wichita, and studied the possibilities for the success of a new bank. While he was in Albuquerque, I introduced him to J. F. T. O'Connor, the newly appointed Comptroller of the Currency, who was in Albuquerque at the time. Knowing that Mr. Chandler was a wealthy man I worked hard to get him interested in buying the bank's assets. On July 10, 1933, Mr. Chandler wrote me saying:

> I had quite a conference with my associates here over the situation. We recognize, just as you say, that Albuquerque offers a great opportunity. It is a Denver of that section and in my mind has a future. However, conditions are such we doubt the advisability or desirability of extending ourselves at this juncture in the banking business.

Albuquerque National Trust and Savings Bank, the name of which was later shortened to Albuquerque National Bank, the only bank in Albuquerque after the collapse of both First National Bank of Albuquerque and its affiliate, First Savings Bank and Trust Company, was quite anxious to gain control of the First National Bank assets. On June 6, 1933, George A. Kaseman, President of Albuquerque National, wrote me a five-page typewritten letter, offering to take over the assets and assume the First National's liabilities and responsibilities upon the outlined terms and conditions. In substance and effect the Kaseman offer was a contemplated merger of Albuquerque National and the remnants of the First National Bank of Albuquerque. After a preliminary statement of the situation, Kaseman in his letter made a statement, the truth of which could not be contradicted: "The depositors of the First National need their money, and in many cases the need is desperate." Among other things Kaseman stated:

> It may be assumed at the outset that any trade we make can and will be carried through, backed by ample resources and a desire and willingness on our part to come to the aid of

this community in general and the depositors of the First National Bank in particular. Let it be understood that the Albuquerque National Trust and Savings Bank is not desirous of making a trade on the basis of profit. Neither do we expect to make a trade at a loss.

Mr. Kaseman was a highly respected citizen of the community, with a long record for useful public service, formerly a member of the Senate in the New Mexico legislature, one time member of the Department of Public Welfare, and looked upon as a public spirited man in every respect, and his offer was worthy of serious consideration. Mr. Kaseman had not been immune personally from heavy financial disaster. In 1924, following the failure of the State National Bank in Albuquerque, in which he had been a large stockholder and a director, he had salvaged enough money to buy with associates the assets of the State National Bank of Albuquerque, then in receivership, and start a new bank. Through W. C. Reid, a long-time Kaseman friend, and as the result of Reid's close friendship with U.S. Senator Holm O. Bursum, the Comptroller of the Currency had expedited the processing of Kaseman's application, and quickly granted a charter to the Albuquerque National Trust & Savings Bank. Depositors and creditors of the insolvent State National Bank had previously accepted a satisfactory percentage of their claims. The new bank, under the direction of Mr. Kaseman and Frederick Luthy, following the failure of the First National Bank of Albuquerque, became the largest and most successful bank in New Mexico, under the name, Albuquerque National Bank.

Attached to the Kaseman letter of June 6, 1933, was a copy of the Albuquerque National statement of June 1, 1933, showing the bank's condition as of that date, with total resources of $3,972,142.30. First National depositors,

Northeast corner of Third Street and Central Avenue in Albuquerque, site of nine-story First National Bank building erected in 1924.

according to the Kaseman letter, would be paid at once in cash seventy-five percent of their deposits, plus an additional percent of any salvage, minus a reasonable amount for handling and collecting. In a personal talk with Senator Kaseman and Mr. Luthy I told them I could not recommend acceptance of the offer for many reasons, principally because it would mean that there would be only one bank in Albuquerque, that there would be no borrowing competition. Senator Kaseman urged a favorable recommendation to the comptroller, because he was strongly in favor of one strong bank for Albuquerque. Notwithstanding my objections to the Kaseman offer, it was my judgment that it should be submitted to the comptroller's office for consideration. I was in Washington on July 6 and had several meetings with officials handling the affairs of stricken banks, among them First National of Albuquerque. The Kaseman offer was thoroughly explored and analyzed; the decision was reached that it should not be accepted for a number of reasons, including the one that Albuquerque was of sufficient importance to justify the existence of at least two national banks, and Senator Kaseman was so notified. He sent me a 775-word telegram urging reconsideration, pointing out the favorable aspects of the offer, but the comptroller's decision remained as it had been handed down. In the meantime what appeared to me to be a more attractive bid for the bank assets was received from Mr. and Mrs. Albert G. Simms and Bartley H. Kinney, all of Albuquerque. They offered, among other things, to pay depositors seventy cents on the dollar in cash at once, and a participation in the net recovery upon liquidation of frozen assets. Mrs. Simms had lived in Albuquerque since her marriage to Mr. Simms on March 9, 1932. Albert Simms and Ruth Hanna McCormick Simms had served together in the

NATIONAL BANK FAILURE 201

71st Congress of the United States, she as a Congresswoman from Illinois, he as the lone Congressman from New Mexico. Mrs. Simms was nationally known, not only as a daughter of Mark Hanna, prominent in Republican politics during the William McKinley era, but as a powerful and influential person in her own right, the widow of Joseph Medill McCormick, publisher of the Chicago *Tribune*. In 1930 she had made an unsuccessful race for United States Senator from Illinois, and for some years published a daily newspaper in Rockford, Illinois.

As part of her offer to purchase the First National assets, along with Bart Kinney, Mrs. Simms agreed to buy $75,000 in common stock. Kinney agreed to invest $25,000 in common stock, and to become president of the bank. Kinney was a successful business man, and in my estimation had the ability to manage the proposed rehabilitated bank. Subject to some modifications and amendments, the comptroller indicated a willingness to approve the Simms-Kinney plan. No doubt that Mrs. Simms was prompted to cooperate with Mr. Kinney in making an offer for the bank assets by a strong desire to be of help to the community and its people in a time of distress. While the details of the Simms-Kinney plan were still under consideration in Washington, Mr. Kinney told me that suddenly out of a clear sky, Albert Simms had telephoned him to say that "Ruth had decided not to go into the banking business and was withdrawing her offer." As a result Mr. Kinney told me he preferred to discontinue his efforts as a possible purchaser of the assets. Hopeful that Albert Simms might be persuaded to reconsider his decision, I wrote and telephoned to him at Rockford, Illinois, where he and Mrs. Simms were on a business visit, in an effort to get them interested once again in banking. From Rockford, Mr. and Mrs. Simms went to Woods Hole, Massachusetts. After consulting with Mr. Kinney, I corresponded with them there by mail, telegraph and telephone urging them to renew and revive their offer. On July 30, 1933, Albert Simms telephoned me from Woods Hole, holding out some slight hope of a change of attitude, but, on July 31, 1933, he telegraphed me as follows: "After careful consideration we find it impossible to comply with your request. Kindest regards to you."

With the Albuquerque National offer unacceptable to the comptroller, and the Simms-Kinney offer withdrawn, a committee headed by Sidney M. Weil, Chairman, and made up of Guy Rogers, Henry G. Coors, Bruce Hanger and others who were working long hours for the rehabilitation of the bank, a campaign was begun to have the depositors themselves invest ten percent of their deposits in common stock in a new banking corporation, which would take over the assets of the First National Bank of Albuquerque, and resume business. Discouraged depositors to a surprising extent signed subscription agreements, and the stock selling campaign proved successful, despite the fact that several large corporations, which might have been expected to go along with the plan, refused to cooperate and insisted on receiving 100% of their deposits. The "lifted assets" had been previously appraised and the Reconstruction Finance Corporation agreed to make a loan on them of $250,000, and to buy $250,000 in preferred stock in the contemplated new banking corporation. When the totals were announced, it appeared that it would be necessary to have the R.F.C. loan increased from $250,000 to $375,000.

During the summer of 1933 the R.F.C. was being besieged by bankers from all parts of the country, clamoring for loans, demanding prompt action on applications, insisting on service of every imaginable type in the fields of finance and commerce. The minor R.F.C. officials having refused to look favorably on our application for the $375,000 loan, I went to Washington and wangled an appointment with Jesse Jones, Chairman of the R.F.C. I explained the Albuquerque situation to Mr. Jones, who was sympathetic, but told me patiently of the pressure and demand for increased loans from many railroads, banks and other institutions, and of his inability to comply with all requests. Jesse Jones on this occasion measured up to my expectations of him and his great ability as an executive. During the few moments allotted to me, he was interrupted several times by assistants in order to communicate important information. He appeared to be carrying on two telephone conversations simultaneously with a receiver held against each ear. Mr. Jones' answer to my request for the $375,000 loan was an emphatic "no." Politely shown out of the R.F.C. offices, I hurried to the Senate Office Building and asked the help of United States Senator Sam G. Bratton, a long-time personal friend. After listening to my problem, the Senator went to the White House to ask the assistance of President Roosevelt. Within an hour, Senator Bratton telephoned me, saying that he had talked to the President, who had told him: "Sam, I'm just leaving for the Union Station where a special train is waiting to take me to Hyde Park; I haven't enough time left now or I would telephone Jesse Jones and ask him to increase that loan. I will rely on your judgment that the bank in your town is a key bank and should be opened. The moment I get to Hyde Park I will telephone Jesse Jones and see what can be done."

Senator Bratton telephoned the next day to say that a White House assistant had told him to have his constituent get in touch with the R.F.C. again, about that "bank loan business." I went at once to the R.F.C. offices, encountering there an entirely different atmosphere than that experienced on the previous visit. I was introduced to an executive who told me that the loan application had been reconsidered and approved for $375,000. Within a short time the application and a new pro forma statement had been submitted.

Now that sufficient stock had been subscribed for, most of which was to be paid for by a shrinking of deposits on an average of ten percent, and now that the R.F.C. had agreed to loan $375,000 on lifted assets, in addition to subscribing for $250,000 in preferred stock, there remained only the mechanics of picking up the broken pieces resulting from the bank's failure, and fitting them together again. The Comptroller of the Currency promptly issued a charter for the new corporation, named First National Bank in Albuquerque. Young men of the community were reluctant to become directors in the new bank, so I invited William C. Thaxton, Silvestre Mirabal and D. K. B. Sellers, all clients of mine, to accept places on the board, and they accepted.

The comptroller had previously ruled that no officer or director of First National Bank of Albuquerque would be permitted to serve as an officer or director of the new bank. The names of several capable men were recommended to the board to be president. In Washington I had called upon Cale W. Carson and had discussed with him the possibility of accepting the presidency. At the time Mr. Carson was a deputy land bank commissioner, busily engaged in important work in trying to rehabilitate farm mortgages held by the Federal Land Banks. I had known "Kit" Carson slightly for several years, through acquaintance with Henry G. Coors, his brother-in-law, formerly of Las Vegas, New Mexico, and a close friend of John M. Raynolds, President of the now insolvent First

National Bank of Albuquerque. At first Carson was somewhat reluctant to accept the call to the presidency of the new bank, but finally decided to take a close-up view of the situation. Accordingly he came to Albuquerque, accompanied by Charles Q. Chandler, a Wichita banker whom I had tried several months before to interest in the bank. Carson and Chandler went over the bank's note case carefully, and studied the general situation. An informal meeting was held of the recently elected Board of Directors of the new corporation, in the course of which the Board offered Carson the presidency at a starting salary of $8,500, which he accepted and handed me a check for $3,750 down payment on a sufficient number of shares of stock in the new bank to qualify as a director. Carson resigned his position in Washington, came to Albuquerque as soon as the necessary arrangements could be made, assumed management of the new bank, fitting well into the community. He used to good advantage years of prior banking experience with the Fuqua banks in Amarillo, Spearman and other places in West Texas, extending credit to customers, new and old, whenever deserved and consistent with conditions, participating actively in all worthy, forward-looking community endeavors. More than thirty-five years have come and gone since I served as Conservator of the First National Bank of Albuquerque, helped rehabilitate it and helped select Cale Wellman Carson as its first president, under whose administration and direction the bank has grown and prospered consistent with the growth and prosperity of the community.

The newly-established First National Bank in Albuquerque opened for business promptly at 10 o'clock on October 24, 1933, the old bank having closed on April 15. Some six months had elapsed between the day the Comptroller had appointed me as conservator, and the reopening. During the entire six months Thomas M. Pepperday, publisher of the *Albuquerque Journal,* had been most loyal to the Raynolds family, and very helpful to me in my work. R. F. (Deacon) Arledge, a star *Journal* reporter, had been given a permanent assignment to cover the bank story and did an excellent job of keeping depositors informed of developments looking toward rehabilitation.

On October 25 I resumed my law practice. On the previous day Tom Pepperday had rolled a cigarette, filled with Prince Albert tobacco, lighted it, took a few puffs, sat down to his ancient Royal typewriter and pecked out with two fingers an editorial, something he rarely did. The editorial, published in the *Journal* of October 25, read as follows:

He Deserves Credit.

While credit is being given for the successful reopening of the First National Bank in Albuquerque, Mr. W. A. Keleher, conservator, should not be overlooked. A native son who has always had faith in Albuquerque and its institutions, he had faith in the possibilities of the reopening and didn't want to see the bank that had served the southwest for so many years pass out of existence. He showed great tact and patience in dealing with the problems as they came up and in the eventual working out of the plan that was put over.

A less persevering man might have given up, but he stuck with the job. He is not connected with the new organization and will not profit personally but he was as highly gratified as anyone with direct interests, in seeing the institution reopened. He deserves the gratitude of the citizens and especially the depositors of the bank for his good work.

CHAPTER THIRTEEN

The Gallup Coal Strike

Now THAT the First National Bank of Albuquerque had begun business under its new name, First National Bank in Albuquerque, with every indication that it would continue indefinitely as a successful, going concern, it appeared that I might resume the practice of law more or less abandoned during the time I had served as conservator. Within a few days, however, I found myself engaged in another public interest project. This time the trouble revolved around a coal strike.

On November 2, 1933, Governor Andrew W. Hockenhull telephoned me from Santa Fe stating that he was naming former Governor Merritt C. Mechem and me as a committee of two to inquire into the causes for the serious labor trouble in the coal fields near McKinley County on the New Mexico-Arizona border, some 140 miles west of Albuquerque. Governor Hockenhull would not take "no" for an answer to his appeal for help in what he described as a crisis in his administration, and I promised to assist him.

Governor Hockenhull wrote me a lengthy letter on November 3, expressing his concern and saying that he was most anxious to get the coal strike settled. The Governor outlined the situation somewhat in detail, saying that fearing public disorder in the coal fields, he had called out the National Guard and that the soldiers were in camps on the outskirts of Gallup under the command of Adjutant General Osborne Wood. The adjutant general was a son of famed General Leonard Wood, prominent in the era of Col. Theodore Roosevelt.

In a general way I was familiar with the strike situation. Although he did not realize it at the time, Governor Hockenhull was asking Judge Mechem and me to participate in a final chapter, in the twilight hours, of the generations old struggle between capital and labor in New Mexico, a state which had never been important industrially. It had been freely charged that the Constitution of New Mexico had been adopted, following the granting of statehood in 1912, under the sponsorship of the big corporate interests, and that it had been drafted by corporation lawyers. Although it was not a coal producing state of importance when compared with Colorado, Pennsylvania, West Virginia, Kentucky and other states, nevertheless, New Mexico had important coal deposits, and production of coal was a significant factor in the state's economy. Important New Mexico coal mining properties included those at Dawson, in Colfax County, at Madrid, in Santa Fe County, and the Gallup field, in McKinley County. The extent of mining in the Dawson field came to the notice of the people of the state in a forceful way on October 26, 1913, when 263 miners lost their lives in an explosion in Dawson Mine No. 2. It was inevitable that the labor unions would become involved with the mines and mining operators in New Mexico. For years, beginning as far back as 1895, the unions and the employer corporations had engaged in an almost continuous feud

THE GALLUP COAL STRIKE 209

over wages and hours of employment, the inherent right of the miners to join a union, the right to be openly identified and known as a "union man." There had been much argument over the check off, the right of weighmen, the company store, and company store money. Local and national labor leaders had fought for years for what they contended was fair play for the miners. The mining companies, so the union organizers claimed, had always closed their eyes to the rights of the miners, had stubbornly refused to budge one inch toward complying with the demands of the men. The deadlock between the miners and mine owners had, over the years, resulted in many strikes in New Mexico.

The 1933 strike, called during the Hockenhull administration, was no different than previous strikes, with one very important exception, at the time only vaguely understood and but little appreciated. In 1933 the federal government, under "New Deal" laws, proposed to take a hand in strike situations, to throw its might on the side of the miners, to see that capital could not and would not turn the screw and pinch the miner's thumb, or bend his elbow until compelled to cry "ouch." For the first time the national government was injecting a bit of moral law into a strike situation.

No one would deny that Governor Hockenhull was an ideal Christian gentleman. The people generally knew he was a staunch member of the First Baptist Church of Clovis, a generous supporter of Baptist missionary work in Mexico. A man with a conscience, he had told close friends that he was greatly troubled over the possibility that he had not acted as a true Christian in sending troops to the Gallup coal field. Accordingly, he was anxious to have Judge Mechem and me expedite our work, and tell him what, if anything, could be done to remedy the situation.

When on September 1, 1933, Governor Hockenhull sent troops into Gallup to "preserve law and order," he knew or should have known that he was signing his own political death warrant. From the day troops were ordered out, miners to a man, and union men generally, classified Hockenhull as a "tool of the vested interests," a "hound dog of capitalism," and political leaders in the Democratic party soon marked him off as a possible candidate for nomination for the governorship of New Mexico. Gallup, center of a vast field of bituminous coal, was no stranger to turmoil. On previous occasions, New Mexico State Militia had camped near Gallup, ostensibly for the purpose of "preserving law and order." The Gallup coal field extended many miles to the west and northwest of the town, reaching into the interior of the Navajo Indian reservation. Gallup had a population in 1933 of 10,500. It had been an important place since 1882 when the Atlantic and Pacific Railroad had built westward toward the Colorado River from Albuquerque. It was in 1933, and ever since has been, the railhead and gateway to the vast and all-important Navajo Indian reservation. For many years prior to 1933, Gallup had enjoyed great economic advantages as the result of its proximity to the coal fields. With much money available to those willing to fight for it, there was keen commercial competition among Gallup merchants. Many business and professional men, ordinarily of good will and even temperament, found themselves, willingly or otherwise, engaged in last ditch commercial and political rivalry, battling and scheming in what appeared to be a life and death struggle over money or property. Railroad and coal mining operations generated payrolls, supplemented by money derived from federal appropriations for Indian purposes. As a result of the economic advantages, money was available in Gallup for those interested in acquiring it.

Many Slav miners had worked in the Gallup coal fields, bringing with them their native heritage and customs, including thrift and an inclination toward hard work. The Slavs were anxious to own real estate, willing to buy bank stock, and deposited money freely on account with merchants and storekeepers, always with an eye to going in business for themselves at some future day.

The Navajo Indian never fully understood Gallup and its devious ways; and Gallup was not particularly anxious at any time to adequately understand the Navajo. Some venturesome Navajos, in Gallup occasionally to buy supplies, unable to speak one word of English, not too much inclined to resist the persuasion and blandishments of the professional bootlegger, found themselves in trouble in a day when it was a federal offense to buy or sell intoxicating liquor to or from an Indian on or off an Indian reservation. As a result, some Navajos, visiting Gallup and wandering about town, awakened from sleep in jail, with a vague and remote recollection of having been arrested hours before on a charge of being drunk and disorderly. Arraigned summarily before a police judge experienced in the ways of the Navajo, the Indian defendant was found guilty as a matter of course and fined a reasonable sum. By a strange coincidence, the trial judge customarily took into consideration, when assessing the fine, the amount of money reported by the arresting officer to have been found on the defendant's person at the time of arrest, and fined him accordingly. Having thus been treated to a bit of Gallup hospitality, the unhappy Navajo, fairly well sobered up by now, and a wiser and sadder Indian, was free to begin his return journey to the Navajo Reservation, a much more friendly country, mumbling to himself, perhaps, the Navajo lines equivalent to Arthur Clough's:

"In front, the sun climbs slow, how slowly,
But westward, look, the land is bright."

On November 4, 1933, Judge Mechem and I held the first session of the investigation in Albuquerque at which we asked the miners to give the background of their grievances. We stated that we had no power to administer oaths, or to compel any person to appear or testify. The first four witnesses represented five locals of the National Miners Union. They were: James Walker, a very intelligent Negro who had worked for the Defiance Coal Company in Gallup for eight years; Juan Ochoa, of Mexican descent who had worked in the Gallup mines for five years; Pete Ricki and Steven Katzman.

Walker, principal spokesman for the union, outlined its contentions, saying that he and his colleagues had been employed in the Gallup area by the Defiance Coal Company, the Gallup American Fuel Company, and the National Coal Company. Walker explained:

> When the National Recovery Act was established some months ago, we understood that it gave miners and other workmen the right to join the local union of their own choice. Two unions, the National Miners Union and the United Mine Workers of America, competed for membership in the Gallup field, in which 750 miners were employed, 600 of whom were said to belong to the National Miners Union, most of the others holding membership in the United Mine Workers. An election was held to see which would be the dominant union. The election resulted in a vote of 426 for the National Miners and 26 for the United Mine Workers. The National Miners Union, having established and won the election, several locals

THE GALLUP COAL STRIKE

were formed under the jurisdiction of that organization, and plans were made to submit to the coal companies in the area a list of grievances and demands for consideration. The Defiance and Gallup American Companies flatly refused to recognize any demands of any union at that time. They decided to start a union of their own. They proceeded to coerce and intimidate the men, to force them to join the company union, which the union men refused to do.

We stated to them: 'You are taking away from us a part of our rights. We are entitled to have a union of our own choice.' To this the company said: 'We will not recognize any union of the men.' A week went by and we again presented our plans to the companies. Their answer was: 'Your plan is no good, and we will not have anything to do with it because it is not a miners' union, but this is a Red outfit.' We knew nothing of any red outfit, but by reading, we found out that they were referring to some existing Russian Society that was protesting against certain things and were called Communists. The company sent word to us: 'You fellows clean up and join the union called "The United Mine Workers of America." ' We refused. We again presented our demands to Defiance, Gallup American and Mutual Companies and then to the Diamond Coal Company, owner of the Allison Mine and Mentmore, but they one and all refused. Then miners from all five companies went on strike and that is how the trouble started, particularly because the companies began to bring in scabs in an attempt to break the strike, and the governor called out the National Guard.

Walker's testimony was corroborated by that of Alejandro Alvarado, Juan Ochoa and Pete Ricki. Ricki stated the following reasons for the strike: "The conditions underground in some of the mines were very bad for the workers. That was the reason we wanted a union. The miners underground had no air. Such air as we have is no good for breathing. Lots of times I have seen men naked working without any clothes on at all and they would be sweating. These conditions brought on a strike, and also because wages were very low and we do not have scales to weigh out the coal we mine."

The functions of a check-weigh man were described by James Walker: "The check-weigh man is the man who weighs the coal on top with the weigh-boss. There are two men. One, the weigh-boss, is paid by the company. The men will select and pay the wages of the other check-weigh man to look after their interests, to see that the coal is weighed correctly by the weigh load." Juan Ochoa, for the National Miners testified that the men complained that the scales weighed incorrectly; that one set of scales hadn't been tested for accuracy for many years, and that the suggestion made by the company to have the sheriff of McKinley County as the only one authorized to test the scales was entirely unacceptable to them. The significance of the demand for a weigh-man, and for scale testing became apparent through Ochoa's testimony. He also stated that miners were paid 51¢ a ton for digging coal, which was reduced 25¢ a ton because of the objectionable weighing process.

Steven Katzman, employed for nine years as a rope-rider in one of the mines, testified that the company he had worked for estimated the weight of the coal he mined instead of actually weighing it out; that the men were not being fairly treated in connection with the disposal of dead weight.

Walker, Alvarado and Ochoa were united in the opinion that the National Guard troops should be removed from Gallup at once. Ochoa said: "The troops should be sent away. There was no cause for them to be sent here in the first place. They hinder union activities. So naturally we cannot function as we should because of martial law."

Concerning the conflict between the National Miners Union and the United Mine Workers, Ochoa testified: "The United Mine Workers of America hasn't been a union of the miners for many years past. They pretend to improve the condition of the miner. Actually they do not."

James Walker described the historical background of the United Mine Workers as follows:

> I belonged to the United Mine Workers for twenty-five years. I saw its obligations and its purpose from start to finish. The United Mine Workers was a union for the mines until in 1912 when John L. Lewis became president and they got several million dollars and they refused to let the rank and file have anything to do with running the union and the men don't want to belong to it any more. Now they are trying to take advantage in Gallup of the National Miners Union, following a consultation with Mr. Mosley, who tried to put down the United Mine Workers in 1903 and again in 1917. Why does Mosely work for them now? It is to try and kill the National Miners Union and then kick the United Mine Workers out also.

When the committee representing the National Miners Union and the committee representing the United Mine Workers of America had finished outlining their positions and stating their grievances, we asked the mine operators to submit testimony. Appearing as a witness for the owners and operators were: George Miksch of the Defiance Coal Company; B. B. Hanger of the Diamond; George A. Kaseman of the Defiance; Sharp Hansen for the Southwestern; Horace Moses for the Gallup American; and H. S. Mills for the Mutual Company. Of the companies operating in the area, the Gallup American was the largest and most important, employing more miners than all other companies combined. Before mining a ton of coal that company had spent $5,000,000.00 above and below ground, installing air conditioning, laying many miles of track, and equipping the mines with the most modern coal digging machinery available.

Judge Mechem summarized for the operators the case submitted on behalf of the miners. He concluded by saying: "Governor Hockenhull has told us he wants to get some practical suggestions for settlement of the strike. We would like to have you state into the record your views in regard to that." Horace Moses, testifying for the owners and operators, said that he was General Manager of the Gallup American Company, which would not recognize or deal with either the National Miners Union or the United Mine Workers. "My instructions are very emphatic, we will not recognize the union. We will shut down first."

That the Gallup American Mines would be closed before the company would recognize or deal with the unions was quite significant. Assuming Gallup American stopped mining coal, it would be only a few days until the Chino Copper Mines near Silver City and the smelter at nearby Hurley would be obliged to shut down because of lack of coal.

Horace Moses urged that we recommend to the Governor that troops be retained in Gallup indefinitely, saying: "If Governor Hockenhull, days ago, had come out with a firm stand, declaring that the troops were going to be in Gallup until law and order prevailed and peace achieved in the field, it would have been only a short time until the strike would have been over." Moses contended that the strikers were being financed from many directions: "The other day I saw where they got $100.00 from Detroit and $60.00 from San Francisco. The Communist party said if we can get a foothold in Gallup, we can force the state; if not, we can go elsewhere. They tried in

Madrid, New Mexico. From Madrid, they went to Raton. From Raton they went to Dawson, and from Dawson to Gallup. Their agitators came to Gallup from Denver and if they get a foothold in Gallup, Gallup will be their headquarters."

The Gamerco management had refused to resort to eviction, Moses said: "We have over 150 houses now occupied by striking miners who are not paying rent. They are getting free rent, free lights and water. When they move they break up our furniture and break out all the window lights." Moses described the situation from a practical standpoint: "We told these miners to get out. We had leases and we couldn't move them. They had a meeting and stayed right there. Had we gone up there into a man's house, tearing down his pictures and other pieces of our own furniture, put them all in a truck and dumped his kids on top of the pile, asked them where they wanted to go, and dumped them out in the streets, because they had no place to go, there would have been an awful hue and cry."

Fred Stetham, Secretary of the Gallup local of the United Mine Workers, testified that he had been employed as a coal digger for fourteen years in Mine No. 51, Central Coal and Coke Company in Pittsburg, Kansas, and as a shot-firer for several years at the Gamerco mines. He testified that he had belonged to the United Mine Workers of America for Kansas years before, and that he had dropped his membership in that state but joined as a new member in Gallup several months before the strike had been called.

Asked about the animosity existing between the National Miners Union and the United Mine Workers, Stetham testified: "The United Mine Workers Union is not a labor union. It is a Communist Party—a subsidiary of the Communist Party." Stetham exhibited a copy of the Gallup local United Mine Workers charter, dated August 24, 1933, several days before the strike was called on August 29, 1933. On the latter date he said 520 men were carried on the Gamerco payroll. As of November 7, 1933, 219 men were still employed in that mine. That the current daily wage had been $4.48, but this would be increased to $4.70 under the new NRA code.

After hearing testimony for four days on the Gallup strike assignment, Judge Mechem and I submitted a report to Governor Hockenhull advising him that four major grievances had precipitated the strike and motivated its continuance: refusal of the companies to enter into collective bargaining; refusal to pay for dead work; failure of the companies to concede a weigh-man; failure of the companies to permit the introduction of the check-off system. We reported to Governor Hockenhull that apparently the companies might be willing to agree to collective bargaining, to pay for dead work, and to allow a check weigh-man, but that they balked at the demand for a check-off, which would allow workers to assign a portion of their wages for an indefinite period of time, to be considered as union dues. On the question of recognizing the union, we advised the Governor that the operators presented a solid front. The answer was a definite and emphatic "no." The operators were a unit, too, on the question of reinstating former employees then on strike. They could regain employment only by making application, so the mine owners claimed, with the right reserved on the part of the operators to refuse to re-employ.

On October 31, 1933, D. C. Jackling, general manager of the interlocking Gallup American Coal Co. of the companies which owned and operated the Chino Copper Company mines near Silver City and the smelter at Hurley, spent a day in Albuquerque. Jackling was traveling in a private car on the Santa Fe Railroad en route from New York to his home in San Francisco. On invitation of Horace Moses, Judge Mechem and I went to the railroad station and talked to Jackling about the possibilities for settling the strike. Jackling, one of the top-flight authorities in the world on copper production, was not particularly disturbed over the Gallup strike. Horace Moses had kept him informed about the situation. He told Mechem and me that he had no particular objection to collective bargaining, as such, but didn't like the check-off. He said he would offer no objection if some arrangement could be made whereby the individual miner would sign an agreement directing the company to pay a specified sum each month to a benefit association which could channel the money to a final destination, the identity of which Gamerco would not scrutinize too closely. By using such a method, Jackling said, a face-to-face meeting with the check-off arrangement could be evaded and avoided. In regard to re-employment of striking miners, Jackling said he would favor giving jobs back to men who had not been obnoxious during the strike, with preference given to men with families.

Concerning wages, Jackling said he would authorize payment of whatever the operators in the Colorado field agreed to pay under the recent ruling emanating from Washington. Jackling was quite firm in his declaration that if Gamerco shut down, causing 350 to 500 men to lose their jobs, then the Chino Copper Mines would also shut down at once, throwing 700 to 800 men out of work.

Although perhaps not aware or conscious of it at the time, the miners and operators identified with the hearing concerning the Gallup strike in 1933 were participating in the events of more than passing historical significance.

The scope of the hearing conducted by Judge Mechem and me at Governor Hockenhull's request was, in a small way, nothing more nor less than a recapitulation of unresolved differences of opinion that had existed between coal miners and operators for some fifty years. There was nothing in the testimony by miner or operator to justify the prediction that within a comparatively short period, the arguments and contentions advanced by the participants would become academic, perhaps moot. Little consideration had been given to the possibilities inherent in the recently enacted federal statutes, eliminating, perhaps forever, most of the points of difference then existing between capital and labor.

The Mechem-Keleher report promptly forwarded to Governor Hockenhull, although prepared at considerable time and effort, proved of no significance or importance in the scheme of things. However, it allowed the Governor time to reappraise the strike situation. Much to his relief, the strong arm of the federal government intervened and saved all concerned from the necessity of a showdown. On October 30, 1933, while the Gallup strike was well under way, and the New Mexico National Guard was on duty in Gallup, an announcement was made from Washington of vast importance to coal operators and coal miners all over the United States. The Anthracite Institute, which represented most of the hard coal operators in the country, filed a code of ethics agreement with the National Recovery Administration in Washington, consenting to the establishment of a 48-hour week, assurance of recognition of labor unions as a party in interest in bargaining, and acceptance in principle of the philosophy of collective bargaining on hours, wages and working conditions. Within a matter of hours, the soft coal operators, through their national organization, agreed to go along with the hard coal operators. The full impact of the agreement was not felt in New Mexico for some days, and the investigation requested by Governor Hockenhull proceeded on what ultimately proved to be a moot basis, simply because power and authority required to maintain and sustain a strike had passed from the states to the federal government, and that power and might would from henceforth be exercised in Washington instead of in the capitols of the individual states.

On or about November 10, 1933, the Gallup strike became a shambles insofar as the mine operators were concerned when the Colorado Fuel and Iron Company announced from its Denver office that the company, then in receivership in the United States District Court in Colorado, would in the near future recognize the United Mine Workers as the bargaining agent for the miners, and that no further attempt would be made to function under the so-called John D. Rockefeller, Jr. Plan, virtually a company-union compromise arrangement, adopted following Rockefeller's investigation on the ground in Colorado subsequent to the so-called "Bloody Ludlow Massacre" involving Colorado Mines and law enforcement officers in a fierce fight which attracted world-wide attention.

In the wake of the news that drastic changes had taken place in the field of capital and labor, the striking Gallup miners appealed for help to the National Labor Board in Washington. The Board responded quickly by sending Major John D. Moore, of 1119 84th Street, Brooklyn, New York, to Gallup to make an investigation into the strike and, if possible, effect a settlement. Major Moore, one of the earliest conciliators in the field, with the prestige afforded him by the National Labor Board and supported by recent federal court decisions, proved successful in getting the operators and miners together on a settlement agreement which was not entirely satisfactory to either side. A so-called "Declaration of Peace and Amity" was signed. The mining companies consented to a new wage scale, patterned after the plan recommended by the NRA. The companies agreed to what one operator described as the "voracious and unpalatable demands of the New Deal," accepted collective bargaining, agreed to pay for dead work, agreed to employment of a check-weigh man, and to a thinly disguised formula for the check-off, including deduction of union dues from a miner's wages.

Overshadowing the coal industry of New Mexico prior and subsequent to 1933 was the threat that oil and natural gas would supplant coal in New Mexico. Before the Gallup strike, important discoveries of gas and oil in San Juan, Lea, Eddy and Chaves Counties, New Mexico, pinpointed that coal was on its way out; and indicated that after all there might be some truth to the claims of the operators that the coal industry was a "sick industry."

Within a few months after the Gallup strike had been settled, the coal industry in New Mexico appeared to be rapidly approaching virtual extinction. Coal had been used from many New Mexico mines for generations on railroads using steam locomotives. One by one, the Santa Fe, Southern Pacific, Rock Island, and other railroads in New Mexico placed their coal burning locomotives on side tracks and operated their equipment with oil burners and diesel engines. The demand for coal dwindled almost to zero. The discovery of natural gas of high BTU content, produced in substantial quantities in southeastern and northwestern New Mexico provided the knockout blow. Coal operators were quick to read the handwriting on the wall, to admit the approaching demise of a long-time flourishing industry. Miners faced the certain loss of their jobs in Dawson, Madrid, Gallup and other coal mining camps. Almost overnight, pipelines were built into almost every important supply point in New Mexico. Natural gas was soon available for fuel in mines, smelters, manufacturing plants and domestic purposes, at a price which eliminated coal as a competitor. Coal mines, which had been important producers for many years, were relegated to the category of wagon mines. Nearly all of the major mines in the Gallup area were shut down and boarded up. The Gallup American property, the most important in the Gallup field, was sold for $250,000, a mere fraction of its value in the years of production.

More than thirty-five years have come and gone since Governor Hockenhull asked Merritt Mechem and me to investigate the Gallup strike. As of 1969, there are many signs that coal is destined to again play an important part in New Mexico's economy. Comparatively few miners are being used today in connection with vast strip-mining projects in the coal fields on the Navajo Reservation in northwestern New Mexico and adjoining northern Arizona. Huge coal excavators dig as much coal in one day as a capable miner could dig in a year in 1933, working with pick and shovel. The federal government, private capital, and the tribal authorities of the Navajo Indians have united in cooperating in finding and developing a market for Navajo Reservation coal. One giant electrical generating plant has been built, and others are in course of construction in the Four Corner country where four states, Utah, Colorado, Arizona and New Mexico converge. Vast quantities of electric power are being sent over modern transmission lines to California, Arizona, New Mexico, Utah and West Texas.

In the light of subsequent and intervening events, the

inquiry requested by Governor Hockenhull, and pursued by Judge Mechem and me, was a sham battle, a demonstration of how capital and labor differed in the not too distant past, and the possibility for capital and labor to cooperate in plans for mutual benefit.

CHAPTER FOURTEEN

Libraries

DURING THE administration of Governor John E. Miles, I was afforded an opportunity of being helpful in acquiring the Paul Van de Velde Library for the University of New Mexico. Dr. George P. Hammond, at the time Dean of the Graduate School of the University of New Mexico, learned that the Van de Velde books were for sale at $20,000, and was very anxious to get them for the University. The difficulty was that the University had not budgeted any money for such an acquisition, and for a time it appeared that the books would be sold either to the University of Texas at Austin, or to the University of California at Berkeley.

When I was in San Bernardino, California, on January 7, 1939, Dr. Hammond wrote me a letter urging me to go to Los Angeles, look at the books, evaluate them, and see if Van de Velde would not sell them on some credit plan. I did so, and enroute to 948 South Figueroa Street, where the books were stored, I happened to meet Judge David Chavez, then Judge of the First Judicial District Court of New Mexico, with residence in Santa Fe, later Chief Justice of the Supreme Court of New Mexico. He accepted an invitation to look at the library with me and, if acceptable, to try and make a deal with Van de

Velde. The books proved to be all that Dr. Hammond hoped for, some 8,000 volumes by Spanish and Mexican writers, badly needed to fill in gaps in the Coronado Library at the University of New Mexico.

Van de Velde had come into possession of the books in a peculiar way. He had been in the Belgian consular service in Mexico City, and while there had conceived the idea of buying books then available, many of them doubtless formerly owned by colleges, convents and schools victimized by the religious persecution. Such acquisition was customary in Mexico during a period of several years in the early '30's. Van de Velde bought the books at bargain prices and shipped them in diplomatic pouches to a blind address in Los Angeles, retrieving them when he retired from the diplomatic services and left Mexico. One of the surprise packages among the Van de Velde books was a complete, well-bound file of the Mexican *Herald,* beginning with the inauguration of President Porfirio Diaz, and ending with revolution which began in 1914.

Judge Chavez and I, although familiar with only a scattering-few of the books, had no doubt but that they should be worth $20,000. We told Van de Velde that we would buy them for the University of New Mexico. Van de Velde had all the canny bargaining talent of his countrymen. He refused to allow the books to be shipped to New Mexico on a rather informal C.O.D. basis. However, he agreed to meet us in Santa Fe, where the State Legislature was in session, and help us lobby an appropriation through House and Senate.

Upon returning to Santa Fe, Judge Chavez and I explained the entire situation to Governor Miles and obtained his promise of help. I was delegated to draw a bill providing for the $20,000 appropriation, which became Chapter 211 of the 1939 Session Laws. The preamble of the bill set forth the objectives, somewhat in detail, and it was not difficult to enlist supporters, especially among the Spanish-American members of the Legislature for the purchase of the books at what subsequently proved to be a very reasonable price. In our efforts to get the bill through the Legislature, Judge Chavez and I made out lists of members each of us was to "lobby."

Before many days we could count noses and be assured of enactment. Judge Chavez had promised to talk to George W. Armijo, all-powerful Speaker of the House, and attempt to interest him in the fate of the bill. Chavez expected a prompt offer of help, but Armijo, it appeared was not too anxious at that particular time to talk about Mexico or things Mexican. He confidentially explained to Judge Chavez his reluctance to be identified or associated with anything that reminded him of Mexico:

> Dave, the other night I had a terrible dream. I thought I was in Mexico City, where I was wined and dined by several wealthy and influential Mexicans. As you well know, I am not much of a man for religious practices, but nominally I am of the Catholic faith through inheritance. Fortunately, before it was too late, I discovered why these Mexicans were making such a fuss over me. They were very anxious, it seemed, to have me apply for membership in the Masonic Order. I explained that I had been familiar for some years with the saying "once a Mason, always a Mason," that I had many friends in my home town of Santa Fe who had been highly honored in the Scottish Rite of the Masonic Order, among them Judge Richard H. Hanna and Rupert F. Asplund, men I respected highly and admired greatly.
>
> I told my Mexican friends that I could not in good conscience go against my Catholic training and background and ask to become a member of their order. When I had finally and absolutely refused their invitation, one of them snapped his fingers. Two burly Mexicans, instantly entered the large room where we were standing, seized me by the throat and

began to manhandle me something terrible. During that ordeal, my body was covered with clammy perspiration, and I was afraid for my life. I tried to scream as loudly as I could, but my voice was only a whisper. Fortunately, just at that time, in one of the really great crises of my life, I woke up. I have been nervous and shaky ever since. So you can see, Dave, and will understand, I am sure, why I am not too anxious to help you on this library proposition.

Despite his night-mare wrestling with Mexican friends, George Armijo finally supported the bill to appropriate the money making it possible for the University of New Mexico to buy the library.

After the bill had been passed, Van de Velde agreed that the University should move the books from Los Angeles to Albuquerque. He would be willing to wait for payment of the purchase-price now that the source of the funds was certain. It then developed that the University had no funds to pay the transportation charges. Explaining the difficulty to Governor Miles, I asked him to authorize the State Highway Department to send a truck, with a driver and helper, to Los Angeles, load up the library and haul it back to Albuquerque. The governor at once telephoned Grover Conroy, State Highway Engineer, asking him to arrange the trip. Governor Miles promised to assume sole responsibility if political enemies claimed that highway employees and equipment had been used for an unlawful purpose. Within two hours a large truck moved out of Santa Fe equipped with tarpaulins to protect the books from rain or wind. Within a few days, the truck, laden with its precious cargo of books, was on the University campus. The books soon became a part of the Coronado library.

Having discounted his claim at an Albuquerque bank, Paul Van de Velde called on me in order to say good-bye and to thank me for my part in the library transaction. He gave me an Indian Christ, carved from native wood in Mexico, with the following note:

Albuquerque
March 12, 1939

Dear Mr. Keleher:
    May this Indian Chief, from Tlacolula, Oaxaca, serve as a reminder of our gratitude for your invaluable help in satisfactorily terminating the library deal.
PAUL AND HARIETTA VAN DE VELDE

Six years after the Van de Velde library incident, I inadvertently became involved in another library acquisition in which I was pleased to be of some assistance. Ernie Pyle, famed Scripps-Howard war correspondent, killed in action at Ie Shima on April 11, 1945, made his home in Albuquerque for many months prior to and during World War II. The Pyle home at 900 Girard Avenue Southeast in Albuquerque is now and has been for more than twenty years known as the Ernie Pyle Memorial Library, a branch of the Albuquerque Library system. The library is a nationally known shrine, dedicated to the memory not only of Ernest Pyle and his wife, Geraldine Siebolds Pyle, but to GI's everywhere. The library was made possible as the result of provisions originally contained in the mutual wills made by the Pyles, furthered by the patient and persevering cooperation of a committee headed by Erna Fergusson, and by the splendid cooperation of the Pyle and Siebolds families. The committee of "The Ernie Pyle Memorial Project," consisted of Erna Fergusson, Chairman, Fred White, W. A. Keleher, Mrs. Ethel Moulton Bond, James P. Threlkeld, Dan Burrows then editor of the *Albuquerque Tribune,* and Keen Rafferty, then Chairman of the Department of Journalism of the University of New Mexico.

The committee was formed in response to a suggestion made by Geraldine Siebolds Pyle, who was anxious to be assured that the wishes of herself and husband in regard to disposition of the home place should be carried out. The committee met with Chairman Clyde Tingley, of the City Commission, on May 8, 1945, at the City Hall. At this meeting it was explained that Geraldine Pyle, Ernie Pyle's widow, had indicated her wish to deed the Pyle home place to the city. It was to be held and used in perpetuity as a memorial library, reserving a life estate in herself, contingent upon the city's written agreement to acquire and convert into a park a tract of land directly across Girard Avenue to the west, containing several acres. Scarcity of money would prevent the city from cooperating at the time, Tingley decided, and the contemplated project was abandoned. Subsequently, the library project became a bit complicated. Geraldine Siebolds Pyle survived her husband by only seven months, at which time it became known that she had changed her last will and testament on December 19, 1944. The change in the will placed the library project in jeopardy. Erna Fergusson's committee held a meeting on December 7, 1945, which was attended by some of the Pyle and Siebolds heirs. The meeting was held for the purpose of seeking a way out of the entanglements which resulted from the execution of Jerry's new will, but no solution was found. Soon after the December 7, 1945, meeting I was asked by Mrs. Mary E. Bales, of Dana, Indiana, Ernie Pyle's famed "Aunt Mary," by William Pyle, Ernie's father, and other members of the Pyle family, to represent their interests in connection with litigation anticipated over the Geraldine Siebolds Pyle will.

The Pyle side of the family contended that Ernie Pyle

and Jerry Pyle had agreed to make and did make mutual wills; that Pyle's will was in effect when he died; that under Ernie's will Jerry had inherited all joint property; that after Ernie's death Jerry had been persuaded by some one or more members of her family to sign a new will, and in so doing entirely disinherited Ernie's side of his family. Inasmuch as all this information concerning this phase of the Pyle affairs was public property at the time, has been available to the public from newspaper accounts and public records on file "In the Matter of the Estate of Geraldine Siebolds Pyle, Probate No. 165, in the District Court of Bernalillo County, New Mexico," it is not believed that any confidential information is presently being disclosed. I was employed by "Aunt Mary" and other Pyle heirs probably because I had done some legal work for Ernie while he was in Africa on a war assignment. I requested Irwin Moise, who had only recently returned to New Mexico after military service and started to practice law in Albuquerque, to become associated with me in representing the Pyle heirs. Irwin Moise, years later Justice and then Chief Justice of the Supreme Court of New Mexico, rendered helpful service in negotiating a satisfactory settlement, preventing what threatened for a time to be tedious and unnecessary litigation. By stipulation signed on May 10, 1946, by some twenty-six Pyle and Siebolds heirs, the assets of the Ernie Pyle and Jerry Pyle estates were divided equitably among them.

To the extent possible under the circumstances, although acting in a dual capacity as a member of the Ernie Pyle Memorial Library Project Committee, and as attorney for some of the Pyle heirs, I encouraged the Pyles to adjust their differences and to cooperate with the Siebolds heirs in the establishment of the memorial library. As a result of prolonged negotiations and mutual concessions, a paragraph was inserted in the settlement agreement providing as follows:

> It is further agreed that the Pyle home in Albuquerque shall be conveyed in proper manner to Ernie Pyle Memorial Committee of Albuquerque, or to the City of Albuquerque, in order that the same may be preserved and maintained as a proper and suitable memorial to the memory of Ernie Pyle and that all of the parties hereto will sign such waiver, or quitclaim deed, as may be required in order to effect the transfer of title to said property for said purpose, either to said Ernie Pyle Memorial Committee of Albuquerque, or to the City of Albuquerque, whichever is determined most desirable or suitable. It is also understood that the furnishings now in the house shall likewise be transferred and remain as a part of the said memorial.

Paige Cavanaugh, a Pyle relative, residing at the time at 400 W. Fairview Boulevard, Inglewood, California, was of much help in negotiating the settlement, particularly in arranging for the establishment of the library. The deed conveying the property to the City of Albuquerque was signed and recorded. The city officials and members of the Library Board cooperated and the memorial library became an established institution on October 20, 1948.

On October 20, 1949, the first anniversary of the establishment, Librarian Elsa Smith Thompson reported 1,056 registered borrowers. There were 5,629 volumes on the shelves. A total of 2,728 visitors signed the guest list, with names of people from almost every country in the world. The twentieth anniversary of the establishment of the Ernie Pyle Memorial Library was observed on October 20, 1968. During the year 1967–1968 there were 3,887 registered borrowers; 67,965 books were circulated. After twenty years the Pyle library is a thriving institution, a living memorial to Ernie and Jerry Siebolds Pyle, evidence

LIBRARIES 233

of the soundness of their joint decision concerning the disposition of their home place. On November 6, 1968, Donald A. Riechmann, Director of the Albuquerque Library system, reported:

> The Ernie Pyle Memorial Library has been and we expect it to continue to be a very busy agency. We are very pleased with this agency, its progress and proud of its history and association. City funds in an adequate amount have been available each year for painting, landscaping and other maintenance, as we wish to protect the Ernie Pyle home for posterity. Many visitors still find their way to the Memorial and they have enthusiastic and favorable comments as they sign the guest book. There were 488 signatures in 1967–1968.

CHAPTER FIFTEEN

Eugene Manlove Rhodes

EUGENE MANLOVE RHODES, famous New Mexico writer, died in Pacific Beach, suburban San Diego, California, on June 27, 1934. Three days later, on June 30, 1934, the remains were taken from the railway station in Tularosa, New Mexico, to the final resting place, excavated in a site two and a half acres in extent, dedicated for that purpose on the ranch property of Mr. and Mrs. Charles Hardin. According to a last request of the decedent, the remains were buried in a grave on the summit of a peak in the San Andres Mountains, a few miles from Tularosa and only a short distance from the place where Rhodes at one time owned a small ranch. Longtime close friends of Gene Rhodes, among them Frank Werden, Robert Martin, Hiram Yoast, and George Curry escorted the remains, accompanied by Mrs. May D. Rhodes, the widow, and her friend and companion, Dr. Mary Turner Riech. A wooden cross, on which had been penciled the words *Paso Por Aqui* (passed by here) was placed on the grave as a temporary marker. The inscription, the title of perhaps his best known short story, had been selected by Rhodes from a message carved on Inscription Rock in the Zuñi Country in western Valencia County, New Mexico, by Juan de Oñate, great explorer and soldier, as he had passed through there in 1605.

Gene Rhodes' interment, high on a mountainside was not in alien soil. Although he did not own at the time of his death a single acre in the millions of acres of land embracing the Tularosa Country, nevertheless symbolically he owned the entire country. On January 20, 1933, some eighteen months before his death, Gene Rhodes from Pacific Beach, California, "64 years old yesterday and not a lick of sense yet," wrote a letter to Dana Johnson displaying unusual sentiment and emotion about the Tularosa Country. In this letter, Gene Rhodes told Johnson:

> I was the only inhabitant in a space in that country as large as Delaware for many years. I laid out the road from Engle to Tularosa—and built it through the mountains with my own hands, my own pick, my own dynamite, fuse caps, my own brains. I began dreaming that straight road from Tularosa to Engle in 1890.

On June 28, 1938, four years after the death of Eugene Manlove Rhodes, I visited his grave in the San Andres Mountains and made a brief entry in a notebook: "Eugene Manlove Rhodes is buried in a little glen, surrounded by pine trees and scrub oak, affording a marvelous view of the San Mateos in the distance. No tombstone, only a marker. His grave enclosed by a barbed wire fence."

Soon after the death of the famous author, writers and artists of Santa Fe directed by Alice Corbin Henderson, poet, and E. Dana Johnson, editor of the *Santa Fe New Mexican,* organized the Eugene Manlove Rhodes Memorial Association. The purpose of the association was to solicit funds in order to buy a bronze tablet for the grave site to take the place of the wooden marker erected at the head of the grave at the time of burial, and to provide money for perpetual care for the grave. The campaign to solicit funds made good progress, but slowed down following Johnson's death on December 15, 1937. Mary Eckles Johnson, Dana Johnson's widow, asked my assistance in the work on January 10, 1941, advising me that the committee had collected more than $900.00 which was in a savings bank account.

At the time I was president of the Board of Regents of the New Mexico College of Agriculture and Mechanical Arts (now New Mexico State University), and in a position to be helpful. At my request, President Hugh M. Milton of A & M, authorized by the board actively co-operated with the Memorial Association and made all necessary manpower and equipment available at once. Co-operation between college and association resulted in the procurement of the bronze marker, the inscription for which had been prepared by William Penhallow Henderson. Henderson, representing the Memorial Association, and Jack Baird, for the college, met several times at the grave-site to make the improvement plans. The Association designated May 14, 1941, as the day for the dedication ceremonies. The *Santa Fe New Mexican* of May 4, 1941, invited everyone in the state to attend the dedication:

> There will be no hand-picked audience. Everyone is invited. All those who knew Gene as a writer; all those who missed knowing him to their everlasting regret; all those who wish to see the records of the beloved New Mexican set in perpetuity at the grave.

I was among those who, in the words of the *New Mexican* "missed knowing Rhodes, to their everlasting regret." For many years I was an interested reader of the Gene

Rhodes serials in the *Saturday Evening Post* when it was edited by George Horace Lorimer, a true friend of the author of the stories. I had talked to Mr. Lorimer on several occasions in Albuquerque while enroute from his home in Philadelphia to the Grand Canyon in Arizona, his then favorite vacation place.

When making his choice of a burial place, Gene Rhodes never dreamed perhaps that not many years would elapse before the federal government would take over almost entire control of the area. At 5:30 o'clock a.m. on July 16, 1945, a bit more than ten years after the death of Eugene Manlove Rhodes, the world's first nuclear device was exploded, described by witnesses as "an incredible burst of light." Trinity Site, scene of the explosion, is some forty-five to fifty miles distance from the Rhodes grave site. For many years to come its remoteness is assured by the United State military.

At the request of Isabel Eckles Johnson and other friends of Gene Rhodes I prepared a bill which was submitted to the 1951 session of the New Mexico Legislature directing the Board of Regents of A & M College to

> . . . expend such sums of money out of public funds of the college, as required from time to time, to cause the grave of Eugene Manlove Rhodes, the fence surrounding it, and the monument erected therein in his memory by the artists and writers of New Mexico, to be maintained in good order and condition, all to the end that the last resting place of one of New Mexico's most valiant sons shall not suffer decay from wind, rain and the passage of time after the family and friends of Gene Rhodes have gone to be with him in the Great Beyond.

Supported in the House by Representative Murray Morgan, of Otero County, and in the Senate by Senator Burton Roach, of Sierra, the bill was enacted into law by the legislature. Known as Chapter 89 of the 1951 Session Laws, the bill was signed by Governor Edwin L. Mechem, an ardent Rhodes fan, born and reared in Otero County, the heart of the Gene Rhodes country. The law subsequently became Chapter 73-26-26, New Mexico Statutes Annotated.

Fully aware of the significance of the Rhodes grave, the military command has been courteous, co-operative and sympathetic in permitting annual pilgrimages to the site and in allowing ingress and egress to authorized representatives of New Mexico State University and other persons having lawful reason to visit the area. The Trinity Site explosion of July 16, 1945, deferred indefinitely the plans of some who anticipated and envisaged easy access to the Rhodes grave site, the possibility that in time it might become a shrine somewhat comparable to the grave site of Robert Louis Stevenson, who had died more than forty years previously, and had been buried on Vaca Peak, in Vailima, Samoa, many thousands of miles distant from New Mexico.

When I visited the gravesite of Gene Rhodes in 1938, his footprints were easy to follow, particularly from Engle, northwestern outpost of the Rhodes country, across miles of rangeland to Tularosa, perhaps his favorite town in all the world. Although many men in the Rhodes country praised him highly, only a few of them, when asked, could say they had read one of his stories, perhaps because most of the men who worked on the range in his day and time were not readers. They were men of action, most of them skilled at breaking a bronco, wrestling down a steer, cutting up a hog, cow or calf, digging water wells. They did well any of the countless tasks required to be done as a matter of routine on a ranch, from baking bread and making pancakes to frying a chunk of freshly butchered meat.

Only one of the several men I interviewed on the range, Watson Ritch, son of W. G. Ritch, would qualify as a Gene Rhodes reader. Educated at Swarthmore, Watson Ritch said that he had read every story Rhodes wrote, and that he had in his library all of the Rhodes' published books. However, Ritch made no claim to being a book lover. A few years previously he had sold hundreds of books from the library of his father's estate to a Des Moines, Iowa book dealer, and to the Huntington Library in California. Watson Ritch's father, W. G. Ritch, had at one time, in the early '80's, served as secretary and acting governor of the Territory of New Mexico. In the last years of his life he was postmaster at Engle, New Mexico where he handed out letters to Gene Rhodes when he called for his mail. Rhodes claimed that Mr. Ritch would pay no attention to his request for his mail unless and until Rhodes would address him as "governor."

In Tularosa, a beautiful town not far from San Andres Peak, Verne Clayton, a lawyer, father of Jan Clayton, a future star in "Showboat" and "Carousel," told of the affection Rhodes had for that place. Verne Clayton and Gene Rhodes had been boys together. Clayton's father, Sweet Clayton, ran a general merchandise store in Tularosa. Rhodes was a regular customer at the Clayton store. Because of a speech impediment, Rhodes pronounced Clayton's given name "Tweet," instead of "Sweet." Verne Clayton told of an experience his father, Sweet Clayton, had with Gene Rhodes about 1900 when Rhodes was young, handsome, strong and ready for any kind of a fuss. Gene and Elijah Cooper, also a young cowboy, well known in the Tularosa country, went on an exploring expedition one summer evening, made their way as uninvited guests into a *baile* in a dance hall in Tularosa's "Dogtown." Sweet Clayton, sleeping soundly in a room in back of his store, was awakened at midnight by pounding and clattering on the front door of the store. Sweet Clayton shouted to the maker of the noise, "What in the hell do you want at this hour of the night?" Sweet Clayton recognized the voice that answered, "Tweet, Tweet, get up and open up the store right away. I want to buy a dozen pairs of brass knucks. 'Lige and I have had a fight at the dance. The Mexicans beat the hell out of us and I want to buy a couple of deadly weapons." Sweet Clayton managed to calm down Gene Rhodes and 'Lige, his companion, persuaded them to forget about seeking revenge at the dance, and to go home.

Several days later Gene Rhodes went to the Clayton store and a bit sheepishly explained the situation to Sweet Clayton. "Tweet, the other night I asked you to order me a dozen pair of brass knuckles. Just cancel that order. Instead, I would like for you to order a carload of the damned things and keep them in stock, and I would like to have you keep the store open all night when I am in town so that I can get a pair of knucks when I need them."

While attempting to pick up the trail of Eugene Manlove Rhodes, several people told me that Robert Martin of Engle had been his closest friend, knew him better than almost anybody else, and advised me to see him. Answering my letter asking for an appointment, Martin invited me to call on him at his ranch near Hot Springs, Sierra County. I visited with him on or about September 10, 1940. Bob Martin, retired rancher, long-time merchant and at that time active as a bank director, talked about his friend from early evening until almost daybreak. Among other things he told me the following:

I met Gene Rhodes for the first time in Engle in 1892. He was wearing store clothes instead of a cowboy outfit. I thought to myself at the time that Gene was a peculiar looking genius, almost a bit eccentric. But before long I knew that the store clothes were deceptive. I realized that Gene Rhodes was more at home on a horse or working on a ranch than any man I had ever known.

Rhodes was an expert, a specialist you might say, in breaking broncos. The wilder the broncos, the more they bucked, the better Gene liked it. He apparently didn't know the meaning of fear. I can see him now as I close my eyes, riding on a favorite big vinegar roan horse on the Bar Cross range. I saw him break lots of horses in battles of skill and will as between man and horse, something he relished greatly. In these contests, Gene relied on his great physical strength and endurance, and extraordinary will-power.

Rhodes liked taking a turn at digging a water well or post holes on the range. Even when on an errand of his own or for his boss, he would stop at the first sign of anybody trying to do a job on the range, drop everything, forget everything else, and help in whatever work was being done.

Gene liked to take over the responsibility of handling the hardest job around a cow camp. I remember the first time he showed up on the Barr Cross Ranch. We were branding a lot of big calves, seven or eight months old. We had to wrestle them down. Without being asked or invited to do so, Rhodes pitched in and helped us, showing great strength and grim determination. He was rather sensitive about some things. If anybody around the ranch made light of him, Rhodes would immediately challenge the offender to a fist fight or a wrestling bout of seemingly terrific significance to him.

Gene was a most generous, open-handed man. He would share his last crust of bread with a total stranger. He was a miserable cook and starved himself out on his own little ranch because of his extreme distaste and dislike for having anything to do with cooking. It wasn't because he was lazy. He was always willing to rustle the firewood for someone else to cook the food. He was willing to handle the pots, pans and skillets.

Nobody ever saw Gene Rhodes take a drink of liquor. But he was tolerant enough to respect the other fellow's views. I knew that because we were bunk mates for years, and I always had a bottle of whiskey in my bedroll, and many times we slept together on the range in the same shakedown, whiskey and all.

I spent several days with Gene Rhodes in California in 1934, just before his death. We talked for hours about old times. Gene told me that he had had more than fifty fights in his lifetime. He asked, 'Bob, why did I have all those fights?' I told him, 'Gene, because you were over-sensitive about some things.'

In the last long talk between us, Gene recalled one memorable fight he had while making his way from New Mexico to New York to get married. He had been getting ready for weeks to leave Engle for the east, but unfortunately got mixed up in a poker game while waiting for his train to arrive in Engle. He lost every dollar he had saved up for his ticket and expenses. He borrowed $35.00 from me. Our conversation on that day was about as follows: 'Bob, have you got any money?' I told him, 'Gene, I've got $35.00; it's about all I've got handy.' Gene said, 'Let me have it; I am going east to get married. If I don't pay you back, go out to the ranch, pick out a good horse for yourself and keep it.'

Rhodes left Engle on a cattle train for Kansas City. Upon arriving at the Kansas City Union Stockyards, he at once looked up Fred Fourchette whom he knew was one of the yard bosses. Fred gave him a job on a cattle train then being loaded with choice fat steers, destined for New York City. The representative of the steer-owners accosted Rhodes soon after the train had left the Kansas City stockyards. He told Rhodes in rather rough language that no nonsense would be tolerated on the trip. At the time Rhodes was resting a bit on top of one of the cattle cars, tired out after having walked on the ground alongside the full length of the fifty-car train, using a prod pole to keep the steers on their feet, instead of lying down, exposed to the risk of being trampled to death.

When Rhodes failed to respond to the agent's provocation, the agent spoke to him, saying in a loud voice, 'Ain't you the bum supposed to be working these cattle?' Rhodes reached for his prod pole and tapped the man gently with it on the side of his head, saying nothing in the process. Rhodes then returned to the caboose at the end of the train. He made a makeshift bed in the caboose by joining two seats together, then stretched himself out and settled down to try to get some sleep. In a few moments the belligerent agent entered the caboose. He took a look at Rhodes, poked him sharply in the ribs with his fist, saying 'Ain't you the —— —— bum they sent up here to work these cattle? They've got to quit sending bums like you up here.' The agent continued, 'You must be the bum who hit me with a prod pole a few minutes ago.'

The agent was a large man, six feet in height, big of bone and heavy set. Rhodes didn't hesitate, but tore into him on the floor of the caboose, using blows and toe-holds he had learned in many years of gouging and fighting in the cattle country. Gene told me, 'Bob, that was the damnedest fight I ever had in my life. When it was over the trainman washed this man up. I had given him a terrible beating. His eyes were half closed; his lips were cut and he was mumbling to himself. The train conductor said that the same man had beaten up other men who were working cattle trains and that the train crew were all glad to see that he had tackled someone who could whip him.' Gene finished the story. 'I got out of the caboose at the next stop, walked up and down the train, using my prod pole to keep the steers up. At the front end of the train I saw my man standing near the tender. I marched up to him and told him, "I am the man in charge of these cattle. The next time you tackle a cow puncher, you had better notify the undertaker."'

At his ranch home on the same occasion, Bob Martin also told me this story:

Frank LePage was night agent and telegraph operator for the Santa Fe Railroad at Engle during much of the time Gene Rhodes lived there. LePage was a busy man with many duties to look after, particularly before and after the arrival and departure of the once-a-night Albuquerque to El Paso passenger train. In addition to his duties as combination baggage agent, ticket salesman, freight and express agent, LePage was the handler of the United States mail. Gene Rhodes had a habit, which annoyed Frank LePage greatly, of sauntering into the depot at any time of day or night acting as if he owned half interest in the place, and asking if the mail from the East had arrived. Rhodes had another exasperating habit of insisting on being told when a train was reported late, why it was late, and always asking why the railroad didn't run its trains on time. Engle post office was not much more than a hundred feet or so away from the railroad right-of-way, opposite the depot. One night Rhodes pestered LePage almost beyond endurance. He first asked about the probable time of arrival of the mail train, then demanded that LePage tell him about what time after the train arrived he expected to carry the mail sack to the post office. Rhodes asked so many "fool question," that LePage took down a Wells Fargo and Co. Express Company shotgun from the gun rack on the wall, pointed it at Rhodes, told him "to get the hell out of here," threatened to shoot him if he didn't get out at once.

Rhodes decided quickly to leave the depot in as orderly and dignified a manner as possible. He started to walk across the roadway, not hurriedly, but not slowly either. Turning around for one last look, Rhodes saw LePage standing in the depot doorway, shotgun in hand, and decided he still meant business. As Rhodes reached the adobe-walled post office, LePage pulled the trigger, peppered the building with bird shot. At almost the same instant, Postmaster W. G. Ritch, a most sedate and dignified character, emerged from the post office door. Bowing low, without looking back, Rhodes tipped his hat politely and said nonchalantly, 'Good evening, Governor.'

As soon as he believed it wise to do so, Rhodes went home, got his six-shooter and returned to the depot, on the lookout for LePage. Thinking that LePage might have gone home, Rhodes went to LePage's house, rapped on the door with his six-shooter, anxious to resume the war. LePage, however, decided he had had enough of Gene Rhodes for one night, refused to go to the door.

My talks with Bob Martin evidenced that, in his opinion, sufficient emphasis had not been previously placed on some of the Rhodes outstanding proclivities and accomplishments which had nothing whatever to do with his literary attainment: his great physical strength, perhaps an inheritance from his father; his extraordinary tenacity; and his ability to take and absorb gruelling physical punishment, his varied combative traits of character. It was easy to see that from Bob Martin's viewpoint, Gene Rhodes would have been victorious as a gladiator, a magnificent soldier, a world champion prize fighter. He failed to understand or appreciate, however, his greatness as a literary person. He did not preserve any of the many letters Gene Rhodes had written to him over the years.

Gene Rhodes left behind him a word picture of himself. "My autobiography," he wrote in a letter several years before his death, "is written in my books, here a little, there a little, but most of it happily forgotten." In "Stepsons of Light" published in the *Saturday Evening Post* of September 11 and October 2, 1920, later published in book form, Rhodes offered testimony of the kind of man he considered himself to be. He had Pete Harkey, an old timer, describe Adam Forbes, the principal character of the story:

> You all knew Adam Forbes. He was a simple and kindly man. He brought a good courage to living, he was all help and laughter. He joyed in the sting and relish of rousing life. Those of you who were most unfriendly to him will not soon forget that gay, reckless, tenderhearted creature. You know his faults. He was given to hasty wrath. To stubbornness. His hand was heavy. If there are any here who have been wronged by this dead man—as I think most like—let the memory of it be buried in his grave. It was never his way to walk blameless. He did many things amiss; he took wrong turnings. But he

was never too proud to turn back, to admit a mistake, or to right his wrong-doing. He paid for what he broke. For the rest—he fed the hungry, helped the weak, he nursed the sick and dug graves for the dead. Now, in his turn, it is fitting and just that no bought hand dug the grave, but that his friends and folk did him this last service and called pleasant dreams to his long sleep.

CHAPTER SIXTEEN

Interest in Regional Writing

DURING THE six years I worked as a reporter on Albuquerque papers, from 1907 to 1913, it was my good fortune to meet and interview a number of well-known literary celebrities of the day, among them Dr. Henry Van Dyke, leading Presbyterian clergyman, whose *Other Wise Man* had tremendous vogue at the time, and for many years thereafter; Owen Wister, author of *The Virginian,* an alltime Western classic; Sir Gilbert Parker, whose *Right of Way* was a widely-read novel on both sides of the Atlantic; and Winston Churchill, of Cornish, New Hampshire, whose *The Inside of the Cup, Mr. Crewe's Career,* and other novels, written at the turn of the century, achieved great popularity.

Dr. Van Dyke impressed me as being a truly spiritual man. Sir Gilbert Parker, enroute to England on a Santa Fe train after a visit in Hollywood, beamed when I told him, in the course of our conversation, that I had read *The Right of Way* more than once, and that it was my favorite book, something I could not truthfully say today. Sir Gilbert, as a parting shot, recommended that I read *The Weavers,* another book he had written, which I read at the first opportunity, but in my then opinion it did not measure up to *The Right of Way.* I recall asking Winston

Churchill the reason for the choice of titles for his books, all of which up to that time at least being dominated by the letter "C." My query prompted the reply by Mr. Churchill that the question was a new one to him, that the title subject had never before been discussed by him, and that he could give me no off-hand satisfactory answer.

Learning that Owen Wister was ill and confined to his room in the Alvarado Hotel while in Albuquerque in 1910, I called upon him several days in succession and was apparently a welcome visitor. Owen Wister told me about some of his western experiences, and I told him about John H. Hicks, of Santa Rosa, New Mexico, a partner of A. A. Jones of Las Vegas, in the ranch and cattle business, who had been pointed out to me on several occasions when in Albuquerque as being the original of the Virginian, the principal character in his novel. I told my new-found friend that the story about John Hicks being the Virginian had been widely circulated in New Mexico, and generally accepted as being the gospel truth on cattle ranches and at story telling time at revival camp meetings. I described John Hicks for Owen Wister as being a rather handsome Southerner, then in his late forties, a typical cowman, who wore a stylish Stetson hat, Western style tailor-made clothes, boots by the best bootmaker in San Angelo, Texas. Mr. Wister told me that he would not like to spoil a good story but that there was no truth, no foundation in fact for the Hicks yarn; he had never met or known Mr. Hicks; that in delineating the Virginian he had no particular man in mind; that the Virginian was a composite character. Mr. Wister told me that he had been in and out of New Mexico several times before writing the story, and recalled particularly that he had visited Deming, spending ten days there on one occasion, a guest at cattle ranches, and looking in at the saloons and gambling houses.

In interviewing people who traveled in and out of Albuquerque, I asked some of them to give me the name of the book that had been important in their lives. In some instances, after interviewing people, I asked them to recommend a book for me to read, preferably one that had been influential in their life work, and if at all possible I read the recommended book. I particularly recall that one man recommended the *Memoirs of U. S. Grant,* and I not only read the *Memoirs,* in a two volume edition, but went on and ploughed through the ten volumes of Hay and Nicolay's *Life of Lincoln.* One man told me to read Dumas. Professor J. C. Monaghan, of Notre Dame University did not recommend any particular book, but advised me to "Read, read, read, write, write, write, speak, speak, speak," if my goal was to be better educated. One man advised me to read Carlyle's *French Revolution,* a two-volume work, which I bought but never read beyond the first chapters.

My father and mother were both readers, and I probably accrued a desire for reading from them. I recall that Mother started me on the road to being a reader by giving me first *Robinson Crusoe,* and later the *Swiss Family Robinson.* For birthdays and Christmas gifts Mother gave me books about George Washington, Patrick Henry, Robert E. Lee and other nationally-known patriots. A persuasive and persistent book salesman sold Mother a "complete set" of the novels of Charles Reade on the installment plan, three dollars down and fifty cents a week "until fully paid for." Mother allowed me to read all of Reade's novels with the exception of *Hard Cash* which she thought "too old" for me. Between ten and twelve years of age, I read all of the Reade novels, excepting the one forbidden. To this day I have never read *Hard Cash.* The Reade novels, among them *The Cloister and the*

Hearth, 'Tis Never Too Late to Mend, A Terrible Temptation, Put Yourself in His Place, and others to me then all absorbing stories, had no particular influence on my life insofar as I can recall. My Father's favorite author was Charles Dickens and *David Copperfield* his favorite Dickens' novel.

With an inclination to read in boyhood, and with newspaper reporting in more mature years, followed by legal training and work as a lawyer, it was perhaps only natural that the time would come when I would have the urge to write.

On July 5, 1929, at the Forty-eighth Annual Session of the Texas Bar Association, held in Amarillo, Texas, I read a paper on "Law of the New Mexico Land Grant," which marked the beginning of my venture into the field of regional historical writing. The New Mexico Bar Association had been invited to the Amarillo meeting as guests of the Texas Bar Association, and many New Mexico attorneys attended the several sessions. My paper was published in the October, 1929 issue of the *Texas Law Review,* on pages 154 to 170. As an indication of appreciation and friendship toward the New Mexico lawyers, the Association voted me an honorary life membership.

In preparing my paper, I had made a study of New Mexico land grants as they had existed under Spanish and Mexican rule, and found that there was a human interest story connected with nearly every grant. I was interested in the extraordinary story of the Peralta-Reavis Grant and began serious study of its ramifications. I examined the files and stacks of papers, documents and transcripts of testimony in this case, contained in several filing cabinets then stored in Santa Fe in the Surveyor General's office which were later transferred to the Bureau of Land Management office. After working on the Peralta-Reavis case for some months, and writing several thousands of words on it, I decided to abandon the task, having reached the conclusion that the Peralta-Reavis story would not be of particular interest to the people of New Mexico.

The pleadings and proofs in the case, submitted to the Court of Private Land Claims demonstrated beyond doubt that the alleged Grant, which measured fifty miles in width for hundreds of miles between Phoenix, Arizona and Tierra Amarilla, in Rio Arriba County, New Mexico, had been an attempted fraud of great magnitude. The evidence showed conclusively that one man, James Addison Peralta Reavis was apparently a scoundrel, a master forger and a swindler. However, Reavis seemed to me to be a character who could not be successfully portrayed as in any way attractive or interesting. The evidence in the case proved that Reavis was an aggressive, indefatigable worker, persistent and persevering, possessing iron nerve, a man apparently without a single observable redeeming trait that I could discover. Having reached the conclusion that I should look further, I stopped work on James Addison Peralta Reavis and the Peralta-Reavis Grant, and devoted effort to the history of the Maxwell Land Grant. I have never regretted that decision.

I had been attracted to the story of the Maxwell Grant because of the scope and immensity of the subject. The story revolved around many people, enveloped a vast area of mountain and plain in Colfax and Taos Counties, New Mexico, extending quite a distance into Southern Colorado, the result of the federal government's action in straightening out the boundary line between New Mexico and Colorado, by act of Congress of 1863. As I proceeded with my study, it became apparent to me that the history of the Maxwell Land Grant had all the ingredients a writer could ask for or a reader desire: cowboys and Indians, mountain men, a gold rush and miners, great herds of cattle, big timber, many high mountains and vast areas of grass land, squatters, a military post and soldiers, ministers of the gospel, people of every kind from all parts of the world. There were also the usual array of lawyers and judges in and about Cimarron, the then county seat of Colfax County, some scheming and conniving, others able and honorable, all thrown together in a crucible of great interest.

With an interesting assortment of characters to write about and much important litigation to be considered, I began work on a narrative which became a book entitled *Maxwell Land Grant*. George Curry, eighty years of age, at the time a patient in the U.S. Veteran's facility in Albuquerque, was my principal source for information, in addition to written records. He furnished me with much local color. I went to Cimarron, Springer, Raton, Rayado, and other places on the Grant, to learn about the geography of the country, to interview available old-timers.

George Curry, with a remarkably retentive memory, was a mine of dependable information. Curry had led a storybook life. He had lived as a boy in Dodge City, Kansas, where he had known Bat Masterson and other noted characters of the day; he had clerked in a store in the buffalo country in Texas in the late '70's; ranched in Lincoln County, New Mexico, during the Lincoln County War years; had been personally acquainted with William H. Bonney ("Billy the Kid"), and had participated actively in crucial events in the Grant troubles in Colfax County. John Curry, his only brother, had been shot and killed at Springer, the then county seat of Colfax County, in a gun battle on March 15, 1885. Curry had been a Rough Rider in Colonel Theodore Roosevelt's regiment in Cuba during the Spanish-American War; Chief of

Police in Manila during the time William Howard Taft served as Governor General of the Philippine Islands; he had been Governor of the Teritory of New Mexico by appointment of President Roosevelt; and he had served in the Congress of the United States after New Mexico had become a state. It would have been difficult to find a New Mexican of his era who could match George Curry's opportunities for adventure and excitement.

The history of the Maxwell Land Grant followed the pattern of most grants: the land had been granted on January 11, 1841, by Manuel Armijo, last governor of New Mexico during Mexican rule, to Carlos Beaubien, a Canadian, and Guadalupe Miranda, a Mexican citizen. The land grant was presumed to embrace 100,000 acres. Lucien B. Maxwell, at the time a resident of Taos, had acquired title to the Beaubien-Miranda tract for a modest consideration and sold it to land speculators, after which the original 100,000 tract was enlarged and extended many fold, by devious means, so that it contained a startling total of 1,793,000 acres. Ejectment suits, temporary and permanent injunctions, and other court actions, some of which went on appeal to the Supreme Court of the United States for final decision, provided a decisive chapter in land grant history. The principal Maxwell Land Grant case, on appeal to the Supreme Court in Washington was considered by the court to be of such importance that three full days were set aside for oral argument of counsel.

On December 12, 1942, thirteen years after I read my paper, "Law of the New Mexico Land Grant" at the Bar Convention in Amarillo, my book entitled the *Maxwell Land Grant,* was published by the Rydal Press of Santa Fe. Bound by Hazel Dreis of Santa Fe, the book sold well and the critics were kind and generous in their reviews.

Encouraged by the reception accorded the *Maxwell Land Grant*, I began work several months later on *The Fabulous Frontier, 12 New Mexico Items*, published by the Rydal Press in 1945. In *The Fabulous Frontier*, an attempt was made to assemble available facts and lore about some of the men who had taken a prominent part in the development of southeastern New Mexico, a vast area originally included in Dona Ana and Lincoln Counties. There were a number of colorful characters to select from in considering subjects for a place in the contemplated book. The men finally decided upon included John S. Chisum, Pat Garrett, Oliver M. Lee, John J. Hagerman, Thomas B. Catron, Charles B. Eddy, Albert Bacon Fall, Albert J. Fountain, and William Ashton Hawkins. I had personally been acquainted with Lee, Catron, Fall and Hawkins. I had seen Pat Garrett one time as he stood with his back against the bar, arms akimbo, in Sturges Saloon in Albuquerque, three years before he was killed near Las Cruces on February 29, 1908. On the occasion on which I had seen him, Garrett was surrounded by a dozen or more men, gazing up at his great height, perhaps out of curiosity or admiration.

In starting work on the book it seemed to me that an important part of it would revolve around the mysterious disappearance of Colonel Albert J. Fountain and his nine-year old son Henry, on January 31, 1896, some forty-five miles east of Las Cruces on the Tularosa highway. I was already somewhat familiar with the Fountain case, having written some years before several thousand words in a manuscript entitled "Fountain and Henry, his Son." While working on the Fountain-Lee phase of the book which became *The Fabulous Frontier* I spent some days in Almagordo, Las Cruces, Hillsboro and other places in southeastern New Mexico. I talked to old timers who had

INTEREST IN REGIONAL WRITING 255

some knowledge of the case and completed such investigation of places and incidents feasible at that late date, almost forty years after the Fountains had disappeared. It was apparent to me after having done considerable preliminary work that Oliver Lee was the one man, above all others, who should be consulted about the case. Lee's close friends told me that I would be wasting my time trying to talk to Oliver Lee; that he had repeatedly refused to discuss it with anyone. I had known Oliver Lee slightly during the years he served in the New Mexico Legislature, had seen him on many occasions in Santa Fe, as he walked to his desk in the Senate, a tall, erect and handsome man, always of dignified appearance and well-groomed, a striking figure. The legs of his trousers were always carefully tucked into tailor-made boots, and ordinarily he wore a knee-length black frock coat, a stylish Stetson hat on his head, white shirt, flowing black tie. It was generally known in and about the Senate chamber that Senator Lee, under the folds of his preacher-like coat, carried a business-like loaded .45.

The description of Oliver Lee, as he appeared while in the Legislature in Santa Fe, then about seventy years of age, recalled to the memory of the old timers the life-like portrait in words Eugene Manlove Rhodes had drawn of him in Chapter 2 of "The Desire of the Moth" published in the *Saturday Evening Post* of February 26 and March 4, 1946. Gene Rhodes was writing about Christopher (Kit) Foy, the principal character of the story, but describing Oliver Lee:

> He was about thirty, above middle height, every mold and line of him slender and fine and strong. His face was resolute, vivacious, intelligent; his eyes were large and brown, pleasant and fearless. A wide black hat pushed back now, showed a broad forehead, white against crisp coal black hair, and the

pleasant tan of neck and cheek. But it was not his dark, forceful face alone that lent him such distinction. Rather it was the perfect poise and balance of the man, the ease and unconscious grace of every swift and sure motion. He wore a working garb now—blue overalls and a blue rowdy. But he wore them with an air that made him well-dressed.

Talking about the Fountain case with Marion L. Fox, at the time editor of the *Albuquerque Journal,* I told him that in my opinion no story about it could be considered complete without some word from Oliver Lee. Mr. Fox volunteered to undertake to try and arrange a meeting between Mr. Lee and me, and to attend it with me. As a result of Mr. Fox's efforts, we met Oliver Lee by appointment in his home in Alamogordo on November 7, 1937. In the beginning of our conversation things were somewhat strained; Oliver Lee was plainly a bit nervous. Before consenting to an interview, Mr. Lee had written to Mr. Fox: "I have never talked about the Fountain case with a living soul, not even to members of my own family, since that day in Hillsboro in 1899, when I testified under oath from the witness stand." Mr. Fox had replied: "Senator, for your own sake and for the sake of your family, you should tell your side of the story before it is too late." During the meeting Mr. Fox sat in an old-fashioned rocking chair in Lee's living room, presiding as a sort of trial judge ready to rule if any questions were asked which might be considered irrelevant. Several times during the interview, Mr. Lee arose from his chair and walked up and down the room, apparently prompted by present recollection of some long forgotten incident. Oliver Lee on that day told a straightforward story. There was no doubt in my mind but that he was telling the truth. Mr. Lee saw that I was making notes, but offered no objection. I finished typing the notes within a few days and gave a copy to Mr. Fox for his consideration, and he told me that in his opinion the work fairly and correctly stated Mr. Lee's position.

Oliver Lee died in Alamogordo on December 15, 1941. By that date I had completed the Oliver Lee chapter of my book. I did not wish to publish it without first submitting it to the Lee family. I sent a copy of the chapter as prepared to Vincent Lee of Alamogordo, one of Senator Lee's sons. I told him of the circumstances under which his father had given me the information, and requested the family's permission to publish it. On September 29, 1943, Vince Lee wrote saying: "The family seemed a bit skeptical about what the reaction would be to your book. I don't know myself, but suppose it will be both good and bad. Since you talked to Dad personally, however, and he had no objection, I can see no reason why the rest of us should."

Having asked the family for a photograph, Vincent Lee sent me a kodak picture of his father taken not long before the Senator's death, showing him standing alongside an automobile. E. L. Blumenschein, Taos artist who had many years before done illustrations for Jack London, Booth Tarkington, George Barr McCutcheon, Willa Cather and other noted writers, took the picture, blocked out the automobile completely, sketched in cowboy boots customarily worn by Oliver Lee. The illustration, an excellent likeness it seemed to me, is shown between pages 226 and 227 of *The Fabulous Frontier*.

Anxious to gather all available facts relating to the Lee case, I went to Hillsboro, at the time county seat of Sierra County, where it had been tried before a jury. I checked the criminal docket and examined the original court papers in Territory of New Mexico vs. Oliver M. Lee, James Gilliland, et al. I asked the county clerk for permission to see the bound volumes of the *Sierra County Advocate,* the only newspaper published in Sierra County at the time of the trial. The clerk figuratively threw up his hands in despair. He told me that the newspapers had been neglected, stacked up for years; that the county commissioners had failed to budget enough money to pay for binding. "All those papers are out there," the clerk said, pointing to a cement block shed in the rear of the courthouse while handing me a key. Unlocking the door I was dismayed to find hundreds of newspapers scattered all over the floor, piled up, loose, without sequence, in confusion and disorder. It was evident no attempt had been made for years to stack the papers in order, or to protect them from insects or wind and weather. Estimating that it would require several men a week or more to sort out the papers, and bring order out of chaos, I was about to lock the door and leave the shed. Obeying a hunch, I stooped down and scooped up an armful of copies of the *Sierra County Advocate* and was delighted to see that the scooped up papers, beginning with the issue of June 25, 1899, and for subsequent weeks, were the very issues which I needed most. The *Advocate* reports of the trial gave me the necessary local color, the feel of the story, and the atmosphere of the trial not obtainable in the formal day to day entries in court dockets. When I returned the key to the county clerk, he assured me that all the old newspapers lying in the shed would be moved to Hot Springs, the new county seat; that all copies of the *Advocate* would be kept safely in a fireproof vault until bound.

Several months later, after the new courthouse in Hot Springs (T. or C.) had been completed and occupied as the official seat of government of Sierra County, I was in that place and asked the same clerk about progress in binding the *Sierra County Advocate* which we had last talked about in Hillsboro. Again, the clerk figuratively threw up his hands in despair and told me: "When the commissioners found out how much it was going to cost to bind those newspapers they decided not to move them to Hot Springs. So we had a big bonfire in Hillsboro, and they all went up in smoke. I'm sorry."

The material for the chapter on Oliver Lee in my book *The Fabulous Frontier* having received family approval, I turned my attention to a contemplated chapter entitled "Thomas Benton Catron." Former Governor Miguel A. Otero had told me some months previously of an incident that had taken place while he was writing *My Nine Years as Governor,* published by the University of New Mexico Press in 1940. Governor Otero said that all four of Tom Catron's sons, John, Charles, Thomas Jr., and Fletcher, called on him in a body at his residence in Santa Fe, having made a telephone appointment the day before. John, the eldest son, was spokesman for the brothers. Otero told me that John Catron began the conversation by saying:

> Governor, we understand you are writing a book on the years covering your administration as governor. We know that you and Father did not get along, politically or personally. You probably had differences of opinion, arguments and misunderstandings. The purpose of our visit today is to tell you that we propose to hold you personally responsible for anything you may say about him that would be derogatory.

According to Otero's version as related to me, he replied to the Catrons:

> Gentlemen, I have never in my entire life allowed any man or group of men to dictate to me or intimidate me. Your father and I were as opposite as the poles. In my book I shall expect to tell the truth about Senator Catron and everybody else mentioned in it. If I do this, there should be no objections. Good day, gentlemen.

Bearing this incident in mind while writing the Tom Catron chapter for my book, I went to Santa Fe by appointment, and submitted the work to Charles C. Catron, an attorney, whom I considered the son with authority to speak for the family. I waited in an outer office while Charles Catron went over the Catron chapter, apparently reading it with care, line for line, word for word. At last he came out from his private office and said to me, "Well, Keleher, it looks to me as if you've got the old man, all right." Several days later I wrote to Catron, asking if he could let me have a photograph of his father, to be used as one of the illustrations in my book. On October 25, 1944, he wrote to me:

> Soon after my father went to the United States Senate he was sent by the Republican Senators to Baltimore, Maryland to scout the Democratic Convention and while he was leaving the convention hall some reporter took a snapshot of him. This snapshot, when enlarged and touched up, was such a marvelous likeness and was so informal that I had a young Italian artist make a portrait from same. After the artist had completed the portrait in the rough, I spent several afternoons with him, giving him the correct coloring for hair, flesh, clothes, etc. This portrait is probably the most natural likeness of my father in existence today. I think it would be well worth your time to let me know the next time you are in Santa Fe and let me show you the portrait. If you agree with me, I will gladly let you take it to have a photograph and cut made from same.

I went to Santa Fe. Charles Catron took me to his home, showed me the Senator's portrait, which seemed to me to be an excellent likeness. A cut for the portrait is shown between pages 106 and 107 of the *Fabulous Frontier*.

In the beginning of my work on the chapter on James John Hagerman in the *Fabulous Frontier*, my principal source was W. C. Reid, an Albuquerque attorney, long time resident of the Pecos Valley, with many years of law practice and public service in Roswell. Mr. Reid had been Hagerman's lawyer for many years, held him in high esteem. He praised Hagerman as a man of exceptional honor and integrity. I had been fairly well acquainted over the years with Hagerman's son, Herbert J. Hagerman, governor of the territory in 1906 and part of 1907. I had seen and talked to Herbert Hagerman on many occasions between 1906 and 1935, the year of his death. Governor Hagerman, in my estimation, was an outstanding citizen, very sincere in his attempts to render exceptional public service. It had appeared to me, however, that Herbert Hagerman lacked fighting spirit; that he had too often shied away from combat when he should have taken a decisive stand and fought back. It had seemed to me, also, that Herbert Hagerman had always thought he was battling alone, while in truth and in fact it always seemed to me he had many good people on his side, although apparently he did not know it.

After he graduated from Cornell University with B.A. and LL.B. degrees, Herbert Hagerman practiced law briefly in Colorado in 1897 and 1898, but was weaned away from the drudgery of the law by the supposedly glamorous life of a diplomat. He was appointed Second Secretary of the American Embassy in St. Petersburg and went to Russia. According to his statement to me, Hagerman, in later life, considered his work at the Embassy more or less a waste of time. He described his life in St. Petersburg in the book *Letters of a Young Diplomat,* published by the Rydal Press in Santa Fe in 1937. Herbert Hagerman gave me a copy of a much more important book entitled *Matters Relating to the Administration and Removal of Herbert Hagerman, Governor of New Mexico, 1906–1907,* published in 1908, inscribed "My good friend, Will Keleher, a rare book from H. J. Hagerman, Mch 24,

1931." Hagerman gave me the book no doubt because I had known many of the men who had been active in political life while he was governor, and he wanted me to know his side of the case. In my opinion, many of the New Mexico politicians who helped ruin Hagerman's public life were political pirates, making up as merry a crew as ever cut a political throat or scuttled a political ship.

On the day he handed me the book, and while discussing its contents, Hagerman told me something about the difficulties he had encountered during the final months and days of his service as Governor of New Mexico. Knowing that serious charges had been filed against him by Republican leaders in New Mexico, and that a petition incorporating the charges, asking his removal from office, was on President Roosevelt's desk awaiting final decision, Hagerman had repeatedly asked Secretary of the Interior James R. Garfield, for permission to go to Washington so that he might see the President personally and to explain to him the falsity of the charges. For weeks Garfield had ignored Hagerman's request for permission for out-of-state travel, but finally authorized him to make the trip to Washington. Upon reaching the capital, Hagerman was dismayed to learn, he told me, that Secretary Garfield was most reluctant to request an appointment for the President to see him. Hagerman told me:

> After sitting around Washington for several days in my hotel room and cooling my heels in halls, corridors, and reception rooms in public buildings, I finally managed to get in to see the President. After a rather cool, very formal greeting, the President started to lecture me as if I were a boy who had disobeyed the rules at a prep school. I was unable to get in one word in my own defense. When the President had ended what I can only describe as a harangue, he told me that he needed no further information in my case, that all necessary investigations had been completed, that he had made up his

mind to ask for my resignation as Governor of the Territory. The President refused to listen to my contention that there was no good reason, as I saw it, for me to resign. I could see, and recognized from the tone of his voice, the setting and atmosphere of the place, that I was getting nowhere with the President. I feared that if I continued to argue with him that he might ring a bell for an usher and have me bodily escorted from his office. The President took me by the arm in a display of friendliness, and walked me toward the door, saying as we approached it, 'Governor, out of respect and consideration for your father, who is my good friend, I will allow you to resign voluntarily. This will save you and your father the embarrassment of a requested resignation.'

According to Hagerman, President Roosevelt, as a farewell gesture of good will, gave him definite instructions on procedure, saying: "Governor, I request that you leave for Santa Fe as soon as you can do so, tonight if possible. On your arrival in Santa Fe you are to write me a letter of resignation on official stationery. I will reply at once by writing you a friendly letter, expressing my personal regret. I have not given much thought as yet to a possible successor, but I assure you I expect to appoint someone who is well qualified and who will get along with the people out there."

Hagerman told me the rest of the story: "I left Washington that night, spending a sleepless night in a Pullman car. I got off the train in St. Louis the next day and bought several daily papers. I was amazed to see my name in the headlines in dispatches from Washington stating that the President had announced that he had accepted my resignation as Governor of New Mexico and would appoint George Curry, of his old Rough Rider Regiment, to succeed me."

Some thirty-two years after President Theodore Roosevelt, to all intents and purposes, according to Hagerman's version, had "fired" Herbert Hagerman, his successor, George Curry, told me of some of his experiences as Governor of the Territory. Curry told of difficulties encountered in trying to get along with the ringleaders of the Republican Old Guard in New Mexico. On this occasion, I showed George Curry the book Hagerman had given me on March 31, 1931. Curry reached for a pen and wrote this message below Hagerman's signature on the autographed copy of the book:

> Gov. Hagerman was an able and good governor, always doing what he thought right and could be classed as a statesman, but a poor politician. We need more of his type in public life. George Curry, Mch. 5, 1939.

On that day I asked Governor Curry this question: "Governor Curry, how long before you were appointed Governor of New Mexico by President Roosevelt did you know that you might get the place?" George Curry replied:

> The Colonel sent me two or three cablegrams in the Philippine Islands over a period of several weeks. In answer to one cablegram I reminded him that politically I had been known in New Mexico for many years as a Democrat; and that if he appointed me governor as he proposed it could embarrass him and might cause trouble for him with some New Mexico politicians. The President cabled back: "I don't mind what your politics are, but if you accept my appointment, I shall expect you to carry out my policies and obey my instructions." I cabled back that I would do the best I could to follow his wishes and instructions in administering the affairs of the office. Without waiting for any more communications from Washington, I started from Manila on the transport *Sheridan* and reached San Francisco in about thirty days.

While writing the chapter on James John Hagerman for *The Fabulous Frontier*, I wrote to Percy Hagerman, Herbert's elder brother in Colorado Springs, asking for a photograph of his father, saying that I proposed to publish a book on some of the men of Southeastern New Mexico who had contributed to its development. Percy Hagerman replied at once saying, "If you are really serious about writing something about my father, I will come to Albuquerque at once." Assuring him that I was indeed serious about such a project, I was pleased when Percy Hagerman arrived in Albuquerque within the next few days. He brought with him much information and a snapshot which showed his father as he had appeared several months before his death.

In the picture between pages 178 and 179 of *The Fabulous Frontier*, James John Hagerman is shown as he stood in a grove of trees planted on his property, once owned by John S. Chisum, a few miles south and east of Roswell, on which Hagerman had built a pretentious residence. Percy Hagerman supplied me with a wealth of material concerning his father's early life, his later successes and failures. No one could have been more faithful or cooperative. On August 7, 1945, acknowledging a copy of the book I sent him, Percy Hagerman wrote:

> Many of the characters of whom you speak in your book were well-known to me, my father first of all, C. B. Eddy, Pat Garrett, W. A. Hawkins, Capt. John Poe, Capt. J. S. Lea and many others. I think you have shown them all in their true light and with a real historical spirit. Naturally I was particularly interested in what you said about my father who was of a very different type from those who preceded him in Lincoln County and most of his contemporaries during the years when he spent most of his time and the greater part of his money in that country. It goes without saying that I have often regretted that he ever saw the Pecos Valley, and yet when one contemplates the final result of his efforts there, one must admit that they resulted in much good for the valley and for the state at large.

For many years I had a casual acquaintance with William Ashton Hawkins, the central figure in one chapter of *The Fabulous Frontier,* and knew him fairly well in the latter years of his life. He was recognized throughout New Mexico as an able and resourceful lawyer. He was counsel for a number of large corporations, entrusted with many important matters which required a wide knowledge of business and finance. He gained a great deal of notoriety in New Mexico, and national fame of sorts, by having the 1903 New Mexico legislature pass a bill which he had prepared while a member of the senate. After its passage the bill was known as "The Hawkins Act." Opponents contended that the law was grossly discriminating in favor of railroad corporations, and very prejudiced against individuals in personal injury litigation. The act was eventually nullified by Act of Congress under the power reserved in the Organic Act of 1852, creating the Territory of New Mexico.

Although my acquaintance with William A. Hawkins was slight, I was well acquainted with John M. Hawkins, a brother, at the time living in El Paso, Texas. For several years prior to going to El Paso, John Hawkins had been an editorial writer for the *Albuquerque Journal.* In 1943 and 1944, when I was corresponding with him, John Hawkins was suffering from an eye ailment, but cooperated with me nevertheless in every way in my efforts to relate the facts of his brother's life, particularly about his early day residence in Silver City and his law practice there, with time taken out occasionally to fight Apache Indians as a member of the Territorial Militia. John Hawkins furnished much information about his brother's work as attorney for Charles B. Eddy, early day railroad promoter, who built a railroad which became part of the Rock Island and Southern Pacific Railway systems.

On August 15, 1945, John Hawkins wrote to me from El Paso, thanking me for sending him a copy of *The Fabulous Frontier,* containing the chapter about his brother, to which he had so generously contributed:

> From your book I have learned much of the region my father helped to bring under our flag, where his three sons lived for more than half a century and learned to love the land and the people. Ninety and nine years ago our father, Corp. Ashton Hawkins, a militia corps member in a backwoods Tennessee town was in Mexico with old rough and ready Gen. Taylor battling Santa Ana at Buena Vista. Twenty years later as Capt. Ashton Hawkins in our own Union Army, he fought to keep the flag waving over the western land he helped to win. Little did he know or dream of half a continent that would be taken to keep and to hold. I am glad you added to my knowledge of what has been happening in the zone where destiny drew me. I thank you for the kindly spirit in which you wrote of my brother and for your courtesy to me.

In undertaking to write about characters of Southeastern New Mexico, I was quite confident that I would have no difficulty in obtaining an abundance of material about Pat Garrett, not only because of the notoriety he had achieved as a result of killing Billy the Kid at Fort Sumner on July 14, 1881, but also because of his participation for many years in public affairs of importance. Both George Curry, former Governor of the Territory, and James M. Hervey, Attorney General of New Mexico during a part of Curry's administration, had known Garrett well and gave me the benefit of their recollections. I soon found out, however, that it would not be an easy task to find much firsthand material about Garrett and his times, particularly about his early years in New Mexico. Apparently, he wrote but few letters and carried on very little personal correspondence with friends.

In my quest for information, I received several letters

from John Nance Garner, of Uvalde, Texas, Vice President under Franklin D. Roosevelt. In reply to my questions Garner wrote that he had known Garrett quite well in the '90's; that they shared a common interest in the breeding and racing of horses; that Garrett had lived in and about Uvalde for several years, that he had returned to New Mexico about 1897 to "vindicate himself." Garner recalled that Garrett, while living in Uvalde, had been active in politics, and that he had helped elect Garrett to a place on the County Commission in Uvalde. In Las Cruces, where Pat Garrett lived for many years, I talked to his daughter, Pauline, at the time a deputy clerk of Dona Ana County, hoping that she might know the whereabouts of her father's correspondence. Pauline Garrett told me that Pat Garrett, Jr., her brother, had been the custodian of the family papers, which had been lost or stolen after the death of Pat, Jr. in Mexico City some years before.

When beginning to write the chapter for *The Fabulous Frontier* on Charles Bishop Eddy, I learned that but few people then living had known him personally, and that they knew little or nothing about the actual facts of his life or of his activities in the cattle business or railroad promotion. Eddy had been prominently identified with work in both fields. He had been an indefatigable worker, particularly in railroad promotion, at times a rival of James John Hagerman. Information about Eddy was so sketchy that it proved difficult to find out for certain his correct middle name. Finally, I found out that Roy A. Prentice, then a resident of Tucumcari, had worked as Eddy's private secretary for several years; and he was kind and co-operative in giving me the benefit of his recollections.

In writing the chapter on Albert J. Fountain, I relied

largely on information given to me by old timers. Other sources were newspapers and court records. For several years Fountain published a newspaper in Dona Ana County. He was a combination lawyer and politician of renown in a colorful era in New Mexico. He was murdered, as was his nine-year-old son Henry, in the Chalk Hills Country, on the edge of the White Sands in present day Otero County, on or about February 1, 1896, under circumstances which have remained an unsolved mystery to this day.

In writing the chapter of Albert Bacon Fall, I had the advantage of knowing personally some facts about his life and career. I had known him for some years and had talked to him occasionally about political affairs. I also had information given to me by George Curry and other old-timers of Fall's day and generation. I made a trip to El Paso from Albuquerque especially to see and talk to Judge Fall while he was a patient in the Beaumont Hospital at Fort Bliss. I had anticipated talking to him about early days in New Mexico. However, he was too ill to do other than to shake hands with me and wish me well. Several years later I acquired in El Paso a collection of papers dealing mostly with the Tea Pot Dome affair, which I gave to the University of New Mexico Library on July 1, 1955, on condition that they should be catalogued, indexed and made available for the use of scholars.

In working on both *The Maxwell Land Grant* and *The Fabulous Frontier,* I had the advantage of writing about men and events still comparatively fresh in the minds and recollections of many people. In writing *Turmoil in New Mexico, 1846–1868,* published in 1952, it was necessary to rely almost entirely on official and semi-official reports, documents and newspaper accounts. As contemplated in the beginning, the book would encompass four major events of particular historical importance and significance to New Mexico: General Kearny's invasion and conquest of New Mexico; the invasion of New Mexico by the Texas-Confederates in 1862; General Carleton's march in 1862 from near Los Angeles, on the Pacific Coast, through the deserts of California and Arizona, to the Rio Grande, near Las Cruces, New Mexico; and Carleton's strange war against the Navajo Indians, their confinement at Bosque Redondo, and subsequent freedom following the signing of a treaty between the Indians and the federal government, negotiated for the United States by General William T. Sherman, of Civil War fame. Prior to writing *Turmoil,* on a trip lasting three weeks, I traveled on horseback to out-of-the-way places on the Navajo Reservation, and later visited or revisited what could be found of several early-day military posts of importance during the Civil War, including Fort Union, Fort Marcy, old and new Fort Wingate, Fort Defiance, Fort Cummings and Fort Fillmore.

The official *War of the Rebellion Series* proved an invaluable source of authentic material on the Civil War years. *Reports of the Commissioner of Indian Affairs* provided many off-the-record touches to illustrate the incidents and happenings on the Indian reservations. While writing on the Indians, it so happened that William A. Brophy, a long-time friend, was appointed Commissioner of Indian Affairs. Commissioner Brophy furnished me with much information and material which might not have otherwise been available to me.

On the lookout for a likeness of Governor Manuel Armijo, the last governor of New Mexico under Mexican rule, I traveled to a number of out-of-the-way places. Inquiry among the people of Lemitar, where the general had lived for years before his death, failed to produce a portrait of a man who had once been Lemitar's most noted character. Actually, many Lemitar people had never heard of General Manuel Armijo and knew nothing of his one-time identification with the town. In Socorro, several miles to the south, I learned that Edward Baca, Court Reporter for the Seventh Judicial District, was the owner of a recognized oil painting of the general, said to have been the work of an itinerant Mexican artist. Baca gave me a picture of the painting, a cut of which appeared between pages 10 and 11 of the book when published. Some months later a fire in Baca's home destroyed the painting.

Through the efforts of United States Senator Carl A. Hatch, and his prestige at the State Department in Washington, I was enabled to get photostats and microfilm of the all-important Magoffin papers, previously for generations considered as classified material in the department's archives. Magoffin, a Kentuckian, had played an important part in the diplomatic maneuvering incident to the attempts of the United States to cause Governor Armijo to abandon his office, thus allowing General Kearny's Army of Occupation to take over New Mexico "without firing a shot." For his suspected participation in the conspiracy, Magoffin was arrested and kept in jail in Chihuahua for months. Magoffin experienced great difficulty in establishing his claim for reimbursement of out-of-pocket expense money for payment for goods lost or destroyed while enroute from Santa Fe to Chihuahua. Freed at last from prison in Mexico, Magoffin asked for a modest $40,000 in settlement for all his claims. A tight-fisted administrator bargained with him and finally he accepted $30,000 "in full of all demands against the United States."

General Edward Richard Sprigg Canby was Commander of Union troops during most of the Civil War period in New Mexico. Endeavoring to learn as much as possible about General Canby's background and antecedents, I corresponded with Henry Seidel Canby, a distant relative, who courteously searched family letters and papers and gave me such information as he could find. On February 14, 1952, Mr. Canby, one of the founders of the *Saturday Review of Literature* (now *Saturday Review*), then at 254 West 50th Street, wrote:

> Your book, which I have read with the greatest interest, gives me for the first time, a clear idea of the situation in which my relative took part. He seems to have been a cautious Quaker in the midst of firebrands who thought little of after-consequences.

While working on *Turmoil in New Mexico*, it seemed important to write somewhat in detail about Dr. Jonathan Letterman, a surgeon in the United States Army, who had participated to a great extent in Navajo Indian tribal affairs during many years of professional service in the Territory, beginning at Fort Defiance in 1854, and had written several papers concerning the Navajos and Apaches.

By a strange stroke of good fortune, Catherine and Madeline Letterman, daughters of Dr. Letterman, came to Albuquerque to reside after having made their home in Italy for decades. The Letterman sisters, then in their eighties, had come to Albuquerque largely because of their friendship with Margaret Keleher, a cousin of mine. Through her I became acquainted with the Lettermans. When told of my interest in their father's identification with New Mexico, they were most cooperative, furnished me with many letters and documents which enabled me to write in an authentic way about their father. Among other things I wrote in *Turmoil,* page 490: "Dr. Letter-

INTEREST IN REGIONAL WRITING 273

man had a most extraordinary career in the United States Army, the details of which would justify an entire volume." On November 24, 1947, the magazine *Time* published an article saying that Dr. Paul R. Hawley, then chief medical officer of the United States Veterans Administration, had nominated Dr. Jonathan Letterman as the "all-time, all American medical officer."

Among the items given to me by Madeline Letterman was the original commission received by her father when first appointed as an assistant surgeon in the Army. The commission, dated March 27, 1850, was signed by Zachary Taylor, President, and attested by George W. Crawford, Secretary of War. With Miss Letterman's consent, on October 27, 1949, I gave the certificate to the chief medical officer of the Letterman General Hospital in San Francisco, who had it framed and hung in the reception room office.

The University of New Mexico Press published my fourth book, *Violence in Lincoln County 1869–1881*, in 1957. I began to write the book in the spring of 1955 following an illness requiring hospitalization and several weeks of recuperation. In writing *Violence* it was my hope that I could find it possible not only to tell the story of the so-called Lincoln County War, but at the same time place William H. Bonney, known as "Billy the Kid," in proper perspective.

Working on *The Maxwell Land Grant*, *The Fabulous Frontier*, and *Turmoil in New Mexico*, I observed the rule which I had established providing that no part of the work would be allowed to interfere with my regular law office practice hours. Compliance with and obedience to the rule had made it necessary for me to do the research and writing on those books outside office hours, at night, on Sundays and holidays. Working late at night, getting to sleep late, and starting to work on the books soon after daybreak, made it possible for me to accomplish a great deal. One day, at a casual meeting on the street, United States District Judge Colin Neblett asked how I was getting along with my writing. Working at the time on *The Fabulous Frontier,* I told the Judge that I thought I was making fairly good progress but would get along much better if I had a hideaway. Reaching into a pocket, Judge Neblett handed me the key to his offices in the Federal Building, northwest corner of Fifth Street and Gold Avenue in Albuquerque, saying, "Here, take this key and make yourself at home in my offices; I don't hold court in Albuquerque very often." Judge Neblett's kindness afforded me the seclusion I needed and speeded up completion of the book. In writing *Violence,* I was relieved for the time being from the duties in my law office, and as a result devoted all the time necessary to try and piece together the "Billy the Kid" puzzle, not entirely put together satisfactorily even to this day. Students of the War and of Billy the Kid have been unable to unearth information adequately answering several important questions about details, among them certainty as to the date and place of Bonney's birth, when, where and how Bonney learned to ride and shoot; how he had developed during his short life extraordinary skills in intelligent and resourceful leadership.

In a way I was fairly familiar with the outline of the Lincoln County troubles and the colorful career of "Billy the Kid." George Curry had told me a great deal of the lore of the country and I had learned much from James Madison Hervey, who had lived in Lincoln as a boy. In later years Hervey was the official reporter for the Lincoln County District Court, and was Attorney General of the Territory during a part of the Hagerman and Curry administrations. Hervey had been well acquainted with Emerson Hough, the writer, when he lived in White Oaks, Lincoln County. Hough had passed on to Hervey some of his recollections of the early days. Some years before beginning to write the book I had talked to one-time Deputy Sheriff John W. Poe, who was present near by the night Garrett had shot and killed "Billy the Kid."

I had talked about "the Kid" in some detail with Charley A. Siringo, whose book *History of Billy the Kid* was published in 1920. On July 30, 1912, Siringo gave me an autographed copy of his book, *A Cowboy Detective,* published in that year in Chicago. The book was dedicated by Siringo, "to my friend, Alois B. Renehan, of Santa Fe, New Mexico, an eminent lawyer, advocate and writer, as a token of appreciation of many kindnesses done." The dedication by Siringo to Renehan was no doubt partly prompted by a desire on Siringo's part to repay Renehan for legal services rendered by Renehan on Siringo's behalf in connection with litigation following publication of *The Saga of Billy the Kid,* by Walter Noble Burns. Burns, a first cousin of Katherine Burns Mabry, wife of Thomas J. Mabry, years later a governor of New Mexico, had been in New Mexico many times while working on his book.

Siringo contended, in and out of court, that in publishing the *Saga* in 1926, Burns had infringed on Siringo's copyright of *History of Billy the Kid,* published six years previously. The court decided, however, that there had been no infringement because most statements of fact in Siringo's book had been known by many people; that such facts had been published prior to 1920; therefore that the facts related in Siringo's book, as a matter of law, were public property and in the "public domain." The Siringo-Renehan friendship was formed and maintained in part, perhaps, because Renehan was himself interested in literature. In 1900, the New Mexico Printing Co., Santa Fe, published his *Songs from the Black Mesa,* dedicated to Renehan's father, "a poet unknown to fame, because he sang for self alone."

In undertaking to write *Violence,* it was my belief that many writers had focused attention unduly on William H. Bonney, had glorified and over-glamorized his life and exploits, and had given him too prominent a place in the Lincoln County War. It was my opinion also that Lew Wallace, governor of the Territory during many torrid "Billy the Kid" days, had not been adequately portrayed. Hopeful of finding material on the New Mexico period in the life of Lew Wallace, I went to Crawfordville, Indiana, his former home. I was disappointed to find that not much was to be learned about Lew Wallace in the records there. Later, Robert N. Mullin, at the time living in Chicago, told me that an important collection of Lew Wallace papers was available at the William Henry Smith Library of the Indiana Historical Society in Indianapolis. Caroline Dunn, librarian at the Smith Library thereafter provided me with photostats and microfilms of many worthwhile letters and documents related to Lew Wallace's participation of the Lincoln County troubles. Senator Clinton P. Anderson arranged with the State Department to make available to me copies of correspondence between John H. Tunstall and his people in England, some of which were incorporated in my book. Tunstall, a young Englishman, who had been inveigled into investing money in Lincoln through the persuasive salesmanship of A. A. McSween, was murdered in cold blood near Lincoln on February 18, 1878.

Through the courtesy and friendship of George Abbott, of Alamogordo, New Mexico, it was possible to incorpo-

INTEREST IN REGIONAL WRITING 277

rate in a part of *Violence,* an exact translation in English taken from the long-lost coroner's jury verdict of July 15, 1881. Some years before George Abbott had told me that he owned the original verdict, which his brother Harold had found when looking for missing documents for the State Land Office, in the basement of the then capitol building in Santa Fe. A photostat of the verdict showed plainly that rats or mice had nibbled away bits of one corner of one sheet of the paper on which the verdict had been written, grim evidence that it had narrowly escaped total destruction.

CHAPTER SEVENTEEN

Conclusion

MORE THAN fifty years have come and gone since that day, August 11, 1915, when I was granted by the Supreme Court the privilege of practicing law in all New Mexico courts. On February 9, 1916, I was admitted by United States Judge William H. Pope to practice in the Federal Court in New Mexico. Before being admitted to practice in either court I subscribed to the required oaths. To the best of my ability I have endeavored since 1915 to comply with them in their full meaning and intent, and to adhere to the traditions of the bench and bar.

I began to practice in New Mexico at the conclusion of a long transition period, extending over almost sixty years between the first days of the Kearny Code and statehood. During all the many years before statehood, the lawyers and judges had done their fair share and more of work in attempting to shape the destinies of the territory. After a long struggle New Mexico had been admitted as a state to the Union in 1912. Fortunately for me, and for other lawyers similarly situated, the New Mexico Statutes, Annotated, a codification of the existing laws of New Mexico, effective June 11, 1915, was published by authority of the New Mexico Legislature, by the W. H. Courtright Company of Denver. The Code was prepared by Stephen

CONCLUSION 279

B. Davis, Jr. and Merritt C. Mechem, assisted by Herbert W. Clark, of the Las Vegas bar, and by Antonio S. Lucero, the first elected Secretary of State of New Mexico. The codification was completed under the general supervision of a legislative committee composed of Louis C. Ilfeld, of Las Vegas, Edward P. Davies, of Santa Fe, and Raymond R. Ryan, of Silver City. Davis, a Las Vegas attorney, later became a judge of the New Mexico Supreme Court, and Solicitor of the U.S. Department of Commerce under Herbert C. Hoover, and still later went from Washington to New York City as Chief Counsel for the Radio Corporation of America. Merritt C. Mechem, at the time of preparing the Code a territorial District Judge, with residence in Tucumcari, was elected after statehood as judge of the Seventh Judicial District, and in 1920 was elected Governor of the state, and served during 1921–1922. The new codification, containing 1,796 pages, replaced the long out-of-print 1897 General Laws of the Territory of New Mexico, which had been prepared under authority of the Legislature by John P. Victory, Edward L. Bartlett and Thomas N. Wilkerson. The 1897 Codification had continued to be used up to the time of promulgation of the 1915 Codification despite the fact that more than sixteen hundred of its sections had been repealed, amended, or had become obsolete.

At the time I began to practice law in 1915, the town promoters claimed a population of 30,000 and predicted a population of 50,000 by 1925. No question but that Albuquerque's growth since 1940 has been the direct result of the establishment here of military facilities, including Sandia Base and Kirtland Field, with their satellite installations, all in turn due to the nearby location of Los Alamos, twenty minutes away by air traffic, an hour and a half distant by highway. A world war was a preliminary for Albuquerque to gain the army installations now located here, but Albuquerque for many years had cherished a partly suppressed ambition to be the home base for military facilities. As far back as the military occupation of New Mexico by the United States forces in 1846, the military authorities recognized the importance of ingress and egress through Tijeras Canyon, an east and west passageway, the only available direct route for many years through the Sandia Mountains. The military also recognized the importance of the waters of the Rio Grande, with its pasturage in the adjacent valleys affording ideal camp sites, with firewood and grazing for livestock. During the Civil War years, 1861 to 1865, the Union Army's high command established and maintained important military forces in Albuquerque, located approximately at today's Central Avenue and Rio Grande Boulevard, for a time under the command of Gen. James H. Carleton, noted for his forays against the Navajo Indians, with troops equipped and provisioned in Albuquerque.

After the Civil War years, the military establishment in Albuquerque was considered obsolete and abandoned. The fighting against the Navajos was subsequently carried on from Fort Wingate, some one hundred forty miles west of Albuquerque. Following the establishment of the New Mexico Territorial Fair in 1882, cavalry from Fort Wingate participated annually in the Fair program by means of practice marches from Fort Wingate to Albuquerque and return, and daily drills and maneuvers on the parade grounds on which Carleton's cavalrymen had maneuvered during Civil War days nearly twenty years before.

The Commercial Club of Albuquerque, predecessor of the present day Chamber of Commerce, anxious to have the Fort Wingate facilities moved to Albuquerque, prevailed upon General J. Franklin Bell, Chief of Staff of the

CONCLUSION 281

Department of Colorado, of Denver, to make preliminary recommendations for the establishment of a cavalry post in Albuquerque, which would mean the elimination of Fort Wingate. The plan went forward to the extent of pinpointing the site, the location being in part occupied today by the twenty-seven-hole municipal Los Altos Golf Course at 7717 East Copper Avenue, in the vicinity of Lomas Boulevard and Wyoming Avenue. In furtherance of the plan the Congress of the United States enacted a law on June 8, 1906, authorizing the federal government to convey to the City of Albuquerque for military and other specified limited purposes a tract of land containing 640 acres described as the south half of Section 17 and the north half of Section 20, in Township 10 North of Range 4 East of the New Mexico Meridian, and the patent was issued in conformity with the Act of Congress. The Congress, on November 23, 1909, authorized the execution of a supplemental patent. At the request of the City of Albuquerque an act was passed on August 16, 1950, lifting the then existing restrictions, but imposing others, allowing the land to be sold contingent upon the money derived from the sale being used to finance a public auditorium to be erected by the city or jointly with the University of New Mexico. Subsequent legislation by the Congress allowed relaxation of the restrictions to an extent which made it possible for the City of Albuquerque to place the land to beneficial use. With the coming of World War II, Albuquerque's dream for the establishment of a cavalry post here was dissipated, but subsequently Albuquerque gained the all-important military installations revolving around Kirtland Field and Sandia Base.

In Albuquerque in 1915, not more than twelve or fifteen lawyers were active in the profession. One judge, Herbert F. Raynolds, former law partner of Alonzo B. McMillen, was the only judge in the Second Judicial District, which at the time was comprised of the counties of Bernalillo, McKinley and Sandoval. Most lawyers still dreaded the pleadings in use at the time, and the court patiently listened to lengthy arguments on demurrers and motions to strike, motions to make more definite and certain, and other like pleadings, sometimes irrelevant, sometimes meritorious, happily done away with years ago. In the early days of my practice much of the important legal business was generated by Spanish-American clients, at that time still owners of fractional interest in land grants, and owners of other valuable property rights. A lawyer with a working knowledge of Spanish held an important advantage over those who had no facility with the language. It was my good fortune to be employed by a number of old time Spanish-American clients, some of whom had never had a favorable opportunity to learn to speak English.

My interest in, and love of New Mexico, particularly Albuquerque, my home town, are, I think, established facts. The people have been friendly, kind and generous to me, and I have tried to reciprocate by helping to make Albuquerque a good place in which to live. I have had the privilege of watching it grow from a Southwestern frontier town of a few thousand people to a beautiful metropolitan city of approximately 300,000 people.

When I was a boy, we used to "go to the mountains." Now in 1969, the mountains have come to us. Residential areas, and ever-expanding shopping centers within a few miles of the Sandias are easily accessible through the medium of freeways and superhighways. Population growth has brought changes to the lineaments of valley and *mesa* as the magnificent panorama of lights at dusk reveals, but the view from the Sandia Crest on a clear day presents

CONCLUSION

no change in the vast perimeter of grandeur which includes glimpses to the east of the Sangre de Cristo and Jemez Mountains, and far to the west Mount Taylor.

For more than fifty years I have been engaged in the general practice of law, and during most of these years I have had the assistance and loyalty of dedicated associates and partners, and am grateful for that assistance and loyalty. At this time I wish to express my gratitude to the memory of Ilda B. Sganzini who was associated with me as secretary and office manager for forty-four consecutive years, and to Ellis Dean Neel, our present office manager who has served forty-one consecutive years.

To my daughter Mary Ann Keleher Rogers and to my four sons, William B. Keleher, Michael L. Keleher, John G. Keleher and Thomas F. Keleher, to all my grandchildren and to my nephew Timothy B. Keleher I bequeath my respect for the law and my love for New Mexico

THE END

Index

Abbott, George, 276
[Abbott], Harold, 277
Academic degrees, Masters, 94; LL.D., 95; Bachelor of Laws, 96
Adams, Judge Benjamin Franklin, 84ff, 91–92
Affidavit Cigars, 115
Alameda, 35
Alarid, 58
Albright and Anderson, 72
Albuquerque, 24; population in 1900, 50; city in 1900, 55; school staff 1907, 62–63; population in 1915, 279; home of military facilities, 280–281
Albuquerque Daily Citizen, 29, 50, 56, 69, 71
Albuquerque, first city charter, 126
Albuquerque government, early housing, 112ff
Albuquerque Herald, 84, 153
Albuquerque Journal-Democrat, 50
Albuquerque National Bank, 197ff
Albuquerque National Trust and Savings Bank, 197ff
Albuquerque Review, 30, 31
Albuquerque School System 1907, 62
Albuquerque Street Railway Co., 14
Albuquerque Sun, 71
Albuquerque Times, 27
Albuquerque Tribune, 177, 229
Albuquerque Volunteer Fire Department, 21
Alvarado, Alejandro, 213
Alvarado Hotel, 58, 77, 79, 82, 248

Anderson, Clinton P., 276
Anderson, George G., 58, 59
Angel, Maroni, 59
Anthony, D. R., 68
Anthracite Institute, The, 220
Arledge, R. F. (Deacon), 206
Armijo, Cristobal, 193
Armijo, George W., 46, 155, 227
Armijo, Justo R., 193
Armijo, Manuel, 253ff, 270–271
Armijo, Nicolas T., 193
Armijo, Perfecto, 153
Armijo, Tranquilino, 46
Atlantic and Pacific Railroad, 15–16
Atrisco, 22
Awalt, F. F., 192

Baca, Edward, 271
Baca, Elfego, 31, 42, 178ff
Baca, Herman, 182
Baca, Jesus, 138, 166, 174, 182
Baca, Justiniano, 138
Baca, Santiago, 16
Baird, Jack, 236
Bales, Mrs. Mary E., 230
Bank of Commerce, 25, 52
Barelas, 35
Barelas Street Bridge, 22
Barnett, Joseph, 50
Bartlett, Edward L., 279
Beattie, Rev. T. C., 33
Beaubien, Carlos, 253ff
Beck, Joseph, 18
Bell, General J. Franklin, 280
Ben Holliday Stage Company, 33

285

INDEX

Bennett, Mrs. H. M. (Laura Biggar), 71–72
Bernardinelli, P. C., 132
Bernalillo, 35
Bernalillo County, 30
Billy the Kid (William H. Bonney), 42, 54, 252, 267, 273ff
Bimson, Walter B., 196
Black, James S., 73, 100ff
Black and Veatch, 127
Bland, 51ff
Bliss, Zenas H., 65
Bluewater, 58; work at, 59ff; settlement of, 59ff
Bluewater Canyon, 60
Bluewater Development Company, 58, 61
Bluewater Valley, 60–61
Blumenschein, E. L., 257
Board of Education, 61ff
Board of Finance, 135ff
Boatright, David H., 114, 118
Bond, Mrs. Ethel Moulton, 229
Books, recommended and read, 249–250
Bosque Redondo, 270
Braden, John, 31ff
Bratini, A., 16
Bratton, Senator Sam G., 70, 169, 173, 203
Bravo, General Ygnacio, 101ff
Brazil, Wayne, 54
Brice, Clarence R., 149ff, 177
Brisbane, Arthur, 79
Brockmier, Henry, 48
Brockmier's Bicycle Shop, 55
Brooks, Belvidere, 58
Brooks, G. L., 52
Brooks, Joseph W., 58
Brophy, William A., 270
Bryan, R. W. D., 124
Bryan, William Jennings, 38
Burke, Abby U., 70
Burke, William S., 68ff
Burks, Martin P., 93ff, 98
Burnett, J. W., 116
Burns, Walter Noble, 275
Burnside, William, 65
Burroughs, John, 152
Burrows, Dan, 229
Bursum, Holm O., 198
Burton, Dr. Solomon L., 115
Butt, Frank, 115

Cabezon, 35
Cananea, Sonora, Mexico, 37
Canby, General Edward Richard Sprigg, 271–272
Canby, Henry Seidel, 272
Capital vs Labor in New Mexico, 208ff
Cardinal Sattoli, 28
Carlton, General James H., 270, 280
Carr, Clark M., 47
Carr, General Eugene A., 47
Carrie Tingley Hospital, 141, 144ff
Carson, Cale W., 204
Cathedral of St. Francis, Santa Fe, 28
Catron, Charles, 259
Catron, Fletcher, 259
Catron, John, 259
Catron, Thomas B., Jr., 254
Catron, Thomas B., Sr., 259
Cavanaugh, Paige, 232
Central Bank, The, 194
Central School Library, 64
Chandler, Charles J., 196ff
Chandler, Charles Q., 196
Chapelle, Archbishop Placidus Louis, 28
Chapman, Francis A., 192
Chapman, Welcome, General Store, 59
Chavez, David, Jr., 130ff, 225
Chavez, Dennis, 130, 142ff, 168, 175ff
Chavez, Felipe, 193
Chavez, Frank, 104
Chicago Tribune, 201
Chihuahua, Mexico, 100
Chino Copper Mines, 216ff
Chisum, John S., 254
Church of Latter Day Saints of Jesus Christ, 59
Church of the Immaculate Conception, 64
Churchill, Winston, 247
"Cinco de Mayo," 57
City Attorney, 116ff
City of Albuquerque vs Otero, 22 N.M., 128, 113
Civil War, 22
Clancy, Frank W., 76, 88–89
Clapp, E. H., 24
Clark, Herbert W., 279
Clark, Leverett, 65

INDEX 287

Clark, J. Reuben, 60
Clayton, E. M., 116
Clayton, Sweet, 239ff
Clayton, Verne, 239ff
Cleaveland, Agnes Morley, 37
Clerk, Board of Education, 62ff
Cleveland, Grover, 69, 117
Coal Fields in New Mexico, 208ff
Cobb, Eddie Ross, 117
College of St. Joseph on the Rio Grande (University of Albuquerque), 95
Collier, George, 46
Collier, May, 46
Collier, Hon. Needham C., 46
Colorado Fuel and Iron Co., 221
Commercial Club, 29, 50, 280
Company G., 34
Congregational Church, 33, 121
Connelly, Henry F., 46
Connelly, Governor Henry F., 46
Constitutional Convention, 30
Cooper, Elejah, 239ff
Coors, Henry G., 202, 204
Corbett, James, 40
Coronado Library, 226
Coulter, Querino, 153
Cowboy Detective, A, 275
Craig, George R., 62
Crawford, George W., 273
Crichton, Kyle, 46, 156
Crichton, Robert, 46
Cromwell Building, 48, 85, 91, 99
Crowded Years, 83
Curry, George, 234, 252-253, 263ff, 274
Curry, John, 252
Cushman, Austin Thomas, 29
Cushman, Charles O., 29
Cutting, Bronson, 138, 178ff
Cutting, Olivia, 184
Cutting, Mrs. W. Bayard, 172

Daily Citizen, The, 69
Davies, Edward P., 279
Davis, John W., 80
Davis, Stephen B., Jr., 279
"Declaration of Peace and Amity," 222
Defiance Coal Company, 212ff
Delgadillo, Demecio, 153
Democratic political machine, Albuquerque 1916, 115ff

Dempsey, John J., 136, 144
de Onate, Rafael Lopez, 82
de Pino, Soledad Sarracino, 153
Diamond Coal Company, 215ff
Dieckman, Otto, 39
Dillon, Richard C., 138, 169
Dodge City, Kansas, 12
Donegan, Rev. Horace W. B., 172
Dreis, Hazel, 253
Dunn, Brian Boru, 170
Dunn, Caroline, 276
Duranes, 35
Durango, Mexico, 100

Eastern Railway of New Mexico, 61
Eddy, Charles B., 254, 266, 268ff
Eight Spot Saloon, 40
El Gallo, 47
Elks Lodge, 21
Ellis Island, Castle Garden, 14
El Paso Bitulithic Company, 24
El Paso Times, 100ff
El Sanador (Francis Schlatter), 34
Embudo, 35
Emerson, H. J., 33
Engel, E. J., 141
Episcopal Church, 30
Equitable Life Assurance Society, 60
Ernie Pyle Memorial Project, 229
Estancia Valley, 24, 25
Eugene Manlove Rhodes Memorial Association, 235ff

Fabulous Frontier, The, 254ff
Fairbanks, Douglas, 137
Fairview Cemetery, 34
Fall, Albert Bacon, 254, 269ff
Farley, James A., 172
Father, trips with, 28ff; illness of, 48
Faulkner, William, 95
Fergusson, Erna, 229
Fergusson, Harvey B., 38
Fergusson Hook and Ladder Co., No. 1, 31, 34
Feud between "New Town" and "Old Town," 25
First Congregational Church, 82
First law suit, 104ff
First National Bank, 18, 50, 52, 54, 89, 163, 192ff
First National Bank of El Paso, 193
First Presbyterian Church, 84
First Regiment, 34

INDEX

First Regimental Band, 20, 34, 56
First Savings Bank & Trust Company, 195
Fitzsimmons, Bob, 40
Flambeau Club, 32, 34
Foraker, Creighton M., 160
Fornoff, Fred, 32, 54
Fort Bridger, 33
Fort Cummings, 270
Fort Defiance, 270, 272
Fort Fillmore, 270
Fort Kearney, 33
Fort Marcy, 270
Fort Smith, Arkansas, 12
Fort Union, 270
Fort Wingate, 60, 270, 280
Faulkes, Rev., 33
Fountain, Albert J., 254ff, 268–269
Fountain, Henry, 254ff, 268–269
Fox, Marion L., 256
Foy, Pat, 45
Freeman, A. A., 179

G. K. Warren Post No. 1, Grand Army of the Republic, 64–65
Gallup American Fuel Company (Gamerco), 212ff
Gallup, New Mexico, 210ff
Galusha, J. R., 116
Gambling, rumors of in southern New Mexico, 149ff
Garfield, James R., 262
Garland, Rufus C., 149
Garner, John Nance, 268
Garrett, Pat, 54, 254, 267ff
Garrett, Pat, Jr., 268
Garrett, Pauline, 268
Geary, Daniel, 193
General Office Building, 19
Gentile, Fr., A. M., 154
Geronimo, 160
Gianotti, Felix, 44
Gila River, 37
Gilbert & Sullivan, 18
Gillenwater, William H., 73
Gladding, James N., 114, 127
Glecker, Charles E., Building, 72
Gold Avenue, importance of, 50
Gold Star Saloon, 41
Gorman, James, 19
Gorry, John, 13
Gorry, Mary Ann, 14
Gorry, Thomas, 14

Governor, attempted third term, 141ff
Graham, Warren, 115, 128
Grand Army of the Republic, 34, 64
Grant, Angus A., 123
Grant's Opera House, 33, 34
Greiner, Thomas S., 30
Gutierrez, Thomas C., 193

Hagerman, Herbert J., 261
Hagerman, John J., 254ff
Hagerman, Percy, 264ff
Hammond, Dr. George P., 225
Haney, Fred, 56
Haney, Willie, 56
Hanger, B. B., 215
Hanger, Bruce, 202
Hanging of, George Smiley, 44; José P. Ruiz, 42–44
Hanna, Mark, 176
Hanna, Richard H., 57
Hannett, Arthur T., 131, 136, 139, 142
Hansen, Sharp, 215
Hardin, Mr. and Mrs. Charles, 234
Harris, Hugh H., 24
Harrison, Dr. George W., 32
Harrison, Margaret Otero, 32
Harrison, Will, 177
Harrison, William Henry, 70
Harsch, Adolph, 65
Harwood, Rev. Thomas, 65
Hatch, Carl A., 129, 173, 271
Hawkins, John M., 266–267
Hawkins, William Ashton, 254, 266ff
Hawley, Dr. Paul R., 273
Hearne, William, 158, 178
Henderson, Alice Corbin, 234
Henderson, William Penhallow, 236
Hendricks, Dr. C. C., 71ff
Hening, Horace B., 66, 73
Henry Lee Ensign Fountain, 124
Hervey, James M., 267, 274
Hewitt, Dr. E. L., 37
Hickey and Moore, 76
Hicks, John H., 248
Hickok, Wild Bill, 12
Hill, Dr. David Spence, 124
Hilton, Archie, 33
History of Billy the Kid, 275
Hockenhull, Andrew William, 133, 135, 169, 207ff
Hoffman, William Dawson, 90

INDEX 289

Holloman, Judge Reed, 118ff, 184
Home, at 303 West Baca, 18, 27, 117; at 323 W. Atlantic Avenue, 16, 19; at 501 W. Fruit, 16
Hope, Dr. Walter G., 158
Hopkins, R. W., 62, 66
Hot Springs (T or C), 141
House of the Good Shepherd, 19
Howerton, Dr. James Robert, 96
Hubbell, Frank A., 123
Hubbell, J. Lorenzo, 42
Hubbell, Thomas S., 42
Huerta, General Victoriano, 101ff
Hughes, Lena, 29
Hughes, Levi A., 196
Hughes, Thomas, 29
Huning Castle, 52
Huning, Franz, 14, 16, 52
Huning, Louis, 193

Ilfeld, Louis, 14, 279
Immaculate Conception Church, 19, 66
Ireland, 11; Athleague, County Roscommon, 14; Kildare, 14
Isherwood, Thomas, 120
Isleta Indian Reservation, 37
Ives, Byron Henry, 18
Ives, Scholarships, 18

Jackling, D. C., 218ff
Jackson, Thomas Jonathan (Stonewall), 95
Jacoby, Harry, 31
Jacoby, John, 31
James Cardinal Gibbons, 28
Jenkins, Dr. Myra Ellen, 37
Jiminez, Anastacio, 104
John D. Rockefeller, Jr. Plan, 221
Johnson, President Andrew, 117
Johnson, E. Dana, 134, 174ff, 235
Johnson, Edward, 65
Johnson, Judge Hezekiah S., 30
Johnson, Mary Eckles, 236
Jones, A. A., 248
Jones, Aristieus A., 97–98
Jones, B. A., 65
Jones, Jesse, 203
Juarez, Mexico, 57, 100

Kansas, Lawrence, 15
Kansas, Lieutenant Governor of, 30
Kansas Territory, 11

Katzman, Steven, 212ff
Kaseman, George A., 197ff
Kearny, General [Philip], 270, 271
Keleher, David, 11ff, 14
Keleher, Daniel, 15
Keleher, Dennis, 11
Keleher, Franklin, 15
Keleher, John G., 283
Keleher, Julia, 16, 96
Keleher, Katherine, 16, 96
Keleher, Lawrence, 16, 35
Keleher, Loretta Barrett, 16
Keleher, Margaret, 272
Keleher, Margaret Scannell, 11
Keleher, Michael L., 283
Keleher, Ralph, 16, 96
Keleher, Thomas Franklin, 283
Keleher, Thomas F., 11, 12, 13
Keleher, Timothy B., 283
Keleher, W. A., City Attorney, 117
Keleher, William, 15
Keleher, William B., 283
Kelly, Marcus P., 66, 71
Kent, Frederick H., 14
Kinney, Bartley H., 200ff
Kirster Brothers, cigar factory, 41
Korber, Jacob, 113
Korber property, 113
La Opinion Publica, 162, 190
Las Cruces, New Mexico, 19
"Law of the New Mexico Land Grant," 250
Lawrence, Douglas Co., Kansas, 11
Lawrence, Willis, 65
Lee Chapel, 93, 97
Lee, Oliver M., 254ff
Lee, General Robert E., 93, 95
Lee, Vincent, 257
Le Page, Frank, 243–244
Lester, Felix H., 114
Letters of a Young Diplomat, 261
Letterman, Catherine, 272
Letterman General Hospital, 273
Letterman, Dr. Jonathan, 272ff
Letterman, Madeline, 272
Lewis, Bob, 159ff
Lexington, Virginia, 95
Lithgow, H. S., 120
Loeb, Henry, 52
Loeb, Jacob, 52
Log Cabin, The, 70
Logan and Bryan, stockbrokers, 48
Long, Professor Joseph Raglan, 98

Lorimer, George Horace, 237
Lucero, Antonio, 279
Luthy, Frederick, 198

Macpherson, Daniel, 64–66
McAdoo, Eleanor Wilson, 82
McAdoo, Ellen, 81ff
McAdoo, Harriet, 79ff
McAdoo, William G., 78ff
McCabe, Robert E., 59
McCanna, Peter F., 98
McClellan, William M., 65
McConnell, Willis, 71
McCormick, Joseph Medill, 201
McCreight, W. T., 52
McDonald, W. W., 65
McDonald, Governor William C., 108, 138
McGhee, James B., 149
McGuinness, John, 31
McGuinness, Michael, 31
McGuinness, William, 14, 293ff
McIntosh (Albuquerque) Browns, 24
McIntosh Hardware Co., 25
McIntosh, William, 24, 25
McKee, Frank, 55
McKinley, William, 39
McKinney, Robert, 166
McLeod, A. H., 186
McManus, Warden John B., 109
McManus, Judge John B., Jr., 109
McMillen, Alonzo B., 85, 123, 128, 281
McNary, James Graham, 193
McSween, A. A., 276

Mabry, Thomas J., 136, 148, 275
Mabry, Katherine Burns, 275
Maddison, T. K. D., 104
Magoffin Papers, 271
Mandalari, Rev. A. M., S.J., 64
Mann, Claude S., 185
Manzano National Forest, 24
Martin, Robert, 234, 240
Martinez, Paddy, 60
Masterson, Bat, 12, 252
Matters Relating to the Administration and Removal of Herbert Hagerman, Governor of New Mexico, 1906–1907, 261
Maxwell Land Grant, 251ff
Maxwell, Lucien B., 253ff
Mechem, Edwin L., 149, 238

Mechem, Merritt C., 207ff, 279
Medina, José, 104
Medler, Edward, 19
Medler, Edward L., 19
Menaul, Rev. John, 89
Merchant, James, 51
Metcalf, W. P., 48, 126
Metcalf and Strauss, 48
Methodist Church, Lead Ave., 18
Metz, Nick, 18
Mexican Herald, 226
Mexico City, 100
Meylert, Colonel G. W., 20
Miksch, George, 215
Mi Señora Santa Ana, 158
Miles, Governor John E., 136, 142ff, 225
Miller, Jaffa, 138
Miller, N. M., 116
Mills, H. S., 215
Milne, John, 63
Milton, Hugh M., 236
Mirabal, Silvestre, 204
Miranda, Guadalupe, 253ff
Mitchell, Albert K., 146
Mogollon, 37
Moise, Irwin, 231
Moore, Major John D., 221
Moreland, Professor W. H., 98
Morgan, Murray, 237
Moses, Horace, 215ff
Motion pictures, first in Albuquerque, 40
Mother, 45ff
Mount Taylor, 23, 60
Mullin, Robert N., 276
Murphy, John C., 65
Murphy, Pat, 23, 45
Mutual Coal Co., 215
Mutual Protection Society Hall, 35

National Coal Company, 212ff
National Guard Armory, 40
National Labor Board, 221
National Miners Union, 212
National Recovery Act, 212
Navajo Indian Reservation, 23
Neblett, Colin, 80, 274
Neblett, William H., 80
Neel, Ellis Dean, 283
New Albuquerque, 14, 25
Newcomer, Ed, 41
New Mexico Militia, 34

INDEX 291

New Mexico Military Institute, 58
New Mexico Museum, 31, 38
New Mexico Printing Co., 276
New Mexico Statutes, annotated, 278
New York, Piermont, 11
New York Times, 172
Nick Sanchez killing, 27
Nordhaus, Robert J., 186

O'Bannon, Daniel, 41
O'Bannon, Patricio, 41
Ochoa, Juan, 212ff
O'Connor, J. F. T., 197
O'Grady, Pat, 116
Old Albuquerque, 23
Old Town, 14, 22, 25, 29
Olmstead & Dixon, 33
Orozco, 101
Otero, Celestino, 158
Otero, Manuel B., 138
Otero, Mariano S., 32, 193
Otero, Miguel A., 166, 168, 259
Owen, Harry P., 158

Pallium, conferring of, 28
Pancho Villa, 101
Parker, Sir Gilbert, 247
Pasó por Aquí, 234
Pearce, Dr. John F., 42
Peña Blanca, 35
Penick, Paul M., 96
Pepperday, Thomas M., 206
Peralta-Reavis Grant, 250–251
Perea, José Leandro, 193
Phi Beta Kappa, 94
Phi Delta Phi, 94
Phillips, Dr. Barney T., 172
Phillips, William, 74ff
Poe, John W., 275
Pohmer, Delores Chavez, 179ff
Pohmer, Francisquita (Mrs. Elfego Baca), 179ff, 187
Pohmer, Joseph, 179ff
Pope, Judge William H., 278
Picket Fence Gate, disappearance of, 39
Pinchot, Gifford, 24
Pitt, Ross, 117
Post, E. J. & Co., 25
Post Office, 50
Post, Tom, 22
Prentice, Roy A., 268
Provencher, Damas, 46

Provencher, Hector, 46
Pyle, Ernie, Library of, 229ff
Pyle, Geraldine Siebolds, 229ff
Pyle, William, 230

Quantrill Raid, 11

Rafferty, Keen, 229
Rancho Seco, 30
Rand, Frank C., Jr., 166
Raynolds, Frederick, 193
Raynolds, Herbert F., 104, 188ff, 281
Raynolds, Jefferson, 193
Raynolds, John M., 195, 204
Raynolds, Joshua S., 89, 193
Reagan, Bob, 33
Reconstruction Finance Corporation, 202ff
Rees, Frank A., 192
Reid, W. C., 198, 260
Renehan, Alois B., 275
Research for *Turmoil in New Mexico,* 269ff
Rhodes, Eugene Manlove, 255
Rhodes, Mary D. (Mrs. Eugene Manlove), 234
Ricki, Pete, 212ff
Riech, Dr. Mary Turner, 234
Riechmann, Donald A., 233
Riley, Dr. Franklin L., 96, 98
Riley, "Gunnysack," 42
Ringland, A. C., 24
Rio Grande, 19, 23
Ripley, Edward Payson, 77
Ritch, W. G., 239, 244
Ritch, Watson, 239
Roach, Burton, 237
Robinson Park, 34
Roches, Guadalupe, 104
Rodriguez, Angelo, 104
Rogers, Guy, 163, 202
Rogers, Mary Ann Keleher, 291
Romero, Sheriff Jesus, 104
Roosevelt, President Franklin D., 140–141, 168–169, 192, 203, 262
Roosevelt, President Theodore, 24
Rosenwald Bros., 38
Ross, Edmund, 116
Ross, Edmund G., 69, 116–117
Rotary Club, 125
Ruiz, José P., 41ff
Ruppe, Bernard, 21

Ryan, Raymond R., 279
Rydal Press, 253, 254, 261

Saga of Billy the Kid, The, 275
St. Anthony's Hospital, 141
St. John's Church, 15, 80
St. Mary's Cadet Corps, 47
St. Mary's Parochial School, 45
St. Michael's College, Santa Fe, 58
St. Patrick's Cathedral, 33
Salazar, José Ynez, 183
San Carlos Indian Reservation, 37
Sanchez, Nicholas J., 27
Sanctuary Society, 47
Sandia Mountains, 24
San Felipe de Neri, Church of, 14, 44
San Felipe Hotel, 19; fire at, 20, 50
San Francisco, 57
San Jose Market, 51
Santa Fe, 28; in 1902, 56
Santa Fe National Bank, 18
Santa Fe New Mexican, 133, 134, 166, 174, 177, 182, 234, 236
Santa Fe Railroad, 11, 61
Santa Fe Railroad Shops, 16
Saturday Evening Post, 237, 245, 255
Saturday Review of Literature, 272
Scharf, G. C., 58
Schlatter, Francis (*El Sanador*), 34ff
Scott-Moore Hose Co., 32, 34
Sears, Roebuck & Co., 30
Seboyeta, 37
Sedillo, A. A., 62
Seibert, James, 65
Seligman, Arthur, 133, 135, 166
Sellers, D. K. B., 204
Seth, Julian O., 139
Sganzini, Ilda B., 283
Sheriff of Bernalillo County, 16, 42
Sherman, Thomas E., 64
Sherman, William T., 64, 270
Shinick, Mrs. Thomas J., 33
Sierra County Advocate, 258ff
Sigma Chi, 94
Silver City, 37
Simms, Albert G., 176, 200
Simms, John Field, 176
Simms, Ruth Hanna McCormick (Mrs. Albert G.), 176, 200
Simpson, Henry, 114
Simpson's Pawnshop, 113-114
Siringo, Charley A., 275

Sister Blandina's Convent School, 180
Sister Ildefonse, 45
Sister Isabella, 45
Sister Mary Alacoque, 45
Sister St. Claire, 45
Sister Seraphine, 45, 47
Sisters of Charity, 45
Smiley, George, 44
Smith, Al, 80
Smith, George, 14
Smith, Joseph, 60
Smith, Stella, 14
Songs from the Black Mesa, 276
Southern California Law School, 91
Southwestern Brewery and Ice Co., 52
Southwestern Coal Co., 215
Spitz, Edward, 14
Staples, Professor Abram Penn, 93
State National Bank of Albuquerque, 192ff
Sterling, Superintendent W. D., 63
Stetham, Fred, 217ff
Stewart, Harry B., 65
Stover, Crary & Co., 13, 30
Stover, Elias S., 13, 30, 65, 193
Street, paving, 24
Streets, important in Albuquerque in 1900, 50
Strong, Frank H., 62
Sturges European Hotel, 21, 25
Sturges, Frank E., 21
Sturges Saloon, 254
Sulzer, J. F., 72
Supreme Court of New Mexico, 29, 119, 127
"Switch School," 45
Switzer, W. F., 115
Swope, Edwin B., 124, 138

Tandberg, John, 116
Taos Valley, 34
TAT (TWA), 82
Taylor, George C., 186
Taylor, President Zachary, 23, 273
"Temporary Emergency School Sales Tax," 139
Territorial Fair, 32
Territorial Fair Grounds, 22
Territorial Supreme Court Reporter, 41
Texas Confederates, 270

INDEX   293

Texas Law Review, 250
Thaxton, William C., 204
Thompson, Elsa Smith, 232
Thompson, John C., 127
Thompson, M. F., 20
Thornton, Territorial Governor W. T., 22
Threlkeld, James P., 229
Tight, William G., 74
Tingley, Carrie (Mrs. Clyde), 136, 141, 147
Tingley, Clyde, 115, 119ff, 130ff, 175, 230
Tom Post's Inn, 29
Tonkin, Allen M., 185
Torlina, John D., 40
Torlina, John D. Shoe & Carpet Store, 31
Trimble, W. L., 51, 52
Trimble, William Lawrence, 52
Trinity Site, 237
Truth or Consequences, 19
Tucker Hall, 95
Tuohy, Fred, 55
Turmoil in New Mexico, 1846–1868, 269ff
Tunstall, John H., 276
Tyler, John, 70

United Mine Workers of America, 212ff
University of New Mexico, 20, 30; Regents of, 73, 124; press, 273
Upson, Ash, 30
Uranium in New Mexico, 60

Van Atta, Dr. J. R., 58
Van de Velde, Paul, Library of, 225ff
Van Dyke, Dr. Henry, 247
Van Soelen, Don, 47
Van Soelen, Theodore, 47
Van Soelen, Virginia Carr, 47
Vaughan, Maurice, 48
Vaught, Jethro S., 169
Vermejo Park, 137
Victory, John P., 279
Vinita, Indian Territory, 12
Violence in Lincoln County, 1869–1881, 273ff
Virginia Military Institute, 95
Volcanoes, 23

Waha, A. O., 24
Walker, James, 212ff
Wallace (Domingo), 51
Wallace, Lew, 276
Wardwell, Sandy, 33
Warren, Archdeacon, W. E., 80
Washington & Lee University, 80, 92ff
Water Supply Co., 69
Wattron, Sheriff F. J., 42
Weber & Fields, 21
Weber, Rev. George J., 82
Weil, Sidney W., 202
Welch, Rev., 33
Wells, Fargo & Co., 33, 50
Werden, Frank, 234
West, Charles, 145
Westerfeld, Henry, 115, 127
Western Union Telegraph Co., work in Albuquerque, 48ff; in Santa Fe, 56; in El Paso, 57ff, 72
Weston, Edward Payson, 76ff
Whatley, Wayne C., 149
Whitcomb, A. M., 34
White, Charles, 18
White, Edward Douglas, 46
White, Fred, 229
White, Mrs. S. W., 18
White Star Line, 14
White, William, 18
Wilkerson, Thomas N., 118ff, 279
William Henry Smith Library, 276
Wilson, Charles F., 162
Wilson, Woodrow, 82
Wister, Owen, 247–248
Women's Relief Corps, 64
Wood, General Leonard, 208
Wood, Adj. Gen. Osborne, 208ff
Woolsey, T. S., 96
Woolsey, T. S., Jr., 24
Wooster, Carrie (Mrs. Clyde Tingley), 121ff
Wooster, George Clark, 121

Yoast, Hiram, 234
Young, Brigham, 60
Young, Frank, 151
Yrisarri, Sheriff Jacobo, 22

Zapata, 101
Zimmer, Clara, 56

www.ingramcontent.com/pod-product-compliance
Lightning Source LLC
Chambersburg PA
CBHW021819300426
44114CB00009BA/244